MODERN LEGAL STUDIES

LAW
AND THE
ELECTORAL PROCESS

by

H. F. RAWLINGS B.A., PH.D.
Lecturer in Law, University of Bristol

LONDON
SWEET & MAXWELL
1988

Published in 1988 by
Sweet & Maxwell Limited of
11 New Fetter Lane, London.
Laserset by P.B. Computer Typesetting,
Pickering, N. Yorks.
Printed in Great Britain by
Page Bros. (Norwich) Limited.

British Library Cataloguing in Publication Data

Rawlings, H.F. (Hugh F.)
Law and the electoral process.
1.   Great Britain. Parliament. House of
Commons. Members. Elections. Law
I.   Title
344.102'7

ISBN 0–421–37640–6

PREFACE

Elections are, self-evidently, important events in the life of political communities. Despite the recent increased interest shown by British legal academics in the general area of Public Law, our electoral law nevertheless remains a neglected topic. One reason for this may be that the Representation of the People Acts have been seen as both highly technical and not obviously relevant to the manner in which the electoral process is actually conducted. I have chosen here to go beyond the boundaries of those Acts, and to take as my focus of study not "electoral law" as such but the electoral process (widely interpreted to include constituency boundary drawing, voter registration, candidate selection arrangements, etc.), discussing various legal and non-legal rules and administrative practices which influence the workings of the electoral system. I have also on occasion tried to assess the implications for the political parties of the interpretations and implementation of the rules by agencies such as the Boundary Commissions and Electoral Registration Officers.

This general approach has taken me in some unexpected directions, although I was saved from revealing the full extent of my ignorance of company law by the timely publication of Dr. Keith Ewing's excellent monograph on *The Funding of Political Parties in Britain*, which has enabled me significantly to reduce my discussion of that topic. The approach also means that I have not attempted to "state the law" as at any particular date (even if I were to accept the epistomological assumptions underlying such a claim) — rather, I have attempted to discuss some legal and non-legal rules and practices as they related to the electoral system up to and including the General Election of 1987. I hope, therefore, that both lawyers and non-lawyers will find the book of interest.

Very many people have assisted me by responding willingly to requests for information. I would wish to mention in particular Mr. Chris Maclean of the Scottish National Party, Mr. Tony Jones of the Green Party and, especially, Mr. Michael Colvin, M.P., who was exceptionally generous and helpful. I am also grateful to Pat Jones, Jackie Williams,

v

Sheila Salisbury and the staff of Trymtype Ltd. for their admirable secretarial efforts on a frequently-amended manuscript, and to my colleage, Keith Stanton, for advice and assistance on "high-tech" matters.

This book was originally to be jointly written with my colleague, Chris Willmore. Unfortunately, illness and her very heavy commitments as a local government councillor and parliamentary candidate precluded her active involvement in the later stages of writing. She has nevertheless kindly allowed me to make use of draft material which she had earlier prepared, and I would wish to acknowledge here the generously offered and very considerable help she has given me. Many practical implications of electoral law would have escaped my notice if I had not had the benefit of her considerable experience as an election campaigner. In view of the fact that I have both used some of her material and have throughout the text referred to the author in the plural, it is particularly important to state that the views here expressed are mine alone.

Finally, I would wish to mention my wife, Gillian Douglas. She read the whole book in draft, made valuable suggestions for improvement and struggled, only partly successfully, to render my prose in gender-neutral language. During my course of writing she also produced our beloved daughter, Isobel. This book is dedicated to them both, with all my love.

October 8, 1987   Hugh F. Rawlings

CONTENTS

OTHER BOOKS IN THE SERIES

TABLE OF CASES

TABLE OF STATUTES

TABLE OF STATUTORY INSTRUMENTS

RULES OF THE SUPREME COURT

INTRODUCTION

(1) FREE ELECTIONS

Within developed Western industrial societies, the existence of a
"democratic" political system is usually identified with effective
legal provision of machinery for "free elections." What is meant
by "free elections," and why are they important? In this book we
broadly follow the description of a "democratic general election"
offered by Butler, Penniman and Ranney for our understanding
of "free elections." According to those authors, a general election
can properly be described as "democratic" if it "largely or
wholly" satisfies six listed conditions:

"1. Substantially the entire adult population has the right to
vote for candidates for office.
2. Elections take place regularly within prescribed time limits.
3. No substantial group in the adult population is denied the
opportunity of forming a party and putting up candidates.
4. All the seats in the major legislative chamber can be contested and usually are.
5. Campaigns are conducted with reasonable fairness in
that neither law nor violence nor intimidation bars the
candidates from presenting their views and qualifications
or prevents the voters from learning and discussing
them.
6. Votes are cast freely and secretly; they are counted and
reported honestly; and the candidates who receive the
proportions required by law are duly installed in office
until their terms expire and a new election is held."

(Butler, Penniman and Ranney (1981), p. 3)

In this book these various principles will be discussed as they
apply to British parliamentary and local elections, and to elections to the European Parliament.[1] Two points should be made

[1] By virtue of the European Communities (Amendment) Act 1986, s.3, references
in earlier legislation (such as the European Assembly Elections Act 1978) to the
"European Assembly" must now be understood as referring to the "European
Parliament." Here the terms "Parliament" and "Assembly" will be used inter-
changeably.

at the outset. First, it is to be noted that a "democratic" election as understood by Butler *et al.* clearly implies substantial satisfaction of the principle "one person one vote," as their first condition demonstrates. On the other hand, the principle "one vote one value" does not appear as a necessary element in a democratic election. We shall examine how far the system created by British electoral law also seeks to satisfy that principle of electoral equality.

Secondly, Butler *et al.* require only that a given election "largely or wholly" meet these conditions in order to be regarded as democratic. A word of warning is appropriate if these conditions are to be used for the identification of democratic electoral systems which provide for "free elections." Their point is properly made if it implies that a reasonable degree of flexibility of judgment is to be used by the observer in deciding whether particular conditions have been met. It is, however, dangerous if it is used as support for an argument that an electoral system as a whole is "democratic" because (say) four or five of the six elements have been satisfied. Mackenzie has emphasised the "systematic" element of electoral systems, the fact that the various components of electoral systems are closely inter-related:

> "Any code of electoral law includes a number of essential sections of almost equal importance; these deal with the qualifications and disqualifications of voters, the division of the electorate into constituencies, the prevention of corruption and intimidation during the campaign, the judicial and administrative provisions for seeing that the law is observed. Each of these sections is meaningless in isolation from the others. A very wide and equal suffrage loses its value if political bosses are able to gerrymander constituencies so as to suit their own interests; there is no point in having an elaborate system of proportional representation if the electors are all driven in one direction by a preponderance of bribes and threats; legal provisions mean nothing if enforcement of the law is left wholly in the hands of those who profit by breaking it.
>
> This is why it is right to speak of 'the electoral *system*'. Procedure for elections is *systematic* in that its parts are inter-dependent; it is impossible to advance on one 'front' without regard to others."

(Mackenzie (1967), p. 19)

The importance of a system of free elections lies in the fact that it confers initial legitimacy upon those who are selected to exercise governmental authority within the state. This, as Mackenzie notes, is the only consistent answer offered by the West to the problem of legitimate power (1967), p. 11). A measure of the efficacy of any given electoral system is the degree of legitimacy which it confers upon those who have succeeded in the electoral contest. This is not to say that legitimacy derived from the electoral process may not subsequently be lost by a given government's conduct of affairs; but it does mean that an incoming government produced by a free electoral process should begin its administration with the benefit of a generally-accepted authority. In this sense, the electoral process provides an essential mechanism in maintaining the continuity of the State.

(2) THE EUROPEAN CONVENTION ON HUMAN RIGHTS

The extent to which the British electoral system is "free" can be measured by comparing its provisions with those stipulations set out by Butler *et al*. An alternative test is provided by examining the extent to which the system meets the requirements of the European Convention on Human Rights. Article 3 of the First Protocol to that Convention provides: "The High Contracting Parties undertake to hold free elections at reasonable intervals by secret ballot, under conditions which will ensure the free expression of the opinion of the people in the choice of the legislature." The drafters of the Convention included this Article as an expression of their firmly-held view that the maintenance of democratic institutions and respect for individual freedoms (with which the Convention was primarily concerned) were inseparable.[2]

The United Kingdom has ratified the First Protocol, and is thus bound by the terms of Article 3. Furthermore, this country has since 1965 accepted the right of individual petition under the Convention, which means that individual citizens may, subject to the conditions set out in the Convention, institute proceedings before the European Commission of Human Rights alleging a breach by their state of Convention Articles. Article 3 of the First Protocol is unusual in that it is formulated neither as an individual right nor a freedom; rather, it requires ratifying states to take positive action. Notwithstanding this formulation, the

---

[2] T.P. Vol. V., pp. 286 *et seq.*

Commission, after some hesitation, has interpreted the Article in such a way as to permit individual petition:

> 'It follows both from the Preamble and from Article 5 of the First Protocol that the rights set out in the Protocol are protected by the same guarantees as are contained in the Convention itself. It must therefore be admitted that, whatever the wording of Article 3, the right it confers is in the nature of an individual right, since this quality consti- tutes the very foundation of the whole Convention."[3]

Following this interpretation the Commission has frequently considered individual petitions alleging a breach of Article 3 (including several from the United Kingdom), and the result- ing jurisprudence has amplified the meaning of the Article in several respects. The European Court of Human Rights, on the other hand, has not had the opportunity to consider Article 3.

The jurisprudence of the Commission may be summarised by saying that Article 3 requires ratifying states to establish electoral laws permitting individuals the right to vote and to be candidates in regular and free elections to bodies possessing a substantial portion of the legislative capacity of the State. The Convention does not imply the adoption of any particular form of electoral system. In particular, there is no obligation to institute a system of proportional representation.[4] Nor does it require that the right to vote or to be a candidate be universally afforded. It is open to a High Contracting Party to impose restrictions on the exercise of these rights, provided that the restrictions are neither arbitrary nor so substantial as to interfere with the free expression of the people's opinion.[5] The requirement of free elections, and their protection, is derived both from the wording of Article 3 of the First Protocol and from Articles 10 and 14 of the Convention itself, which guarantee freedom of speech and freedom from discrimination.

This bare summary demonstrates that the Commission has laid stress very much on the matters which Butler *et al.* iden- tify as the essential elements of a democratic election. It is with these principles in mind that we must now consider the structure of the British electoral system.

---

[3] *W, X, Y and Z v. Belgium*, Appls. 6745 and 6746/74.
[4] *X v. U.K.* Appl. 7140/75, 7 D. & R. 95; *Lindsay* v. *U.K.* Appl. 8364/78, 15 D. & R. 247.
[5] *W, X, Y and Z v. Belgium*, n. 3 above.

(3) THEORIES OF REPRESENTATION

Bogdanor has observed that "The electoral system which a country adopts depends more upon its political tradition than upon abstract considerations of electoral justice or good government." (Bogdanor and Butler (1983), p. 2). The dichotomy between tradition and "abstract considerations" may not be quite so clear-cut as is here implied; certain of the eighteenth and nineteenth century theories of representation, based upon such abstract considerations, have become part of the political tradition of this country and have been influential in determining the structure of the British electoral system. Before analysing that structure in detail, it is therefore necessary to review those theories in outline (see generally, Birch (1964) and (1971)).

At the risk of gross over-simplification, it might be said that theories of political representation seek to provide answers to two questions: what is to be represented, and how is it to be represented? It should be said that treating these questions independently of each other may lead to a distorted account of the theories under discussion, but for present purposes it is useful to keep them separate.

(a) What is to be Represented?

In Professor Birch's view, three distinct theories of representation can be identified in post-medieval English political thought. These he characterises as Tory, Whig and Radical theories. The Tory theory conceived of the Member of Parliament as a representative of his community, an analysis which perhaps involved a rather idealised view of social organisation in earlier times:

> "Each shire was a unit of the nation, bound together by its common court, its common judicial and administrative organisation. The county was an organised body of men, a *communitas*...If we turn to the towns of the Middle Ages...we find...a community of life, thought and feeling unattainable under the complex conditions of modern society."

> (Brown (1899), p. 70)

Communities, whether of shire or borough, being the units of social organisation, it was natural that they should also be the units of electoral representation: "The ancient idea of representation (was) of communities, of organised bodies of men, bodies which, whether called boroughs or counties, constantly act as wholes and have common rights and duties..." (Maitland (1963), p. 363). By the beginning of the present century, as Brown (above) clearly recognised, concepts of "community" were increasingly difficult to reconcile with the realities of modern urban life, and it may appear strange that any theory of community representation continues to be influential now. Two recent examples will demonstrate the continuing relevance of that idea to the structure of the modern electoral system. In 1977 Mr. Michael Foot (somewhat ironically, in the light of subsequent litigation later to be discussed) declared his belief

> "that constituencies have an organic unity, and I would not like to see them hacked about time after time. I do not think that is good for democracy either. If there is a little loss in mathematical accuracy in order to preserve a rather greater organic unity in the constituencies, I think that is a gain for democracy itself."[6]

This proposition enabled Mr. Foot not to accept as an inherently obvious conclusion the contention that Northern Ireland should receive additional Parliamentary seats to bring its seats/voters ratio more into accord with that prevailing elsewhere in the United Kingdom.

Mr. Enoch Powell has also demonstrated an attachment to the idea of community representation:

> "The House (of Commons) is a geographical representation of the Kingdom. We come here sent from our respective places. We do not have a mass poll of the citizenry to elect a Government or a Prime Minister: instead the electorate of the several places send one person to Parliament, to use his discretion on their behalf. That is one of the profound characteristics of the House of Commons... Indeed it is the reason why the House of Commons has its name. It is the House of the 'communities'..."[7]

This perception of the House as "in a sense, a congress of constituencies"[8] led Mr. Powell in 1985 to oppose the extension of postal voting to those resident abroad who no longer retained ordinary residence in United Kingdom constituencies.

[6] (1977–78) H.C. 70–ii, p. 25.
[7] Hansard, H.C. Deb. Vol. 69, col. 783.
[8] Hansard, H.C. Deb. Vol. 72, col. 197.

These examples illustrate the potential relevance of Tory theory to our present electoral system. That theory argues for community representation, and hence for geographically-determined representation (as Mr. Powell points out), in preference, if necessary, to strict electoral equality among voters and constituencies (Mr. Foot); and it insists upon voters being connected or related in some not insubstantial way to the constituency within which they may exercise their right to vote. As will be seen, each of these ideas has to some extent been carried through into our electoral law.

Whig representation theory, although markedly different from that of the Tories, shared with it an acceptance of geographically-defined constituencies as the appropriate unit of Parliamentary representation. But this did not imply an acceptance of a theory of representation of the community. Rather, the Member of Parliament was to represent constituency *interest* as he identified it, and his function was to promote the national interest in a deliberative process of reconciliation of constituency interests (Judge (1980)). This theory led Whigs to argue that the extent of the franchise did not greatly matter, since the principle of "virtual representation" guaranteed protection of the interests of the unenfranchised by those MPs who had (because of constituency responsibilities) concerned themselves with the interests of the trade or industry or type of farming in which such unenfranchised individuals happened to be engaged (Birch (1964), pp. 23–24, and (1971), p. 51).

In contrast to these traditional theories, Radical representation theory argued for the establishment of popular sovereignty through manhood (and, much later, adult) suffrage, an argument initially advanced upon the basis of natural rights and subsequently by reference to utilitarian ideas (Birch (1964), Chap. 3). These proposals were originally linked with demands for "equal constituencies" this being a feature both of the Levellers' claims in the seventeenth century and of the Chartists' in the nineteenth. However, after the Reform Act of 1832 (an Act not noticeably influenced by Radical ideas—see Brock (1973)) it came gradually to be accepted that M.P.s should represent *individuals* rather than interests or communities (Birch (1964), p. 52), and it was recognised that there was a certain inconsistency in maintaining a system of geographically-defined constituencies under a theory of individual representation. For this reason, some Radical opinion, led by J. S. Mill, enthusiastically embraced the proposals for a new electoral system advanced by Thomas Hare, the chief novelty of which was the abandonment of geographically-defined constituencies:

> "To get a fair representation of opinions in the House of Commons...it would be necessary to scrap the whole system of geographical representation in favour of an electoral system in which the total number of voters would be divided by the total number of seats in order to establish an electoral quota. Candidates would be able to campaign on a national basis and any candidate who got the required quota of votes would be elected...In this way, any viewpoint that was supported by the required quota of electors would acquire a spokesman in Parliament, even though these electors were so spread about the country that they composed no more than a tiny minority in any given area."
>
>   (Birch (1971), pp. 89–90. See further, Brown (1899)).

This aspect of the Radicals' case was not, of course, accepted. Indeed, so deeply has the concept of geographically-defined constituencies become entrenched in Britain that those who today argue for reform of the electoral system in the United Kingdom almost unanimously advocate the introduction of proportional representation in multi-member (geographic) constituencies, rather than the so-called "party list" systems in operation in Holland and Israel which do not necessitate the drawing of separate electoral areas. Thus we find in the present British electoral system an acceptance of Tory (and Whig) ideas on the need for geographically-defined constituencies but we also find, as a result of legislation enacted between 1832 and 1985, the incorporation into that system of Radical ideas as to the scope of the franchise. The reconciliation of these ideas has been a matter of some difficulty when the redistribution of Parliamentary seats is attempted.

(b) How is it to be Represented?

The answer to this question proposed respectively by Tories, Whigs and Radicals was intimately related to their perceptions of what was to be represented. For Tories, committed to a theory of community representation, Members of Parliament were to be responsible for representing the grievances of their communities to the King. This duty, in the Tory view, necessitated constant communication with those communities, and they accordingly advocated frequent elections to Parliament. Their political opposition to the Whigs' Septennial Act 1715, which extended the life of the House of Commons to a maximum of seven years as against the three years provided for by the Triennial Act 1694, was expressed in these terms (Birch (1964), pp. 26–27). The same process of reasoning led Radicals to favour frequent elections. M.P.s were to represent the opinions of their constituents, who could ensure that this was achieved by a regular and frequent process of election. Hence, the Chartists called for annual elections, as did Bentham and James Mill from their very different philosophical position (Birch (1964), p. 46).

The Whigs' attitude contrasted strongly with these. In Whig theory the M.P., once elected, was pre-eminently concerned with the identification and advancement of the *national* (as distinct from *individuals'* or *constituents'*) interest. As Edmund Burke put it, the chosen candidate was "not a member of Bristol, but he is a member of *Parliament*," concerned to promote the national interest in a place "where, not local purposes, not local prejudices ought to guide, but the general good resulting from the general reason of the whole." Two consequences followed from this. First (as Mr. Powell observed in the passage previously quoted), the M.P.'s duty was and is to exercise discretionary power on behalf of constituents, rather than under their dictate. Secondly, if M.P.s were to be concerned primarily with the national interest, they should not be subjected to frequent elections, for fear that they become improperly subservient to, or controlled by, their constituents' opinions (which, of course, was what the Radicals advocated).

How far is this idea reflected in the *incidence* of elections under our electoral system? So far as elections to the House of Commons are concerned, the Whigs resisted the Tory attempt to restore the Triennial Act, and it was ultimately a Liberal government that amended the Septennial Act. The maximum duration of a Parliament is now only five years, a period set by the Parliament Act 1911. The explanation for this change lies less in any acceptance of an alternative theory of representation than in the need (perceived for political reasons) to provide a counterweight to the main provisions of the 1911 Act, which strengthened the position of the House of Commons *vis-à-vis* the House of Lords in the legislative process. To this extent the consequences of the original Whig theory have been modified rather than the theory itself rejected. Indeed, the M.P.'s independence required by that theory has been retained. Proposals for a further reduction, to four years, in the maximum duration of a Parliament seem to be based less on explicit acceptance of an alternative theory of representation than on a somewhat cynical (and, it is submitted, naive) belief that such a reduction would give a Prime Minister "much less scope than now for electioneering manoeuvres" (Hood Phillips (1970), p. 54).

If the frequency of elections to Parliament remains partly justified by Whig representation theory, the incidence of local government elections is confused by the fact that there is no agreement as to which theory of representation is appropriate in this context. Reviewing the position in 1969, the Royal Commission on Local Government in England was undecided whether its proposed main councils should be elected quadrennially or triennially (with, in the latter case, the option of yearly elections "by thirds"—see Byrne (1985), p. 100). The former would allow an authority a "better chance to work out and put into effect a coherent policy for its area" (free, by implication, of short-term electoral pressures); the latter might be preferred as offering electors a better opportunity "of passing judgment on the authorities responsible for local government services."[9] This conflict between different theories of representation was resolved by the Local Government Act 1972, which provided that county councils should be elected *in toto* every four years; that metropolitan districts should be elected "by thirds," providing for an election of one-third of the council each year (other than a county council election year); and that non-metropolitan districts should have the choice of "whole council" elections or election by thirds. Most such authorities have opted for "whole council" elections. The Committee on the Conduct of Local Authority Business has recently recommended that a uniform system of quadrennial elections be instituted for all authorities.[10]

So far as by-elections are concerned, the demise of the theory of "virtual representation" after 1832 means that all areas are now entitled to continuous representation on their own account, and elections to fill vacancies must not be unduly delayed. The timing of parliamentary by-elections is now governed by an inter-party understanding that seats will not be left vacant for longer than three months, or four months in

---

[9] Cmnd. 4040, paras. 472–473.
[10] Cmnd. 9797, para. 7.30.

special circumstances.[11] Within that period of time it is for the party whose candidate previously held the seat to decide when to move the writ for the by-election. (For the particular problems arising out of the wholesale resignations of Northern Irish Unionist M.P.s in 1985, see Boulton (1986).) The Recess Elections Act 1975 provides a procedure for the Speaker, under specified conditions, to issue a writ for election to a vacant seat where this arises during a Parliamentary recess. So far as local government elections are concerned, a local election has to be held within 35 days of the event giving rise to the election, but the formal notice of election need only be issued 25 days before the date of election.[12] By-elections for vacant seats in the European Parliament must be held within six months of the vacancy occurring.[13]

In summary, we may say that the present electoral system reflects Tory ideas in the existence of geographically-defined constituencies, which sit uneasily with Radical ideas as to the representation of individuals' opinions rather than community grievances; it reflects Radical ideas as to the scope of the franchise; and (more hesitantly) it reflects Whiggish ideas as to the incidence of parliamentary elections, if not local government elections. In the following chapters we will examine aspects of this structure in more detail.

---

[11] See Cmnd. 5500, Speaker's Conference on Electoral Law.

[12] Local Government Act 1972, s.89, as amended by Representation of the People Act 1985, s.19(6)(c); Local Elections (Principal Areas) Rules (S.I. 1986 No. 2214).

[13] European Assembly Elections Act 1978, Sched. 1, para. 3.

Part One
THE SPATIAL CONTEXT OF ELECTIONS

1. PROBLEMS OF DELINEATION OF ELECTORAL AREAS

(1) INTRODUCTION

A commitment to election from geographically-determined units is one of the fundamental features of the British electoral system. The proper delineation of the territories to be represented is therefore an important factor in maintaining the fair working of the electoral system. What is a "proper" delineation will be determined to a considerable degree by its compatibility with the ideas underlying our commitment to representative government based upon adult suffrage. As the Vivian Committee wrote in 1942:

> "The essential basis of representative Government in this country is that the main representative body of the legislature should consist of persons elected under conditions which confer upon them an *equal representative status*. It is also a fundamental principle of our Parliamentary system that representation should be... *territorial*. Both these features appear to us to be of the greatest importance. It follows from them that seats must be assigned to a series of local areas or communities each of which contains as equal as may be a share of the total number of persons to be represented."[1] (emphasis in original)

But what if communities *cannot* be assigned in such a way as to produce broad electorate equality between constituencies? Should we disregard area boundaries and community ties in the delineation of electoral areas in order to achieve that broad equality, or should we, at the expense of partially sacrificing some hypothesised "one vote one value" principle, respect those ties and boundaries and accept some inequality in electorate numbers between constituencies (a situation known to political scientists as "malapportionment")? In attempting to reconcile the Radical demand for adult suffrage in equal electoral areas with more traditional conceptions of territorial representation, the British electoral system contains within itself

[1] Cmd. 6408, para. 64.

15

a tension and instability which is most obviously manifested on the occasions of the redistribution of parliamentary seats.

For the problem of delineation arises primarily as a problem of *redistribution*. Internal population movements within the country necessitate a regular redistribution of Parliamentary seats to maintain some measure of electoral equality. The same movements may, over a longer time span, necessitate local government boundary changes in the interests of efficient administration, and consequential amendments may need to be made in local electoral arrangements. Any such alteration is likely to have political repercussions. The principal population movements in Britain have been outward from the larger towns and cities to suburban areas and now to rural areas (see Hall (1987), "Britain is returning to the green fields and to the coast"). The Labour Party, which retains its greatest support in the big towns and cities, will benefit disproportionately from *infrequent* and *limited* redistributions which only partially reflect those population movements. This "political repercussions" aspect of re-delineation of electoral areas brings into focus the question, who is to propose or effect redistribution, and are they to be politically-motivated or subject to political influence?

(2) AGENCIES OF REDISTRIBUTION

Gudgin and Taylor (1979), p. 122 identify three possible types of decision-making agency which might be used to delineate electoral boundaries. In *partisan* decision-making, a feature of the American electoral system, the power to redistribute lies within the hands of the party in government, which can draw constituency boundaries in such a way as to optimise its own electoral chances. This is the process known as "gerrymandering." A gerrymandered redistribution may, but need not, depend upon malapportionment of the electorate in order to produce the desired result (see, for example, Busteed (1985), p. 16). The United States Supreme Court has been active in striking down as unconstitutional redistributions based upon malapportionment,[2] and has in an important recent decision opened up the possibility of review of gerrymanders even if the disputed electoral districts meet the "one person one vote" test.[3] Problems of proving such a gerrymander will, however,

[2] *Baker* v. *Carr* 369 U.S. 186 (1962); *Wesberry* v. *Saunders* 376 U.S. 1 (1964); *Reynolds* v. *Sims* 377 U.S. 533 (1964) provide the starting points.
[3] *Davis* v. *Bandemer* 106 S.Ct. 2797 (1986).

be considerable where malapportionment does not obviously appear.

Bi-partisan redistribution operates by a process of negotiation between the parties. As Gudgin and Taylor point out, a danger of this approach to redistribution is that the interests of voters are liable to be excluded from consideration (Gudgin and Taylor (1979), p. 131). Equally, of course, the interests of minority parties are likely to be sacrificed in a big party redistribution "carve-up"; this is a particularly important factor to bear in mind in Britain, where it is arguable that the national two-party system is under threat and in any event there are significant regional parties with legitimate interests to be taken into account.

In these circumstances, recourse may be had to the third alternative, delineation by a *non-partisan* agency, usually operating under pre-determined redistribution rules. The extent to which that agency will be free of direct political influence may be a matter of dispute. The redistribution rules, for example, may have to be the subject of negotiation between the political parties, although they will in all probability exclude any overtly political considerations. Alternatively, leading parties may be permitted to nominate representatives to membership of the agency, although overt party participation may serve to undermine the perceived neutrality of the agency which can give its recommendations considerable weight.

Before 1885, decisions as to parliamentary constituency redistribution were made on a partisan basis. The occasions for redistribution arose in 1832 and 1867. As Le May says, "one of the prizes for carrying a reform Bill (on suffrage) was that the successful Ministers had in their own hands the consequent reshaping of constituencies" (Le May (1979), p. 140). The redistribution of 1884 marked an important change in this pattern. The predominantly Tory House of Lords refused to pass Gladstone's suffrage Bill (equating the borough and county fran-chises) without a redistribution first being agreed between the parties. The ensuing Redistribution of Seats Act 1885 was the product of extended discussions between senior Liberals and Conservatives, and this bi-partisan plan for redistribution was presented to the House of Commons as virtually incapable of amendment by backbenchers of either party. Two features of the plan merit attention. First, it was agreed that greater attention should be paid to assigning seats according to population, and the county seats, in particular, were redrawn with this in mind (Seymour (1915), p. 513). This was, however, achieved without crossing important local government boundaries (Butler (1963), p. 214), and in so far that those boundaries represented traditional community divisions, regard continued to be had to ideals of community representation. On the other hand, the second feature was quite incompatible with the traditional conception of community representation. Since 1265, with few exceptions, electoral areas had been represented by two M.P.s. The 1885 plan provided predominantly for single-member constituencies:

> "Almost every electoral district was now an artificial one, formed by boundary commissioners whose object was to create constituencies of roughly comparable size. For the first time it could clearly be seen that parliamentary constituencies were merely artificial creations formed to give a basis of legitimacy to the politicians at Westminster rather than local communities."

> (Hanham (1971), p. 26)

The 1918 redistribution followed the bi-partisan approach of 1885. Terms of reference for Boundary Commissioners were agreed by party leaders meeting together as a Speaker's Conference on Electoral Law, and these were subsequently approved, with minor modifications, by the House of Commons (Pugh (1978), pp. 77–78, 108–109). The redistribution was achieved with minimal disagreement (Pugh (1978), p. 126). The uncontroversial nature of the 1918 redistribution significantly influenced the Vivian Committee when in 1942 it produced its Report on Electoral Machinery.[4]

(3) THE BOUNDARY COMMISSIONS

(a) The Parliamentary Commissions

The establishment of permanent Boundary Commissions to delineate Parliamentary constituencies was recommended by the Vivian Committee in 1942 and enacted in 1944 in the House of Commons (Redistribution of Seats) Act. The Committee had been primarily concerned to argue the case for *permanent* Commissions; the case for a non-partisan agency operating under politically-agreed rules had been won by the success of the 1918 redistribution. However, the fact that the 1918 redistribution had involved the cumbersome machinery of a

[4] Cmd. 6408.

Speaker's Conference, and that no boundary changes had been effected since 1918, was a source of concern. Furthermore, although redistribution in 1832, 1867, 1885 and 1918 had in each case accompanied franchise reform, it was not inevitably the case that the two should go hand in hand:

> "Redistribution might conceivably follow a drastic revision of the Parliamentary franchise which disturbed the balance of constituencies, or a recasting of the whole constituency system itself. But there can be no such justification for a converse rule that a revision of electoral law in general should invariably attend a redistribution."

(para. 94)

Redistribution should therefore proceed on a regular basis independent of franchise reform.

Nor were the occasions for redistribution to be left to the initiative of Parliament. Rather, the Committee recommended that a review of constituencies (and any necessary redistribution) be conducted during the normal life of every Parliament, under specific statutory powers (para. 98). The reviews should be conducted by four Boundary Commissions, having responsibility for each part of the United Kingdom. The Commissions would have a common Chairman, the Speaker of the House of Commons, who would provide a "contact with the legislature and authoritative experience of the Parliamentary system" (para. 101). This method of political input was to be preferred to including party nominees within the membership of the Commissions, for fear that the nominees might be unable to divest themselves of their party allegiances sufficiently to act impartially (para. 102).

The 1944 Act followed the Vivian Committee Report in all important respects, and the present-day Commissions are constituted largely as envisaged by the Committee.[5] Each Commission has the Speaker as its Chairman, although in practice the holder of that office never participates in the deliberations of the Commissions.[6] This means that the Commissions lack that direct input from the political world which the Vivian Committee considered important, a fact which has led some to argue that senior political figures, such as Privy Councillors, might be permitted a fuller participation in the

[5] See now, the Parliamentary Constituencies Act 1986, ss.2–3 and Sched. 1.
[6] (1986–87) H.C. 97–I, p. iv.

Commissions' work, perhaps to replace the Speaker as Chairman.[7] The need is to achieve the right level of political consciousness within the Commissions as to the implications of their proposals without endangering their non-partisan status. At present, it may be thought that the "completely and utterly apolitical"[8] Commissions do not meet that standard. The Speaker does not serve and the remaining members of the Commissions, who are High Court judges or appointees of the Home Secretary and Secretary of State for the Environment (or their Scottish, Welsh or Northern Irish equivalents) are not expected necessarily to have had political experience. Appointments to the Commissions are, however, made after consultations with the political parties,[9] and at least one Commissioner has apparently not been reappointed on the ground of his political unacceptability to one or more parties.[10]

Under the 1944 Act, the Commissions were required to conduct periodical reviews of Parliamentary constituencies, and to submit reports on any proposed redistribution "not less than three or more than seven years from the date of the submission of their last report" (section 4(2)(*b*)). As Butler has pointed out (Butler (1955), p. 128), this statutory latitude was intended to enable the Commissions to meet the Vivian Committee's recommendation for a boundary revision once in the life of each four- or five-year Parliament. Experience of the Commissions' early work soon led to the view that extensive redistributions should not be undertaken so frequently (Butler (1955), pp. 143–145) and in 1958 the 1944 Act was amended so that future Commission reports were to be presented not less than 10 or more than 15 years from the date of last submission.[11] The implications of this may be considerable. Frequent redistributions are unsettling on local political organisations and may occasion annoyance among voters; nevertheless, the longer the period between reviews, the greater the likelihood of significantly unequal constituencies developing. Quite apart from the electoral unfairness which will be produced, it must also be recognised that an extended period between redistributions may have a differential political impact; as was previously mentioned, the predominant population movement in Britain is away from the larger towns and cities, where the Labour Party

---

[7] (1986–87) H.C. 97–I, p. 65.
[8] *Ibid.*
[9] (1986–87) H.C. 97–I, p. 93.
[10] *Ibid.* p. 97.
[11] See now, the Parliamentary Constituencies Act 1986, s.3(2).

has its greatest strength. The longer the period between reviews and redistributions, the greater will Labour benefit and the greater will be the loss to those parties who poll well in suburban and rural areas (Bromhead (1986)).

This problem might be met by the more frequent use of the power to conduct interim reviews. By virtue of section 3(3) of the Parliamentary Constituencies Act 1986 (which substantially re-enacts provisions first introduced in section 4(3) of the 1944 Act), a Boundary Commission may "from time to time submit to the Secretary of State reports with respect to the area comprised in any particular constituency or constituencies...". This power has been used primarily to align Parliamentary constituency boundaries with changed local government boundaries,[12] but there would be no legal objection to a more wide-ranging review. Quite apart from the problem of defining the appropriate area for review, however, the Commissions might become vulnerable to political attack if it came to be believed that the results of interim reviews were redistributions carrying a differential political impact, and so it may be that caution in the use of the interim review power is justified.

The Commissions' statutory duty on review is to submit reports to their relevant Secretaries of State showing the constituencies into which they recommend that each part of the United Kingdom should be divided, in accordance with the redistribution rules now to be found in Schedule 2 to the 1986 Act. Additionally the Commissions are required to recommend names for the constituencies so delineated, and to state "whether they recommend that it should be a county constituency or a borough constituency."[13] This last duty is important. As will be seen in our discussion of election campaigning, the maximum election expenditure permitted by law is rather higher for a "county constituency" than for a "borough constituency." There is, however, no definition of these terms in electoral law, and the classification is left to the Commissions' discretion. The Commissions for England and Scotland have adopted a practice, where a proposed constituency "contains more than a token rural element," of recommending that it be designated a county constituency[14]. This means that small boroughs are included in county constituencies. There may be good reasons for maintaining the county/borough classification of constituencies for election expense

---

[12] (1986–87) H.C. 97–I, p. 24.
[13] 1986 Act, s. 3(4).
[14] (1986–87) H.C. 97–I, pp. 43, 81.

purposes, but it is unsatisfactory that no proper statutory criteria are available to guide the Commissions in their recommendations on this.

(b) The Local Government Commissions

Permanent arrangements for amending local government boundaries following population movements were not established until 1972.[15] The Local Government Boundary Commissions for England and Wales established by the Local Government Act 1972 are concerned with the review of boundaries "in the interests of effective and convenient local government."[16] Parallel provision is made for Scotland by section 13 of the Local Government (Scotland) Act 1973. The Commissions are further entrusted with the review of the "electoral arrangements" of principal local government authorities, these including not only "the number and boundaries of the electoral areas" into which a given authority's area is to be divided, but also the number of councillors who will constitute the council and the number of councillors to be elected from each electoral area, which is to be named.[17] The two functions of the Commissions are obviously related, in that the drawing of new boundaries "in the interests of effective and convenient local government" will frequently have implications for an authority's "electoral arrangements," but in any event the Commissions are required to conduct reviews of electoral arrangements at 10- to 15-yearly intervals.[18]

So far as the boundary delineation aspects of "electoral arrangements" are concerned, the Commissions are required to divide the counties (regions in Scotland) into "electoral divisions" and the districts (both metropolitan and non-metropolitan) and London boroughs into "wards."[19] The principles of delineation are to be found in Schedules to the 1972 and 1973 Acts. Responsibility for the division of the smallest units of local government, parishes or communities, lies principally with the district councils of which the parishes or communities form a part. Again the principles of delineation are to be found in enacted Schedules.

The position in Northern Ireland is different in several important respects. By virtue of the Local Government (North-

---

[15] For arrangements before that date, see Cmnd. 4040, Research Appendix I, "Local Government Boundaries since 1888."

[16] Local Government Act 1972, s.47(1), s.54(1).

[17] 1972 Act, s.78; 1973 Act, s.28.

[18] 1972 Act, ss.50(2), 57(2); 1973 Act, s.16(2).

[19] 1972 Act, s.6; 1973 Act, s.5.

ern Ireland) Act 1972, a Local Government Boundaries Commissioner is to be appointed in 1981 and in each tenth year thereafter to review the number, boundaries and names of the districts and the number, boundaries and names of the wards into which each district is divided (section 50). The principles of redelineation are set out in Schedule 4 to the Act. These differ in some minor respects from those applicable on the mainland. More important for present purposes, however, is that district council elections in Northern Ireland have since 1972 been conducted on the basis of proportional representation.[20] This necessitates the grouping of wards to create an electoral area from which several candidates may be elected. This function is performed by a District Electoral Areas Commissioner acting under statutory powers[21] and within guidelines which lay down how wards are to be grouped. Thus, in this procedure the Boundaries Commissioner divides the districts into wards, and the District Electoral Areas Commissioner groups those wards into two or more electoral areas from each of which several candidates are elected. The process of grouping will inevitably be controversial, particularly in Northern Ireland where political divisions run so deep as to preclude the easy identification of community interests across ward boundaries.[22]

---

[20] Seè Local Elections (Northern Ireland) Order 1985, (S.I. 1985 No. 454).

[21] District Electoral Areas Commissioner (Northern Ireland) Order 1984, (S.I. 1984 No. 360).

[22] See the debate on the groupings proposed for the Northern Irish local elections of 1985: Hansard H.C. Deb. Vol. 71, cols. 815–834 (January 21, 1985).

2. REDISTRIBUTION: RULES AND PROCESSES

In this chapter we examine the rules and processes of constituency delineation and redistribution in respect of local government, parliamentary and European Assembly elections. Although we shall concentrate on the parliamentary aspect, it is convenient to begin with the delineation of local government electoral areas.

(1) LOCAL GOVERNMENT

As we have mentioned, the Local Government Boundary Commissions for each part of Great Britain have the dual responsibility of defining, "in the interests of effective and convenient local government," the boundaries of the principal authorities created by the 1972 and 1973 legislation, and of settling the electoral arrangements which are to operate within those authorities. The English Commission has indicated that the primary considerations it will have in mind in determining what effective and convenient local government requires in particular instances are the wishes of local inhabitants, the patterns of community life, and the effective operation of local government and associated services.[1]

Within the areas thus defined, the Commissions' duty, as interpreted by the House of Lords in *London Borough of Enfield* v. *Local Government Boundary Commission for England*,[2] is to determine the appropriate number of councillors required for effective and convenient local government. The English Commission, but neither the Scottish nor the Welsh, has established guideline "bands" in respect of each category of authority to assist in determining councillor numbers; thus, London boroughs ought to have 50–70 members, whereas shire counties might have 60–100.[3] The determination of council size raises difficult problems, since the Commission must balance considerations of efficiency (which argue for smaller numbers of

---

[1] The Local Government Boundary Commission for England's Programme 1978–83, DoE Circular 33/78—and see Annex B to the Circular for a fuller exposition of what these considerations entail.

[2] [1979] 3 All E.R. 747, H.L.

[3] For details, see Cmnd. 9797, para. 7.33.

councillors) with the needs of a representative democratic system of local government, which requires that electoral units within a given local authority's area be not unduly large if an individual citizen's choices are to be given any significant weight.

Once the number of councillors for an authority has been broadly determined, the Commissions are required to divide the authority's area into electoral units. A complicating feature in this process is that for some authorities multi-member constituencies are mandatory, for others they are optional and for yet others they are forbidden. For county councils there is no difficulty. Each electoral division must return one member, and the number of electoral divisions will equal the number of councillors deemed necessary for effective and convenient local government. Metropolitan districts, on the other hand, are divided into wards returning a number of members divisible by three. The practice invariably is to have three-member wards rather than the six- or nine-member wards which would be legally permissible. Shire districts and London boroughs are divided into wards which may, but need not be, multi-member. The maximum number of members elected from a London borough ward is three, but there is no such limit for the shire districts and a small number of wards for these councils return four or more members. The explanation for these variations owes more to history than to logic or to the requirements of local democracy, and the Widdicombe Committee has recommended that a uniform system be introduced to provide for one councillor for every electoral ward or division in England and Wales.[4] Scotland has enjoyed such a system since 1975. In Northern Ireland wards are grouped to return between five and seven members elected by way of proportional representation.

The relevance of "numbers to be elected" to the drawing of ward boundaries lies in the fact that Schedule 11 of the 1972 Act (and, for Scotland, Schedule 6 of the 1973 Act) incorporates a requirement of electoral equality for counties, districts and London boroughs respectively. This requirement takes priority over the establishment of easily identifiable boundaries or the maintenance of local ties.[5] Thus, in multi-member wards "the ratio of the number of local government electors to the number of councillors to be elected shall be, as nearly as may be, the

---

[4] *Ibid.* para. 7.30.
[5] See the *Enfield* case, n. 2 above. Local Government Act 1972, Sched. 11, paras. 3(2), (3).

same in every ward of the district or borough"[6] and in the single-member electoral divisions for county councils "the number of local government electors shall be, as nearly as may be, the same in every electoral division of the county."[7] It is to be noted that the achievement of broad electoral equality is to be attained "having regard to any change in the number or distribution of the local government electors of the (district or borough or county) likely to take place within the period of five years immediately following the consideration" of the authority's electoral arrangements.[8] This enables the Commissions to adopt a rather more forward-looking approach to electoral area delineation than is the case with the parliamentary Commissions, whose empowering statute has no equivalent provision. The implications of this will be considered in due course.

In drawing district and county electoral divisions in England and Wales and electoral divisions of regions and districts in Scotland, the Boundary Commissions are required not to divide smaller local government units. Thus in England, parish wards must lie entirely within district wards, and unwarded parishes must lie entirely within district wards. In the same way, county electoral divisions must lie entirely within a single district, and in constructing such divisions regard must be had to the boundaries of the wards of the districts in the county. The observance of these rules of respect for the boundaries of smaller local government units is, under the statute, of equal importance to that of securing broad electoral equality. To this extent the preference afforded to broad electoral equality over the establishment of easily identifiable boundaries and the maintenance of local ties[9] is mitigated, since these latter factors are directly relevant to the drawing of the boundaries of small local government units, which boundaries are to be respected.[10]

---

[6] Local Government Act 1972, Sched. 11, para. 3(2)(*a*).

[7] *Ibid*. para. 1(2)(*a*); for Scotland, where single-member electoral divisions are the rule, see Local Government (Scotland) Act 1973, Sched. 6, para. 1(2)(*a*), and para. 2, which permits departure from the requirements of para. 1(2)(*a*) "where special geographical considerations appear to render a departure desirable." There is no equivalent provision for Wales, to which the full rigour of para. 1(2)(*a*) presumably still applies.

[8] 1972 Act, Sched. 11, para. 1(2); 1973 Act, Sched. 6, para. 1(2). For an account of the problems which this requirement imposes, see the English Commission's Report 413 (May 1981), especially at para. 19.

[9] n. 5, above.

[10] See generally, Sched. 11.

Thus far we have spoken of the process of delineation as a problem for the Commissions, and this in law is the case. However, there is a significant additional element to incorporate into the account. The practice has developed of inviting local authorities to prepare draft schemes of delineation for submission to the relevant Commission. The Commission is not bound by any aspect of the submission, but it seems likely that such draft proposals may go far to structure the debate as to what new electoral arrangements in a given area may be desirable. The problem with this is that proposals may be advanced that reflect the perceived interests of the majority party in a council, rather than of the council as a whole. A former Home Secretary has recently observed that "The LGBC should ensure that the recommendations for new ward boundaries provided by local authorities are carefully vetted. Narrow political input is well-known to emanate from this source."[11] It is not clear how far the over-stretched and under-resourced Commissions are able to undertake this vetting, although the *Enfield* case provides one example of a majority party's proposals, presented in the name of the Council, being rejected by the Commission in favour of minority parties' alternative suggestions.[12] The problem is exacerbated by the fact that district councils have primary responsibility for determining parish boundaries and parish wards.[13] As we have seen, these boundaries must be taken into account in constructing district ward boundaries, and again the possibility arises of proposals being advanced other than purely "in the interests of effective and convenient local government." Thus, partisan delineation may be a significant problem under the present legislation: " . . . one recognises that local authorities draw the local wards, and they will tend to reflect the interests of the authorities concerned—and that has been an open secret for a long time . . .".[14]

The procedure envisaged by the legislation[15] is that the Commissions are required to take such steps as they think fit to bring to the attention of interested parties the fact that a boundary review is to take place in a given area. In particular the Commissions are required to consult councils affected by the review, and it is in this context that the possibility of partisan proposals may arise. Draft proposals must be made available for

---

[11] Mr. Merlyn Rees, in (1986–87) H.C. 97–I, p. 56.
[12] [1979] 3 All E.R. 747, H.L.
[13] 1972 Act, s.48(8).
[14] Mr. G. Bermingham, M.P., (1986–87) H.C. 97–I, p. 67, para. 198.
[15] 1972 Act, s.48(8).

inspection at council offices, and interested persons must be informed of their content. Where a Commission indicates an intention to modify any proposals recommended by a district council, such modifications must again be made available for inspection and attention drawn to their content[16]—a noteworthy provision, which underlines the importance to be attributed to district council proposals by providing a specific procedure to be followed where those proposals (but not those of any other parties) are to be modified. Individual Commissioners or Assistant Commissioners may be appointed to hold local inquiries or carry out consultations or investigations in the area.[17]

At the conclusion of the procedure, a report and proposals, the contents of which must be made available locally, are submitted to the Secretary of State. The Secretary of State may, if he thinks fit, give effect by order to any proposals made by the Commission, but if he chooses to modify those proposals, no order may be made until after the expiry of six weeks from the day on which the proposals were submitted to him. Such modifications will be very rarely made, since frequent use of the power to modify will attract allegations of partisan misuse of power (although, as previously mentioned, a partisan element will not infrequently already have been incorporated into the proposals presented to the Secretary of State). Where county district or London borough boundaries are affected by the terms of the Secretary of State's order, or where any of these are proposed to be abolished, the order is subject to Parliamentary approval by way of the negative resolution procedure.[18]

(2) PARLIAMENTARY CONSTITUENCIES: THE RULES

The rules determining the redistribution of parliamentary seats are now to be found in Schedule 2 to the Parliamentary Constituencies Act 1986. They have been amended in a number of important respects since first enacted in the Third Schedule to the House of Commons (Redistribution of Seats) Act 1944. That Act broadly followed the recommendations of the Speaker's Conference on Electoral Reform and Redistribution of Seats,[19] and as such reflected substantial consensus among the political

---

[16] 1972 Act, s.60(4). The 1973 Act has no equivalent for Scotland.
[17] 1972 Act, s.65, 1973 Act, s.19.
[18] 1972 Act, s.51, 1973 Act, s.17.
[19] Cmd. 6534 (1942).

parties. Subsequent amendments have not always been the subject of such general agreement, and the litigation initiated in 1983 by Mr. Foot as Leader of the Labour Party[20] evidenced considerable unhappiness at the interpretation given to the amended rules by the Boundary Commission for England.

(a) The Electoral Quota

The concept of the electoral quota is crucial in assessing the operation of the rules. In general terms the quota provides a "target figure" for numbers of electors in each consitituency which Commissions should aim for in drawing up new constituency boundaries. According to rule 8:

(a) the expression "electoral quota" means a number obtained by dividing the electorate for that part of the United Kingdom by the number of constituencies in it existing on the enumeration date,

(b) the expression "electorate" means
(i) in relation to a constituency, the number of persons whose names appear on the register of parliamentary electors in force on the enumeration date under the Representation of the People Acts for the constituency,
(ii) in relation to the part of the United Kingdom, the aggregate electorate as defined in subpara. (i) above of all the constituencies in that part,

(c) the expression "enumeration date" means, in relation to any report of a Boundary Commission under this Act, the date on which the notice with respect to that report is published in accordance with section 5(1) of this Act.

Two matters should be noted here. First, the definition of "enumeration date" (the date at which the total number of electors is computed, by reference to the number of entries in the register of electors) ensures that the final decisions of the Boundary Commissions will already be out of date. The number of electors is assessed on the date, under section 5(1) of the 1986 Act, that a Commission gives notice of intention to undertake a review. Commissions are not permitted to take into account changes in the numbers of electors which may occur during the progress of a review, nor do they have the power, as the Local Government Boundary Commission does, to have regard to likely electorate changes in ensuring years.

[20] *R.* v. *Boundary Commission for England, ex p. Foot* [1983] 1 Q.B. 600.

The result of this can be seen particularly clearly in the Third General Review of English constituencies; for various reasons this took seven years to complete (Barnes (1985)), so that the redistribution effected in 1983 consequent upon that review was based on electorate numbers from 1976. During that period the electorate grew by nearly one-and-a-half million. The earliest date at which the English Boundary Commission will be entitled to submit fresh proposals for redistribution will be 1993 (a period of 10 years from 1983). Thus, due both to the definition of "enumeration date" and to the extended interval between reviews introduced by the House of Commons (Redistribution of Seats) Act 1958 (see above), at least three General Elections in England will be fought on the basis of 1976 electorate figures. In Scotland and Wales, on the other hand, because their Commissions commenced their reviews (and therefore took their enumeration dates) in 1978 and 1981 respectively, so as to co-ordinate submission of their Final Reports with that of the English Commission, the degree of obsolescence of their electorate figures is obviously smaller. Be that as it may, the overall failure of the electoral system to keep up to date with population movements provides the Labour Party with a disproportionate political benefit, as the system fails to respond to the consistent movement of voters away from the big towns and cities where Labour polls most strongly. It is true, however, that the English Commission in 1976–1983 attempted to give constituencies where there were strong indications of likely growth (due to the development of New Towns, for instance) the smallest electorates in the area, thereby giving room for growth towards the electoral quota. In the *Foot* case, Webster J. considered that this practice was permissible as within the Commission's judgmental discretion.[21]

The second point to note with respect to rule 8 is this. The rule requires the calculation of four different electoral quotas, one for each part of the United Kingdom. Thus the calculation of the electoral quota for Wales will be achieved by dividing the electorate registered within Wales on the enumeration date by the number of Welsh constituencies existing on the enumeration date. The 1944 Act, following the Speaker's Conference recommendation, envisaged the calculation of a British electoral quota (and a separate Northern Irish quota) by dividing the British electorate as a whole by the total number of constituencies in Britain. The 1958 Act amended this by introducing the provision

---

[21] See n. 20, above—Divisional Court judgment, January 5, 1983 (unreported).

now to be found in rule 8. The reason for this will be discussed below.

(b) Seat Numbers: A Celtic Preference?

We now consider the content of the rules. Rule 1 prescribes the number of seats to be awarded to each of the four parts of the United Kingdom and rules 4 to 6 offer guidance as to how constituency boundaries are to be drawn. Rule 7 permits a departure from the requirements of rules 4 to 6 in certain specified instances.

Rule 1 provides:

1. (1) The number of constituencies in Great Britain shall not be substantially greater or less than 613.
   (2) The number of constituencies in Scotland shall not be less than 71.
   (3) The number of constituencies in Wales shall not be less than 35.
   (4) The number of constituencies in Northern Ireland shall not be greater than 18 or less than 16, and shall be 17 unless it appears to the Boundary Commission for Northern Ireland that Northern Ireland should for the time being be divided into 16 or (as the case may be) into 18 constituencies.

Thus, for Scotland and Wales the rule provides for a minimum number of seats, but no maximum; for Northern Ireland a target number with a specified degree of tolerance above or below that number; and for England, by reading rule 1(1) together with rules 1(2) and 1(3), a target figure of 507 seats (613–(71 + 35)) which must not be substantially exceeded or undershot. The target figure for England would, however, in theory be reduced if Scotland or Wales received seats above their minima, as these would count against the target figure for Great Britain of 613. The present figures for the United Kingdom, following the 1983 redistribution are: for England 523; for Scotland 72; for Wales 38; and for Northern Ireland 17.

Rule 1 presents very considerable problems. The provisions for Scotland and Wales incorporate what might be termed a "Celtic preference," in that each country is guaranteed a minimum number of seats regardless of numbers of qualified electorate. Were Scotland, Wales and Northern Ireland to be treated together with England on a uniform United Kingdom basis, the result would be, on 1985 figures, that the number of

Scottish seats would be reduced by 12, the number of Welsh seats by 6, Northern Ireland would lose 1, and England would gain 19.[22] Scotland, which enjoys the greatest over-representation, has an average constituency electorate some 20 per cent. smaller than that which obtains in England.[23]

The reasons for the existence of this Celtic preference are unclear. The Speaker's Conference of 1944 recommended its retention, and we may assume that the protection of Scottish and Welsh interests was included as part of political bargaining, only the results of which were ever reported. Nevertheless, some protection of English interests was incorporated into the proposals in an indirect way. The Conference recommended, and the 1944 Act included, a provision whereby the electoral quota was to be calculated on an all-Britain basis, dividing the British electorate by the number of constituencies in Britain.[24] The quota thus obtained would then be divided into each country's population, determining the number of seats to which it was entitled. Nevertheless, in both the 1947 and 1954 reviews the English Boundary Commission chose to calculate the quota by dividing the existing number of English constituencies into the total *English* electorate. The effect of this in 1954, given the disproportionate concentration of the British population into England, was to provide England with the same number of seats (506), with new and higher electoral quotas for each constituency. Had the proper procedure been followed, an all-British electoral quota would have been calculated that would have given England 519 seats. Thus, the proper procedure would have gone some way to ameliorating the Celtic preference incorporated into rule 1, by awarding to England an increasing number of seats *vis-à-vis* Wales and Scotland. This increase would have been justified by reason of the fact that England's population was growing faster than that of Scotland or Wales, due in part to migration from those countries into England.

This was the background to *Harper* v. *Home Secretary*.[25] The plaintiff sought declarations that the report of the English Boundary Commission did not comply with the redistribution rules, and that it was accordingly not a "report under the Act." He further sought a declaration that the Home Secretary was not

[22] (1986–87) H.C. 97–I, p. 10.
[23] (1986–7) H.C. 97–I, p. 17 (Home Office memorandum to the House of Commons Select Committee on Home Affairs) Annex B.
[24] House of Commons (Redistribution of Seats) Act 1944, Third Sched., r. 8(1)(*a*)(i).
[25] [1955] Ch. 238.

bound to submit to Her Majesty in Council any draft Order implementing the report's recommendations, and claimed interim injunctions restraining the Home Secretary from making such a submission until after a specified date. An interim injunction was obtained at first instance, but on appeal it was held that the court had no jurisdiction to issue injunctions in cases of this kind. Questions as to whether the Commission had followed the correct procedure, it was held, were matters for Parliament rather than for the courts. We return to this aspect of the case below. The Court of Appeal further held that it was in any event unable to detect any error in the Commission's approach. This, with respect, is incorrect, since the Commission clearly misinterpreted and misapplied the rules in the 1944 Act—although whether that would have entitled the court to hold that the Commission's report was not "a report under the Act" is perhaps more doubtful. Be that as it may, the report stood, England was awarded 506 seats rather than the 519 to which it should have been entitled under the terms of the 1944 Act, and the Celtic preference established by rule 1 was thereby further emphasised.

Notwithstanding the Court of Appeal's decision, it appears to have been found necessary to regularise the practice adopted by the English Commission by amending the 1944 Act. As has already been mentioned, the 1958 Act, by section 3, therefore introduced the method of calculation of four different electoral quotas, one for each part of the United Kingdom. This is the present system. The result may be disproportionately to disadvantage the Conservative Party. The Celtic preference encapsulated in rule 1 probably favours Labour (which polls well in Scotland and Wales), and the smaller number of English seats following the change in method of calculating the electoral quota harms the Conservatives.

As we have pointed out, rule 1 introduces a minimum number of seats for Scotland and Wales respectively, but no maximum. Obviously any increase above the minimum will further accentuate the Celtic preference. Both Scottish and Welsh Commissions have adopted a policy, so far as possible, of regarding the minima set out in rule 1 as target figures.[26] The effect of this can be seen in the four redistributions which took place between 1950 and 1983, which resulted in a total increase of one seat to Scotland and two seats in Wales (all of which were added in the 1983 redistribution). The adoption of a rigid policy

[26] (1986–87) H.C. 97–I, pp. 53, 83.

to this effect would not be lawful,[27] but as the 1983 redistribution demonstrates, there is no evidence that this error has been committed. Nevertheless, the Commissions will clearly be well advised not to allow an excessive growth in Welsh and Scottish constituencies, given that the seat minima set out in rule 1, even if not exceeded, still incorporate a substantial measure of over-representation.

So far as Northern Ireland is concerned, between 1944 and 1979 its Boundary Commission was required to produce 12 constituencies at each redistribution. In United Kingdom terms this led to substantial under-representation, but this, it was said, was justified on the basis that the province possessed its own devolved legislature at Stormont, and so the Ulster population did not require the same degree of representation at Westminster. Following the suspension of Stormont in 1973 this degree of under-representation could not continue, and section 1 of the House of Commons (Redistribution of Seats) Act 1979 introduced what is now rule 1(4) of the 1986 Act. On a strictly proportionate United Kingdom basis, on 1985 figures, Northern Ireland would be entitled to 16 seats, whereas to put it on the same representation basis as Wales would require that it be awarded 18 seats.[28] Any reintroduction of legislative devolution to Northern Ireland would presumably require that rule 1(4) be amended to reduce the number of Ulster seats.[29] As against that, it must be admitted that neither the Scotland Act 1978 (which provided for legislative devolution) nor the Wales Act 1978 (which did not so provide) allowed for any reduction in those countries' Westminster seats. The Northern Ireland Act 1982, which provided for a form of "rolling devolution" which could have extended to some legislative matters, did not deal with the issue of Westminster seats either. The present number of 17 Ulster seats seems not unreasonable.

(c) Seat Delineation: Local Government Boundaries and the Electoral Quota

The principal rules determining how the boundaries of each seat should be delineated are rules 4 and 5:

    4. (1) So far as is practicable having regard to rules 1 to 3
            (*a*) in England and Wales

---

[27] R. v. *Port of London Authority, ex p. Kynoch* [1919] 1 K.B. 176.
[28] (1977–78) H.C. 70–ii, paras. 120–121.
[29] (1986–87) H.C. 97–I, pp. 59, 71–72.

> > (i) no county or any part of a county shall be included in a constituency which includes the whole or part of any other county or the whole or part of a London borough,
> > (ii) no London borough or any part of a London borough shall be included in a constituency which includes the whole or part of any other London borough,
>
> (*b*) in Scotland, regard shall be had to the boundaries of local authority areas,
>
> (*c*) in Northern Ireland, no ward shall be included partly in one constituency and partly in another.
>
> (2) In subpara. (1)(*b*) above, "area" and "local authority" have the same meanings as in the Local Government (Scotland) Act 1973.

5. The electorate of any constituency shall be as near the electoral quota as is practicable having regard to rules 1 to 4; and a Boundary Commission may depart from the strict application of rule 4 if it appears to them that a departure is desirable to avoid an excessive disparity between the electorate of any constituency and the electoral quota, or between the electorate of any constituency and that of neighbouring constituencies in the part of the United Kingdom with which they are concerned.

Thus, rule 4 establishes a principle of respect for local government boundaries, and rule 5 is concerned with the achievement of equal constituencies in terms of numbers of electors. The reconciliation of these two principles has presented some of the greatest difficulties in the processes of redistribution.

The 1944 Act, following the Speaker's Conference recommendation, clearly allocated primacy to the achievement of equal constituencies over the principle of respect for local government boundaries. Rule 4 in the Third Schedule to that Act provided: "So far as is practicable having regard to rule 1 of these rules, the electorate of any constituency . . . shall not be greater or less than the electoral quota by more than approximately one quarter of the electoral quota." Rule 5 provided "so far as is practicable, having regard to the foregoing rules" for respect for local government boundaries, and was thus clearly expressed to be subordinate to the requirements, *inter alia*, of rule 4. However, in 1947 the House of Commons (Redistribution of Seats) Act was passed "to relax the rules set out (in the 1944 Act) . . . so far as they relate to the electoral quota." The relaxation was achieved by repealing rule 4 and replacing it by a new rule 5A, in the terms of the present rule 5. The effect of this was to reverse the priorities between the principles of equal constituency electorates and respect for local government boundaries. The argument advanced by the Home Secretary (of a Labour government, it should be noted) for this reform relied upon traditional Tory theories of representation:

> " ... the (English and Welsh) Commissioners had found themselves gravely handicapped by the strict mathematical formula within which their activities have been confined, and therefore the present Bill has been introduced in an effort to make the future representation of this House more in accordance with the historic precedent of representing communities than would have been possible under the Act of 1944."[30]

As Craig (Craig (1959) pp. 28–29) has pointed out, the Commissioners only found themselves "gravely handicapped" by according primacy to the principle of respect for local government boundaries which Parliament had disavowed in 1944. As with the calculation of the electoral quota, the 1944 Act was amended to reflect Commissioners' practice, rather than it being insisted that the Commissioners observe the 1944 rules. In this way, the gradual movement towards the Radical demand for "one vote one value" in equal constituencies was halted.

The relationship between what are now rules 4 and 5 of the 1986 Act was at the heart of the case brought by Mr. Michael Foot in 1983.[31] The Boundary Commission for England completed a general review of English constituencies in 1982 and was preparing to submit its report and recommendations to the Home Secretary. Mr. Foot sought orders restraining the Commission from submitting its report, on the ground that the Commission had failed to give proper weight to the principle of equal representation found in rule 5. This was sought to be demonstrated by citing the very considerable discrepancies between constituencies which the Commission was about to recommend. It was therefore argued either that the Commission had misconstrued the rules, or had, in its application of them, exercised its discretion unreasonably. As to the construction of the rules, the Court of Appeal was quickly able to dismiss Mr. Foot's contention:

[30] H.C.Deb. (1946–7), Vol. 430, col. 77, quoted in Craig (1959).
[31] *R.* v. *Boundary Commission for England, ex p. Foot* [1983] 1 Q.B. 600.

"It is clear, in our judgment, that . . . the requirement in rule 4 that 'so far as is practicable' constituencies shall not cross county or London borough boundaries must be regarded as taking precedence over the requirement in rule 5 concerning the size of the electorate for each constituency. This appears from the facts that (1) rule 4 is on its face not qualified by reference to rule 5, whereas rule 5 provides that the electorate of any constituency shall be as near the electoral quota as is practicable having regard to the foregoing rules, which of course include rule 4; and (2) the second limb of rule 5 authorises departure from rule 4 only in the circumstances there specified . . . The requirement of electoral equality is, subject to the second limb of rule 5, subservient to the requirement that constituencies shall not cross county or London borough boundaries."[32]

What arguments can be advanced for allocating primacy to a principle of respect for local government boundaries over a principle of equal constituency electorates? As we mentioned, the 1947 amendments were justified on the basis that "community representation" was likely to be facilitated. This assumes that local government boundaries are based upon "communities," yet, as we have seen, the criterion for the drawing of such boundaries has been since 1972 the achievement of "effective and convenient local government." This may, but need not inevitably, be co-extensive with the boundaries of "community," even if that very nebulous concept could be defined and identified in modern Britain (see Rowley 1975, for criticism of the English Boundary Commission's use of the term "community" in its 1969 Report).

An argument more recently advanced justifies the present position by reference to the changing role of the Member of Parliament. It is said that the M.P. nowadays is extensively involved in constituency case work (for a general discussion, see Rawlings (1986)), and that this particularly concerns local government affairs: "Three-quarters of my mailbag is local authority matters, it is housing, it is paving stones, it is dog droppings. That is the life blood, the contact, now for a Member of Parliament."[33] From this it is argued that if an M.P.'s constituency overlaps local government boundaries, the M.P.'s role will be made considerably more difficult in that he will have to deal with two or more authorities on behalf of his

[32] [1983] 1 Q.B. 600, 622 (Sir John Donaldson M.R.).
[33] (1986–87) H.C. 97–I, pp. 91–92 (Mr. Jeremy Hanley M.P.).

constituents.[34] This argument, it is submitted, is extremely weak. It overlooks the predominantly two-tier structure of local government which will inevitably lead most M.P.s to have dealings with two local authorities anyway, since an M.P.'s caseload will never be exclusively concerned with matters which are the responsibility of only one tier of local government. The argument is admittedly rather stronger in respect of the London boroughs, which have, since the abolition of the Greater London Council in 1985, exercised a very wide range of powers, but even here a London M.P. might expect to have cases requiring him to deal with agencies such as the Inner London Education Authority or the joint authorities set up to deal with fire and civil defence and waste disposal.[35]

Perhaps the most compelling argument for the principle of respect for local government boundaries is that it enables the Boundary Commissions more easily to do their job. The English Commission, for example, is faced with the division of England into over 500 constituencies. The requirement that county boundaries be not crossed (save in exceptional circumstances to avoid "an excessive disparity" between neighbouring consti-tuencies or between a constituency and the electoral quota) enables the Commission to draw constituencies within the relatively small and defined areas of the counties, rather than across England as a whole (or some Commission-designated region of it). Thus, the operation of rule 4, so far as the English Commission is concerned, serves to make its task easier by allowing it to treat England on a patchwork basis.[36] This is a strong argument. Radical demands for equal constituencies must take account of pragmatic claims of convenience of administration. But the point must not be over-emphasised. If it were to be shown, for example, that the Commission, in the interests of convenience of administration, had adopted an inflexible policy against crossing county boundaries in any circumstances, that would, in the light of the second limb of rule 5, be improper. An allegation that the English Commission had fettered itself was advanced in *Foot's* case, but failed on the facts.[37]

In contrast to the English Commission's obligation to respect county and London borough boundaries (save to avoid "an excessive disparity"), the Scottish Commission's duty is merely

[34] *Ibid.* p. 91.
[35] *Ibid.*
[36] (1986–87) H.C. 97–I, pp. 11–12.
[37] [1983] 1 Q.B. 600, 631–632.

to have regard to the boundaries of local authority areas—rule 4(1)(*b*). This relatively relaxed restraint was introduced by Sched. 3, para. 1 of the Local Government (Scotland) Act 1973. Its effect is to allow the Scottish Commission a greater discretion than is available to the English and Welsh Commissions, but the Scottish Commission has attempted to avoid crossing regional boundaries. District boundaries have not, however, been regarded as significant barriers in the drawing of equal constituencies.[38] The Northern Irish Commission has even greater flexibility under rule 4, in that *its* obligation is merely to avoid crossing the boundaries of the smallest electoral units, the wards. This has enabled the Commission to work to a maximum tolerance figure of 10 per cent. above or below the electoral quota for each constituency.[39] In contrast the English Commission's recommendations in 1982 included the proposing of constituencies in excess of 30 per cent. above or below the electoral quota. Even if it is accepted, on pragmatic administrative grounds, that *some* regard must be had for local government boundaries in constituency delineation, it is not obvious why the weight of that regard should differ as between the various parts of the United Kingdom, since the result may well be to produce a greater degree of electoral maldistribution in some parts of the country than in others. Some amelioration of the restraints placed upon the English Commission might, however, be achieved by their more easily finding that disparities between neighbouring constituencies were "excessive," and that they were thus justified in making proposals to cross county or London borough boundaries. As the Court of Appeal made clear in *Foot's* case, this would be a matter for the subjective judgment of the Commission, and thus only very rarely susceptible to judicial review.[40]

Quite apart from this, it may be asked why particular respect should be paid in England to the boundaries of the London boroughs when the boundaries of local authorities in other metropolitan areas are not to be so respected? The effect of rule 4(1)(*a*)(ii) in the 1983 redistribution was to give London four more seats than it would have been entitled to on a strict application of the electoral quota to the Greater London area.[41] The rule requiring respect for all borough boundaries which had

---

[38] (1986–87) H.C. 97–I, p. 41.
[39] *Ibid.* p. 12.
[40] [1983] 1 Q.B. 600, 623.
[41] (1986–87) H.C. 97–I, p. 29. The seats were Bromley, Barnet, Bexley and Greenwich.

been found in the 1944 Act was relaxed by Schedule 29, para. 28 of the Local Government Act 1972, save that it continued to apply to London borough boundaries. There seems no reason why London should continue to be favoured in this way. The House of Commons Select Committee on Home Affairs in 1987 drafted paragraphs in its Report on Redistribution of Seats recommending that the provision in rule 4 requiring respect for London borough boundaries should be repealed. These paragraphs were deleted from the final Report on the majority vote of the Conservative members of the Committee.[42] It may not be coincidental that of the four seats created by the operation of rule 4(1)(a)(ii), three are safely held for the Conservative Party.

(d) Seat Delineation: Geographical Considerations

Rule 6 of the constituency redistribution rules provides:

> 6. A Boundary Commission may depart from the strict application of rules 4 and 5 if special geographical considerations, including in particular the size, shape and accessibility of a constituency, appear to them to render a departure desirable.

This rule was first introduced by the House of Commons into the 1918 redistribution rules, the object being to ensure full representation of under-populated agricultural areas (Pugh (1978), pp. 108–109). As Taylor and Johnston point out, redistribution criteria in a number of countries frequently are biased in defence of rural areas:

> "it is a convenient way by which formerly dominant groups and areas can maintain their political power long after their numerical majority has been lost to new areas of population growth."
>
> (Taylor and Johnston (1979), p. 360)

Given this history, it is perhaps not surprising that the Commissioners in the 1947 and 1954 reviews were markedly more generous in granting representation to the rural counties than to the boroughs. As Dr. Butler has pointed out, this was effectively to discriminate against the Labour Party and in favour of those parties (principally the Conservative Party) which polled well in rural areas (Butler (1955), pp. 136–137). In 1948 Parliament responded to the English Commission's pro-

[42] (1986–87) H.C. 97–I, p. xii.

posals favouring the counties by inviting it to recommend 17 additional borough seats, perhaps to the advantage of the Labour Party (Nuffield (1950), pp. 4–5). The 1954 review, presented to a predominantly Conservative Parliament, was allowed to stand. More recently the English Commission has not been prepared to justify a policy of relying on rule 6 to differentiate between rural and borough constituencies in general terms.[43]

The invocation of rule 6 is therefore now limited to particular situations of very scattered rural populations. Any attempt in such situations to draw constituency boundaries containing numbers of electors approaching the electoral quota would produce extremely large constituencies, which M.P.s would find difficult to service. Inevitably it is the Scottish Commission which has most occasion to pray rule 6 in aid, because whereas the area of Scotland is 60 per cent. that of England, its population is only 11 per cent. that of England,[44] and geographical circumstances have led to the development of small population centres scattered over wide and inaccessible areas. Even with the use of rule 6, it is the case that the eight largest constituencies in area terms in the United Kingdom are all in Scotland.[45] In contrast the English Commission in 1983 invoked rule 6 only in respect of three constituencies, in Cumbria, Lancashire and Northumberland.[46] Thus there is again in rule 6 the possibility of a Celtic preference over and above that provided for in rule 1. The Scottish Commission, however, has attempted to avoid further increases in Scottish representation:

"...there is a significant difference between the approach...of the Scottish and English Commissions to rule 6. That arises because...rule 6 provides: 'A Boundary Commission may depart from the strict application of the last two foregoing rules,' nothing else. Therefore, we take the view that we have been provided with a minimum of 71...and that allowance has already been made for that factor in giving us that number. Therefore, although we apply rule 6, we do it, if necessary, at the expense of squeezing other areas."[47]

---

[43] See, for example, the 1983 Report, Cmnd. 8797–I, Chap. 2, paras. 20–21.

[44] (1986–87) H.C. 97–I, p. 42.

[45] *Ibid.*, p. 46.

[46] Cmnd. 8797–I, para. 20.

[47] (1986–87) H.C. 97–I, p. 52 (Lord Davidson).

Thus, by treating the rule 1 figure of 71 seats as a target which already encompasses an element for "rule 6 seats," the Scottish Commission avoids an excessive growth of seats justified on the basis of rule 6. In contrast, the Welsh Commission, in 1983, felt constrained to recommend two additional seats on the basis of rule 6, but was unwilling to "squeeze" other constituencies (in fact, create constituencies with larger electorates) in order to keep to the figure of 36 seats which was set in 1950.[48]

It has recently been argued that improvements in communications have diminished the need for the retention of rule 6.[49] The Select Committee on Home Affairs rejected this proposal, rightly it is submitted, since the abolition of rule 6 would require the creation of constituencies so large in area as to be unacceptable on both practical and political grounds.[50] Provided always that rule 6 is not used further to enhance the Celtic preference, it serves a useful purpose, notwithstanding that some electoral maldistribution must ensue from its operation. Here again, demands for equal constituencies must take account of the consideration of practical convenience.

(e) Seat Numbers: an Inevitable Increase?

Since the redistribution rules were first formulated in 1944, the number of seats in Great Britain has increased from 591 to 633. As we saw, in 1948 Parliament requested the creation of 17 more seats in order to align more closely the electoral quotas in county and borough constituencies. In addition to that, however, there are two other factors which lead to increases in seat numbers. First, rule 8(a) requires the Commissions to calculate the electoral quotas for each part of the country by dividing that part's electorate "by the number of constituencies in it existing on the enumeration date." This means, for example, that when the English Commission in 1983 agreed to recommend three additional seats on the basis of "special geographical considerations" under rule 6, those seats, rather than being regarded as a temporary requirement, became incorporated into the formula for calculating the electoral quota in the future. Thus the *base figure* for the number of seats in each country continually increases, as seats awarded for special reasons become part of the normal complement—and any seats awarded on top of that

[48] *Ibid.* pp. 83–84.
[49] *Ibid.* p. 59 (Mr. Merlyn Rees).
[50] *Ibid.* p. vii.

base figure in turn become incorporated into the base for future reviews.

The operation of rule 5 also incorporates a seat-inflating element:

> "When determining the number of seats which should be allocated to a particular area, such as a county or London borough, it is convenient to calculate the so-called 'theoretical entitlement' to seats by dividing the electorate of the area by the electoral quota. If the number of seats were then determined by rounding the 'theoretical entitlement' *to the nearest whole number,* then the total number of seats in England would have been close to the figure of 516 which was used to determine the electoral quota. However, what Rule 5 actually says is that the boundaries should be chosen so that the electorate in the constituency should be *as near the electoral quota as possible.* This sometimes gives a higher answer. As an example, chosen merely to illustrate the arithmetic, the County of Buckinghamshire had an electorate in 1976 of 359,497 and the electoral quota was 65,753. Thus the theoretical entitlement, ie the electorate divided by the electoral quota, was 5·467 seats. If this were rounded down to five seats then the average electorate would be 71,899, whereas with six seats the average electorate would be 59,916. But the latter figure is nearer to the quota than the former. Thus in order to get as near to the quota as possible, as required under Rule 5, Buckinghamshire should have six seats rather than five and the theoretical entitlement of 5·467 needs to be rounded up instead of down. Each time that this happens, the number of seats will be increased."[51]

Any such increase will again be incorporated into the base figure for future redistributions.

It may be asked why there is no similar inflation in seat numbers in Scotland. The answer is that the Scottish Commission, having taken the minimum seat entitlement in rule 1 as a target figure, compensates for the creation of extra "rule 6" seats by the "squeezing" of other seats.[52] Furthermore, the Scottish Commission does not interpret rule 5 as requiring a "rounding-up" of numbers of seats as the English Commission did in 1983

[51] Boundary Commission for England, Third Periodical Report, Cmnd. 8797–I, Chap. 2, para. 7.
[52] See text to n. 47, above.

in respect of Buckinghamshire, for example, because it gives considerable weight to the target figure of seats in rule 1, and tries to avoid exceeding it.[53] Thus, in this respect, the divergent interpretations given to rule 5 by the English and Scottish Commissions lead to an increase in the number of English seats and a standstill in the number of Scottish seats. To this extent, the Celtic preference inherent in rule 1 is mitigated.

The House of Commons Select Committee on Home Affairs has expressed considerable disquiet about the inbuilt tendency to growth in seat numbers in England. It has proposed that rule 8 be amended so that the electoral quota is calculated not by dividing the electorate by the existing (and ever-growing) number of constituencies, but by fixed divisors. The divisors suggested are for England 515, for Scotland 66, for Wales 36, and for Northern Ireland 17. Rule 1 would also be amended, to provide the Commissions with guidance as to how many additional seats might be awarded in consequence of the operation of rules 5 and 6. The rule would provide that in England the number of constituencies would not be substantially more than 523; in Scotland, not substantially more than 72; in Wales not substantially more than 38; and in Northern Ireland, as now, not more than 18.[54] This proposal has much to commend it, in that the provision of fixed divisors ensures that the base figure for the number of constituencies in each part of the United Kingdom will remain constant, regardless of any Commission's proposals at any review to increase the seat numbers because of rules 5 or 6. Furthermore, the amendment to rule 1 would provide the Commissions with guidance as to how much scope Parliament intended for additional seats in its provision of rules 5 and 6. As against that, the amendment would have the effect in practice of preventing the English Commission from increasing the number of English seats, and so further mitigating the Celtic preference.

(3) PARLIAMENTARY CONSTITUENCIES: THE PROCESS

(a) Provisional Recommendations

The first step taken in drawing constituency boundaries is to determine the number of seats to which a given area is entitled. The areas are "given" by the statutory requirement of respect for county boundaries and London borough boundaries in

---

[53] (1986–87) H.C. 97–I, p. 48.
[54] *Ibid.* p. vi.

England and Wales, and by policies of respect for regional boundaries in Scotland and for county boundaries in Northern Ireland. Within an area thus identified, the electorate for that area is divided by the relevant electoral quota computed in accordance with rule 8 of the redistribution rules, and the result of that division produces a preliminary seat "entitlement" for that area. Obviously this will rarely produce a whole figure, and so rounding up or rounding down to a whole figure is undertaken. In England this will normally be to the nearest whole figure, but this is not an inviolable rule, as the previously-cited example of Buckinghamshire in the 1983 redistribution illustrates. In Scotland and Wales a fairly consistent pattern of rounding-down is to be expected, given these Commissions' determination not to allow a growth in the number of seats beyond the minimum set out in rule 1 of the redistribution rules. The relatively tight margin of tolerance in Northern Ireland, which is to receive not less than 16 nor more than 18 seats, would equally result in a pressure to round down.

Once the preliminary seat entitlement for an area has been determined, the relevant Commission must draw up provisional recommendations for constituency boundaries within that area. It is the settled policy of all the Commissions (although only the Northern Irish Commission is statutorily so required) to use the local government district electoral wards as "building bricks" to create individual constituencies. The English Commission has justified this as follows:

> "In general the local political party organisations (are) based on the district wards and those wards frequently (represent) a community with interests in common. Any division of wards between constituencies (is) likely to break local ties, disrupt political party organisation and be confusing to electors. The boundaries of wards (are) legally defined and (will) cause no problems when describing constituency boundaries. Nor (will) there be any difficulty in preparing electoral registers for parliamentary elections."[55]

This is doubtlessly all true. Nevertheless, the use of wards as building bricks is open to the objection that their boundaries are vulnerable to gerrymandering by political parties operating through district councils under their control, and we expressed concern above as to how far the Local Government Boundary Commission was able to restrain such action. It is certainly the

---

[55] Cmnd. 8797–I, Chap. 2, para. 18.

case that the parliamentary Boundary Commissions take no notice of this.[56]

The construction of constituencies by use of contiguous wards affords the Commissions a most extensive discretion, even given the obligation to produce constituencies "as near the electoral quota as is practicable" in accordance with rule 5. Johnston and Taylor, for example, calculate that in 1983 there were 9,949 different ways of dividing Sheffield's 29 district wards into that city's six-constituency entitlement, allowing for deviation from the electoral quota of not more than 12 per cent. (Johnston and Taylor (1986), p. 142). There is no statutory guidance as to how such discretion is to be exercised, and Waller has criticised the English Commission for failing in 1983 to establish any consistency of approach:

> "Quite frequently when presented with similar problems different recommendations were made in different counties. For example, where a city was slightly too large to have one seat, a variety of solutions were adopted. In Oxford ... the city was divided down the middle along the lines of the Rivers Cherwell and Thames, and each half diluted with territory from rural and suburban areas outside the city. In the other ancient English university town, Cambridge ... , two wards were chipped off the edge leaving a recognizable unified Cambridge constituency. In other comparable cases, the Oxford example was followed in Colchester, Reading and Luton, but the Cambridge type of solution was adopted in Ipswich."

> (Waller (1983), p. 197)

Obviously, these decisions have substantial political consequences. The dilution of inner-Luton wards by the addition of rural and suburban wards will favour the Conservatives in that area, whereas the preservation of Ipswich free of rural influence advantages Labour. Taylor and Gudgin have argued that although Boundary Commission decisions are not *intentionally* partisan, their *effects* are usually the same as would ensue from an explicitly gerrymandered redistribution in the interests of the majority party (Taylor and Gudgin (1976); and see also, Taylor and Johnston (1979), pp. 408–414). This arises, it is argued, because there are (statistically) many more acceptable solutions favourable to the majority party than there are not, and

[56] (1986–87) H.C. 97–I, pp. 30–31.

Commissions are therefore more likely to recommend a solution favourable to the majority party. This statistical bias should be seen in the context of the possible manipulation of ward boundaries to favour majority parties to which we have referred. The case for the existence of non-partisan agencies of redistribution such as the Boundary Commissions then has to rely on the perceived fairness of their procedures rather than on the outcomes of their work. In this sense the Commissions serve as an important legitimating agency for the electoral system, which *appears* politically neutral.

(b) Local Inquiries

Once a Commission has determined its provisional recommendations for any area, these are to be publicised and copies made available for inspection. Notice is also to be given "that representations with respect to the proposed recommendations may be made to the Commission within one month of the publication of the notice" and the Commission is required to take such representations into account.[57] There is a discretion to hold a local inquiry into representations, save that if any objection is received either from a body of 100 or more affected electors or from an "interested authority" (an authority "whose area is wholly or partly comprised in the constituencies affected by the recommendation"), then a local inquiry *must* be held.[58]

Local inquiries constitute an important part of the constituency delimitation process, and it is surprising to note that they do not appear to have been the subject of any academic investigation. Inquiries are chaired by Assistant Commissioners, barristers appointed by the Home Secretary at the request of the Commissions. Appointees are required not to have played any prominent part in political activities, and the various political parties are relied upon to make representations about proposed individual appointments.[59] The same criticism may be made of these Commissioners as has been made of the Commissions themselves, that their immunity from the political process has been taken to such lengths as on occasion to produce unfortunate practical consequences:

> "...when you have an Assistant Commissioner...who has never been to the area before, who has not been

---

[57] Parliamentary Constituencies Act 1986, s.5(2).
[58] *Ibid.* s.6(1), (2).
[59] (1986–87) H.C. 97–I, pp. 30–31.

involved in the discussions of the first report of the Boundary Commissioners, who has no staff to help him and is coming *de novo* into an area, I fail to see how any Assistant Commissioner can possibly comprehend what is going on there. The fact that he is non-political and certainly was non-political in every possible way is the reason why we had such a daft redistribution of the (Leeds) area . . . We could have had a much better report if we had had people who knew the area, which is different from being politically motivated."[60]

Inquiries under the Act are unusual in that no statutory procedure has been laid down to prescribe their conduct, and much is left to the presiding Assistant Commissioners. There is no obligation upon objectors to submit detailed alternative proposals in advance of inquiries and adjournments of inquiries are possible at the discretion of Assistant Commissioners to facilitate fuller consideration of novel proposals advanced at the inquiry itself. Nor is participation in local inquiries restricted to those who have registered objections in the short time period available. It is again within the presiding Assistant Commissioner's discretion as to who shall be heard, and the English Commission's view (which is no doubt reflected in the instructions provided to Commissioners) is that any interested person should be encouraged to participate.[61]

The purpose of the local inquiry is to obtain further information which will enable a Commission to reach a better decision, more in accord if possible with local sentiment. No attempt is made to defend the terms of provisional recommendations save that at the commencement of each inquiry a statement of reasons for the provisional recommendations is read out by the Assistant Commissioner.[62] The conduct of the inquiry must be such as to afford objectors a fair hearing and permit full and proper consideration of their objections. In the *Gateshead* case the Assistant Commissioner, by further amplifying and commenting upon the Commission's provisional recommendations, appeared to preclude himself in advance from considering the merits of arguments in favour of an additional constituency for the county of Tyne and Wear, and the applicants sought to have his report quashed. The Court of Appeal held that although his preliminary statements were at the very least ambiguous, the

[60] *Ibid.* pp. 65–66.
[61] Cmnd. 8797–I, Chap. 1, para. 23.
[62] *Ibid.* para. 25.

Assistant Commissioner had in fact given full consideration to these arguments before rejecting them, and that therefore the applicants had not been treated unfairly.[63]

In the absence of any systematic study of local inquiries, it is not possible to be more specific about the identity of objectors to provisional recommendations. It may be assumed that local political party branches are actively involved. The English Commission observed in respect of the 1983 local inquiries that

> "The representations received in writing or at local inquiries have, sometimes, clearly been inspired solely by political motives. In addition there have been submissions at some inquiries that the boundaries of constituencies should be drawn so as to produce a particular political result."[64]

What is not known is how far the registering of objections and the advancing of alternative schemes of redistribution are inspired by the national headquarters of the major political parties, or whether this is left to the initiative of local party organisations. Nor is it known whether representations made by interested local authorities reflect majority party concerns or more general considerations, as was the position in the *Gateshead* case itself.

The reports of the Assistant Commissioners after local inquiries had been conducted were clearly of considerable significance to the final form of the redistribution in England in 1983. The English Commission "set out with the view that if the Assistant Commissioner's recommendations were in accordance with the statutory requirements and carried local support, then we would accept them. We have consistently applied this policy."[65] According to Waller, the attitude of many Assistant Commissioners in 1983 was one of "minimum disturbance"; existing constituencies were to be modified in as limited a manner as possible, in contrast to the Commission's rather more radical remoulding of the constituencies proposed in its provisional recommendations (Waller (1983), p. 198). In some cases substantial amendment to the provisional recommendations was recommended and acted upon, in order to minimise the changes to existing constituencies.

In only a very limited number of cases did the English Commission make use of its discretion to order a further inquiry

---

[63] *R.* v. *Boundary Commission for England, ex p. Gateshead B.C.* [1983] Q.B. 638, C.A.

[64] Cmnd. 8797–I, Chap. 1, para. 27.

[65] *Ibid.* para. 26.

after publication of revised recommendations.[66] This power was given to the Commissions by the House of Commons (Redistribution of Seats) Act 1958 after complaints that in the 1955 redistribution the English Commission had not infrequently adopted revised recommendations which amounted virtually to new proposals, but which were not made the subject of further local inquiry (Butler (1955), pp. 130–131). The English Commission's policy in 1983 was not to order further local inquiry unless "the crucial point in issue had not been properly discussed at the (first) local inquiry," a situation which the Commission described as "naturally . . . somewhat unusual."[67] Mr. Merlyn Rees M.P. has expressed concern about this policy in the context of the redistribution in Leeds:

> "Only two objections were made to the proposals for the then South Leeds Constituency; yet this proposal was overturned a short time later. Following this there was no opportunity to question publicly the revised report. This must not be allowed to happen again."[68]

Given, as Waller points out, that the Assistant Commissioners operated primarily as a moderating element on the English Commission in 1983, it is not surprising that the Commission did not feel compelled to order further inquiry in most cases. Nevertheless, this approach, when taken with the policy of complying with Assistant Commissioners' reports where possible, indicates the very considerable importance which devolves upon Assistant Commissioners in the redistribution process.

(c) Final Recommendations and the Role of Parliament

Once the Commissions have considered the reports from local inquiries and have finalised their recommendations, these are to be reported to the Secretary of State, whose duty it is "as soon as may be" to lay the report before Parliament together with the draft of an Order in Council "for giving effect, whether with or without modifications, to the recommendations contained in the report."[69] Where modifications are proposed, the Secretary of State must lay before Parliament a statement of the reasons for these.[70] The draft Orders must be approved by Affirmative

---

[66] Parliamentary Constituencies Act 1986, s.6(3).
[67] Cmnd. 8797–I, Chap. 1, para. 29.
[68] (1986–87) H.C. 97–I, p. 57.
[69] Parliamentary Constituencies Act 1986, s.3(5).
[70] *Ibid.* s.4(2).

Resolution by both Houses before submission to Her Majesty in Council, who "may" then make an Order in the terms of the draft.[71] Once this has been done,

"The validity of any Order in Council purporting to be made under this Act and reciting that a draft of the Order has been approved by resolution of each House of Parliament shall not be called in question in any legal proceedings whatsoever."[72]

The formal role envisaged for Parliament in this process is substantial but in practice it is significantly less important than might appear. This is because Parliament is virtually bound to accept Commission recommendations *in toto*. It is true that in 1948 the Government, having received the English Commission's recommendations and having introduced a Bill in their terms, asked the Commission to prepare proposals for 17 further urban seats. As Butler has pointed out, this request occasioned considerable controversy at the time, and was largely responsible for the difficulties which the English Commission got into in 1954 over seat numbers (Butler (1955), p. 127). But, in any event, on that occasion the original recommendations came before Parliament as a Schedule to a Bill, and were thus capable of amendment in the ordinary way. Recommendations which are presented to Parliament, as they now are, in the form of draft Orders in Council, may, under the rules of the House of Commons, normally only be rejected or accepted; they may not be amended unless specific provision is made in the principal statute authorising this and no such provision is made in the present context.[73] Therefore, in both 1954 and 1983, Commissions' recommendations were approved without amendment, although in each case they were the subject of extensive complaint as to detail.

The reception of the 1969 recommendations occasioned extensive controversy. The Commissions reported their recommendations to the Home Secretary in April 1969. Notwithstanding the obligation "as soon as may be" to lay the recommendations before Parliament, nothing was done until June, when they were laid but without attendant Orders in Council. Instead a Bill was introduced implementing the proposals in part, and providing immunity to the Home Secretary for any action for

---

[71] *Ibid*. s.4(4), (5).
[72] *Ibid*. s.4(7).
[73] See generally, Erskine May, *Parliamentary Practice* (20th ed.), p. 617.

breach of statutory duty. The Bill failed to pass the House of Lords, and an elector in an affected constituency sought mandamus requiring the Home Secretary to lay a draft Order in Council before Parliament in accordance with what is now section 3(5) of the 1986 Act. The application was withdrawn on the Home Secretary giving an undertaking to lay the Orders before Parliament.[74] This he duly did, together with a recommendation to Parliament to reject it. This was done, and the General Election ensuing shortly thereafter was fought on the 1954 boundaries, therefore providing Labour with an advantage by virtue of the fact that certain of its inner-city "rotten boroughs" had not been redistributed away. Given that Labour benefits disproportionately from fighting elections on "old" boundaries, it is perhaps not surprising that Conservative-dominated Houses of Commons approved the 1954 and 1983 sets of recommendations without difficulty, whereas the 1948 and 1969 proposals were the source of considerable difficulty for Labour, with General Elections scheduled to take place shortly after their implementation. The 1969 recommendations were implemented by the Conservatives in 1970 soon after they took office.

(d) Judicial Review?

The recommendations for redistribution advanced in 1954, 1969 and 1983 all produced litigation by individuals aggrieved either at the substance of the proposals or (in 1969) at their non-implementation. Given that the role of Parliament in respect of redistribution proposals is inevitably limited, the courts may be the only source of redress for the aggrieved. What scope is there for judicial review of the redistribution process? The history of the litigation referred to does not indicate that the courts have an extensive role to play, for in none of them was the applicant's argument accepted (although in 1969, as previously mentioned, the case never proceeded to judgment).

The first set of problems which a potential litigant may face are procedural. To illustrate these, and to consider how far they may be overcome, it is helpful to consider the various points in the redistribution process when such a litigant might choose to initiate his action. The first point in time will be during the preparation of the recommendations by the Boundary Commission. This was the tactic adopted in *R. v. Boundary Commission for*

---

[74] *R. v. Home Secretary, ex p, McWhirter, The Times*, October 21, 1969.

England, ex p. Foot,[75] where the applicant sought an order prohibiting submission of the recommendations to the Home Secretary on the ground that these had been prepared on a misunderstanding of the redistribution rules and would be *ultra vires*. Quite apart from the merits of that argument, the applicant was faced with two problems. First, given that the recommendations had yet to be published, on what evidentiary materials could he proceed? In *Foot*, it was argued that the Commission's intended report could be inferred as likely to be *ultra vires* on the ground that, on the evidence of the Commission's proposals (whether as originally framed or as revised following inquiries) and the Commission's reaction or non-reaction to suggestions that those be altered, the final report would be one which did not comply with the statutory requirements.[76]

The weakness of this position is illustrated by Sir John Donaldson's judgment in the Court of Appeal. Dealing with contentions that certain of the Boundary Commission's proposals could not possibly be justified as proper exercises of its discretion, Sir John Donaldson said that the court did not have before it the totality of evidence available to the Commission. For all that the Court of Appeal knew, particular proposals might have been advanced on the basis of an application of rule 6 of the 1986 Act, special geographical considerations, which justified a departure from electoral equality under rule 5.[77] Merely to demonstrate considerable inequalities of electorate between constituencies (which was all that the applicant *could* demonstrate, not himself having seen an explanation of the proposed recommendations) could not lead the court to infer *ultra vires* action on that ground alone. In fact, as we now know, the English Commission did *not*, save in three exceptional circumstances, invoke rule 6 in support of its proposals,[78] but both the applicant and the Court of Appeal were wholly ignorant of that because the action had been initiated before publication of the recommendations.

The second procedural problem is that of standing. In the *Foot* case the applicants were respectively the Labour Party leader, the Parliamentary Chief Whip and the party's General Secretary and National Agent. Nevertheless, in Oliver L.J.'s view, these positions were not such as to endow the applicants with

---

[75].[1983] 1 Q.B. 600, C.A.
[76] See Oliver L.J., in his unreported Divisional Court judgment.
[77] [1983] 1 Q.B. 600, 634.
[78] Cmnd. 8797–I, Chap. 2, para. 20.

sufficient interest that applications for judicial review might be maintained. They came to the court in no greater position than that any other elector in England seeking to ensure fair representation in Parliament.[79] With respect, this seems an unduly blinkered approach. It is true that the formal rules of the constitution exhibit an almost total blindness to the role of parties in the government system (and electoral law, especially in respect of campaigning, provides a good example of that), but it is surely taking matters too far to assume that the Leader of Her Majesty's Opposition is in a matter of this kind in exactly the same position as an ordinary citizen. It is submitted therefore that Webster J.'s approach, which afforded standing to the applicants on the basis of the importance of the matter being brought to court,[80] is to be preferred.

However this may be, the *Foot* case illustrates the evidential problems which may arise if an over-hasty challenge is mounted to proposed recommendations. It may therefore be in the interest of potential litigants to wait until the Commission's report is presented to the Home Secretary. Two possibilities may then arise, depending upon the litigant's view of the recommendations. He may wish the recommendations to be enacted expeditiously, or he may wish them to be withdrawn. The first situation arose in 1969, when a litigant sought mandamus to require the Home Secretary to comply with his duty to lay the report before Parliament "as soon as may be."[81] Again the issue of standing will apply here. There is some authority for the proposition that the interest to be demonstrated by the applicant for mandamus must be of a more substantial kind than for the other prerogative orders, perhaps in the sense that the applicant must be able to demonstrate an expectation of benefit if the duty sought to be enforced is actually performed.[82] If this is so, to whom does the Home Secretary owe his duty to lay the Commission's report before Parliament? If, as was contended in 1969,[83] it is owed to the Crown or to Parliament, an elector may have difficulty in

---

[79] n. 76, above.

[80] Following R. v. *Inland Revenue Commissioners, ex p. National Federation of Self-Employed* [1982] A.C. 617. The Court of Appeal in *Foot* expressed no view on the standing point: [1983] 1 Q.B. 600, 634.

[81] R. v. *Home Secretary, ex p. McWhirter, The Times,* October 21, 1969.

[82] See the *National Federation* case, n. 80 above, *per* Lord Wilberforce, at 631, but see Lord Diplock at 641, and R. v. *Felixstowe JJ, ex p. Leigh* [1987] 2 W.L.R. 380, 394 (Watkins L.J.).

[83] *McWhirter,* n. 81 above.

demonstrating sufficient interest, but a Member of Parliament might be an appropriate litigant.

The converse case, where the litigant seeks to prevent implementation of the recommendations, may also present procedural difficulties. Until recently it had been well-established that injunctive relief against a Minister of the Crown was not available, due to the provisions of section 21(2) of the Crown Proceedings Act 1947:

> "The court shall not in any civil proceedings grant any injunction or make any order against an officer of the Crown if the effect of granting the injunction or making the order would be to give any relief against the Crown which could not have been obtained in proceedings against the Crown."[84]

But it has now been held[85] that the incorporation in 1977 of the declaration and injunction into the application for judicial review procedure[86] has resulted in those remedies being available to the same extent as are the traditional prerogative orders, and it is indubitably the case that mandamus will go to an officer of the Crown.[87] Furthermore, the effect of R.S.C. Ord. 53, r. 3(10)(*b*) is to make interim relief available to the applicant for judicial review who is seeking an injunction. It may follow from all this, therefore, that there is no procedural bar to the litigant who wishes to enjoin the Home Secretary from laying a Boundary Commission's recommendations before Parliament, and that interim relief to that effect would be available in support. Such a conclusion would, however, depend upon the courts being willing to apply the (first-instance) *Herbage* decision in the constitutionally-sensitive area of Parliamentary seat redistribution.

Suppose, however, that the Home Secretary has laid the Commission's report before Parliament. May a litigant, even at this late stage, seek judicial review? The answer, as appears from *R.* v. *Her Majesty's Treasury, ex p. Smedley*,[88] is that he may. The case was concerned with the designation as a "Community Treaty" of an Undertaking entered into by the British Government to make supplementary budgetary payments to the European Community. This designation can be achieved by

---

[84] See *Merricks* v. *Heathcoat-Amory* [1955] Ch. 567.
[85] *R.* v. *Home Secretary, ex p. Herbage* [1986] 3 W.L.R. 504, Q.B.D.
[86] See now, Supreme Court Act 1981, s.31(2).
[87] See, for example, *Padfield* v. *Minister of Agriculture* [1968] A.C. 997.
[88] [1985] Q.B. 657, C.A.

Order in Council, save that a draft of the proposed Order, under
section 1(3) of the European Communities Act 1972, must first
be approved by both Houses of Parliament. A draft was duly
laid before both Houses, but before it could be considered the
applicant in judicial review proceedings sought a declaration
that the Undertaking could not in any event constitute a
Community Treaty within section 1(2) of the 1972 Act, and that
any subsequent Order in Council so designating it would be
ultra vires. The merits of that argument need not concern us.
What is of interest here is the Court of Appeal's approach to the
procedural issues raised by this apparent interference with
Parliamentary proceedings, in defiance of established constitutional conventions. The point is dealt with most fully by Slade
L.J., who drew attention to "the somewhat limited role"
accorded to Parliament in such procedures:

> "This role is analogous to a power of veto. If it withholds its
> approval from this draft Order in Council, the Order cannot
> be made. If, however, the approval of Parliament is given,
> Her Majesty in Council is left with a discretion whether or
> not to make the Order. There is no possible question of the
> court seeking or being able to control the exercise of the
> Parliamentary power of veto. However, I can see no reason
> why the exercise of the last-mentioned discretion given to
> Her Majesty in Council should not be open to attack in the
> courts by the process of judicial review . . . Equally . . . I can
> see no good reason why a decision by the courts given at
> the present stage and relating to the proposed exercise of
> the discretion of Her Majesty in Council should be said to
> usurp or interfere with what I conceive to be the function of
> Parliament in this present context, namely that of deciding
> whether or not to exercise what is in substance a power of
> veto . . . "[89]

The true constitutional relationship between court and Parliament could be expressed in the proposition that

> "where some administrative order or regulation is required
> by statute to be approved by resolution of both Houses of
> Parliament, the court can in an appropriate case intervene
> by way of judicial review before the Houses have given
> their approval . . . "[90]

---

[89] [1985] Q.B. 657, 672.
[90] *Ibid.* relying on *R. v. Electricity Commrs.* [1924] 1 K.B. 171, 231 (Younger L.J.).

and declaratory relief will in principle be available.[91] It is submitted that this judgment can equally be applied to the Parliamentary process in respect of Boundary Commission recommendations, since that statutory procedure does not differ from what was discussed in *Smedley*. If that is correct, then there can be no procedural difficulty in an applicant seeking judicial review in the period between the laying of a draft Order in Council before Parliament to implement Boundary Commission recommendations and the consideration of that draft by each House. Again this is subject to the qualification that courts might be reluctant to become involved in the constitutionally sensitive area of redistribution, especially where, even more than was the case in *Smedley*, overtly party-political issues would probably be involved.

What of the position after the Houses have approved the draft? In *Harper* v. *Home Secretary*[92] an injunction was sought restraining the Home Secretary from submitting the draft Orders to Her Majesty in Council. The application failed, both because the Court of Appeal (wrongly, as we have previously submitted) could discern no error in the English Boundary Commission's calculation of the electoral quota, and because section 21(2) of the Crown Proceedings Act 1947 appeared to preclude the issue of an injunction to an officer of the Crown. *Herbage's* case[93] has demonstrated that the latter objection may no longer be applicable, but it does not follow from this that judicial review would now be available in such circumstances. First, the House of Lords has made it clear that it is not appropriate to review a Ministerial decision on the grounds of "*Wednesbury*—unreasonableness"[94] where a statute requires the House of Commons to approve a Minister's decision before he can lawfully enforce it. In such circumstances the Minister is only accountable to Parliament for any allegedly perverse consequences of his decision.[95] That reasoning has particular force in the present context (which assumes legal action *after* Parliamentary approval of draft Orders), since "the representation of the people has traditionally been the special concern of the Commons, and . . . it would be imprudent for the courts to

---

[91] See also R. v. *Boundary Commission for England, ex p. Foot* [1983] Q.B. 600, 634 on this point.
[92] [1955] Ch. 238, C.A.
[93] [1986] 3 W.L.R. 504.
[94] *Associated Picture Houses* v. *Wednesbury Corporation* [1948] 1 K.B. 223, C.A.
[95] R. v *Secretary of State for the Environment, ex p. Nottinghamshire County Council* [1986] A.C. 240, H.L.(E).

interfere" (De Smith (1955), pp. 284–285). Secondly, even if scope is left for review on grounds of illegality rather than irrationality, it is strongly arguable that an applicant (providing he could establish standing) should in any event be denied a remedy on the ground of undue delay, since opportunities for challenge would already have arisen before Parliament considered the draft Orders.[96]

Finally, challenges to the validity of any Order in Council, once made, are likely to be defeated by the provisions of section 4(7) of the 1986 Act, previously quoted (p. 51). Although the courts have in recent years been increasingly prone to limit the effect of statutory provisions ousting judicial review,[97] it nevertheless appears that this subsection will operate to exclude review of the *vires* of an Order in Council based upon a Boundary Commission's recommendations. The use of the formula "purporting to be made" appears well-designed to defeat an *Anisminic*-type argument that a flawed Boundary Commission report is not a "report under the Act" upon which Orders in Council could properly be based.[98] Furthermore, for the reasons of constitutional propriety previously mentioned, it is submitted that it would not be appropriate for the courts enthusiastically to seek out ways of circumventing the ouster so as to attack Orders in Council which have already received Parliamentary approval.

Nevertheless, the *Smedley* case shows that there is in principle an opportunity to seek judicial review well before a Boundary Commission's recommendations become encased in the protective concrete of an Order in Council. We must therefore now consider the basis upon which such an attack might be mounted, and its likelihood of success. Complaints alleging a breach of natural justice might conceivably be advanced in respect of the conduct of local inquiries, but it is less certain that the whole of a Commission's set of recommendations might be held to be vitiated by procedural impropriety. In any event the Commissions have recently placed considerable importance upon consultations with the political parties,[99] and maintenance of this policy will go a long way to meet any arguments based upon natural justice.

This leaves over as grounds of attack misconstruction of the redistribution rules or their unreasonable application. These

---

[96] See generally, *R. v. Stratford-on-Avon D.C., ex p. Jackson* [1985] 1 W.L.R. 1319.
[97] *Anisminic v. Foreign Compensation Commission* [1969] 2 A.C. 147, H.L.(E); *Re Racal Communications* [1981] A.C. 374, H.L.(E).
[98] An argument advanced in *Harper's* case, n. 92 above.
[99] See Cmnd. 8797–I, Chap. 1, para. 31.

were the arguments advanced in *Foot*. It is submitted that future applications for judicial review are likely to be just as unsuccessful as was the *Foot* case, even if the evidential problems which the applicant there faced can be overcome. There are two reasons for this. The first is the interpretation which the Court of Appeal gave to what is now rule 7 of the redistribution rules, which is in these terms:

> 7. It shall not be the duty of a Boundary Commission to aim at giving full effect in all circumstances to the above rules, but they shall take account, so far as they reasonably can,
>
> (a) of the inconveniences attendant on alterations of constituencies other than alterations made for the purposes of rule 4, and
>
> (b) of any local ties which would be broken by such alterations.

This rule was introduced by section 2(2) of the 1958 Act to meet criticisms that in the 1955 redistribution, the Boundary Commission for England had been guilty of excessive devotion to numbers (Butler (1955), p. 135), that established boundaries had been subject to major change in order to achieve relatively small changes in constituency electorates. Rule 7 was therefore designed to exempt a Commission from rigid adherence in particular to rule 5, allowing discretion to depart from the principle "as near . . . as practicable" of observance of the electoral quota in the circumstances specified in rule 7.[1] This was not, however, the interpretation advanced by the Court of Appeal in *Foot*. Rejecting an argument that the dispensation to depart from the redistribution rules was available only in the circumstances specified in the second half of rule 7, Sir John Donaldson M.R. said:

> "We consider that the function of the first limb is to do just what it says viz. to relieve Boundary Commissions from the duty to give effect in all circumstances to the rules, with the result that, although plainly Boundary Commissions must indeed have regard to the rules, they are not strictly bound to give full effect to them in all circumstances. The word 'but' has a role to play because it points the contrast between the dispensation in the first limb of the subsection, and the mandatory requirement in the second limb, that

[1] See Cmnd. 8797–I, Chap. 2, para. 26.

> Boundary Commissions shall nevertheless take account of
> the matters specified in the second limb."[2]

This led his Lordship to the conclusion that "the practical effect
is that a strict application of the rules ceases to be mandatory so
that the rules, while remaining very important indeed, are
reduced to the status of guidelines," a conclusion which, as his
Lordship truly observed, placed a "very substantial obstacle in
the way of judicial review of a decision of a Boundary
Commission to make any particular recommendation in a report
to the Home Secretary."[3]

It is submitted with respect that it cannot be correct to
interpret rule 7 as reducing all of the rules 1–6 to mere
"guidelines." Rules 2 and 3 certainly cannot be so categorised:

> 2. Every constituency shall return a single member.
> 3. There shall continue to be a constituency which shall
>   include the whole of the City of London and the name
>   of which shall refer to the City of London.

It is surely the case that a failure by a Commission to observe
either rule would *ipso facto* be ground for judicial review, since
no discretion is afforded under them and their observance is
mandatory. Be that as it may, this aspect of the *Foot* judgment
serves to reinforce a second reason for concluding that judicial
review will but rarely be available in respect of Boundary
Commission recommendations. This reason is the scope of a
Commission's discretion.

As Oliver L.J. observed in his Divisional Court judgment in
Foot's case, the history of the redistribution legislation since 1944
demonstrates that the legislative purpose has throughout been
to confer a progressively wider discretion upon the Boundary
Commissions. This is seen not only in the relaxation afforded in
1958 by what is now rule 7; it may be demonstrated by the
abolition of the "twenty-five per cent. rule," whereby depar-
tures from the electoral quota in respect of particular constituencies were tolerated only within (plus or minus) 25 per cent. It
can equally be seen in the repeal of the requirement to observe
borough boundaries in England, and in permitting the Scottish
Commission merely to have regard to local authority boundaries. Furthermore, there has always been an entitlement to
depart from certain of the rules if it appears to a Commission
that "special geographical considerations" render this desirable.

[2] [1983] Q.B. 600, 623.
[3] At 624.

Again, rules 4 and 5 are to be observed "so far as is practicable," but rule 5 may be departed from if a Commission considers a departure "desirable to avoid an excessive disparity." This statutory language, when taken together with the legislative history, establishes a highly-discretionary regime which, it is submitted, invites only the most limited judicial review. This would be the case even without the arguably incorrect interpretation of rule 7 which the Court of Appeal arrives at in *Foot*. We therefore conclude that, although many of the *procedural* obstacles to judicial review of Boundary Commission recommendations may have been removed, the scope of discretionary powers which have been allocated renders it unlikely in the extreme that a court will feel able to hold either that the rules ("guidelines") have been misconstrued such as to justify judicial intervention, or that the discretionary powers have been used unreasonably in the *Wednesbury* sense.

This conclusion should be read in the light of our preceding arguments asserting the effective absence of Parliamentary control over the redistribution process. The position we reach is that the Boundary Commissions are effectively free of any serious external restraint in presenting their recommendations, and that this central element in our system of representative government is dependent in large part for its effective working on the administrative integrity of a relatively small number of officials acting under the general direction of part-time Commissioners. To this we should also add the important role of the Assistant Commissioners who conduct local inquiries (without any statutory rules of procedure), since their conclusions are treated with the greatest respect and incorporated into a Commission's final recommendations unless there is very good reason not to do so. Seen in this light, the edifice of Parliamentary government in Britain appears to rest upon somewhat insubstantial foundations.

It may finally be noted that the system which we have described, with all its imperfections, is nevertheless wholly compatible with Article 3 of the First Protocol to the European Convention on Human Rights. The *Travaux Preparatoires* demonstrate that Article 3 was adopted in its present form to ensure that it imposed no obligation upon signatory states to establish any system of proportional representation.[4] Accordingly, the Commission has repeatedly held that simple majority systems

---

[4] T.P., Vol. viii, p. 14.

of election are compatible with the Convention.[5] As was said in one case,

> "Article 3 of the First Protocol gives an individual right to vote in the election provided for by this Article. This is not the same as a protection of equal voting influence for all voters. The question whether or not equality exists in this respect is due to the electoral system being applied. Article 3 of the First Protocol is careful not to bind the States as to the electoral system and does not add any requirement of 'equality' to the 'secret ballot.' "[6]

All that the Convention therefore requires is that an electoral system provides an opportunity for the free expression of the opinion of the people in the choice of the legislature. An electoral system whereby the numbers of votes securing the election of a candidate must necessarily be higher in some constituencies than others will not be held to infringe this principle unless the discrepancies are of such a degree as to be arbitrary, or disproportionately favour one party over others. Although legitimate criticisms of the British electoral system can be made, it could hardly be argued that its imperfections are such as to negate the political rights of citizens which are protected by Article 3.

(4) EUROPEAN ASSEMBLY CONSTITUENCIES: RULES AND PROCESS

The first direct elections to the European Assembly (now known as the European Parliament) took place in 1979. The allocation of seats among the member-states of the Community was agreed by negotiation within the Council of Ministers in 1976. The United Kingdom, in common with Italy, France and West Germany, was awarded 81 seats. (See Taylor and Johnston (1979), pp. 362–368.) The allocation of seats and the organisation of elections within each member-state was left to domestic law and election machinery; in the United Kingdom, the responsibility for drawing Assembly constituency boundaries was given to the parliamentary Boundary Commissions, save in the case of Northern Ireland where boundary-drawing was not necessary, for reasons to be discussed.

---

[5] App. 7140/75, *X* v. *United Kingdom*, 7 D. & R. 95; App. 8364/78, *Lindsay* v. *United Kingdom*, 15 D. & R. 247; App. 8765/79, *Liberal Party* v. *United Kingdom* 21 D. & R. 211.

[6] App. 8941/80, *X* v. *Iceland*, 27 D. & R. 145 at 150.

The United Kingdom is unusual among European Community member-states in not providing for domestic elections based upon some form of proportional representation. Although the Community is committed by Article 138 of the Treaty of Rome to adopt a uniform electoral procedure for elections to the Assembly, that has not yet been done, and both the 1979 and 1984 Assembly elections in Great Britain were fought on the traditional first-past-the-post basis.[7] In 1984, supporters of the SDP-Liberal Alliance unsuccessfully sought a declarator and interdict in Scottish proceedings on the basis that the first-past-the-post system was in breach of their (asserted) enforceable Community rights to a non-discriminatory electoral system. Interdict was refused on the ground that the balance of convenience lay against a public official (the Returning Officer for the constituency in which the petitioners were registered to vote) being restrained from performing his public duty under the European Assembly Elections Act 1978 when the Act had not yet been demonstrated to be *ultra vires* the Treaty of Rome. Furthermore, reference to the European Court of Justice of questions as to the meaning of Article 138 and the requirements of Community law on elections would be made only if the precise issues in dispute had first been clarified by adequate pre-trial procedures. That had not been done.[8]

Although, therefore, the Assembly elections in Great Britain have proceeded on the basis of the traditional simple majority (first-past-the-post) system, in both 1979 and 1984 the elections in Northern Ireland were conducted on the basis of proportional representation, the constituency for which was the whole of the province. The object of this arrangement was to attempt to secure some representation for Catholic/nationalist opinion, and this was in fact achieved. The introduction of proportional representation for one part of the United Kingdom only was the subject of criticism by Ulster Unionist opinion, and in *Lindsay* v. *United Kingdom* the leaders of the British Ulster Dominion Party complained to the European Commission of Human Rights of a breach of Article 3 of the First Protocol to the Convention. The Commission held that no breach had occurred. Even if it could be assumed in the complainants' favour that the European Assembly was part of the United Kingdom's "legislature" to

---

[7] See the Second Report from the House of Commons Select Committee on Direct Elections to the European Assembly (1975–76) H.C. 515, at paras. 14–18, for discussion as to which electoral system to adopt for Assembly elections.

[8] *Prince* v. *Younger* [1984] 1 C.M.L.R. 723 Ct. of Session (O).

which Article 3 applied, the introduction of different electoral systems for regions within the same country was not a breach of the Article:

> "Article 3 of the Protocol only lays down that the conditions of the elections must be so as to ensure the free expression of the opinion of the people. A system of Proportional Representation will lead to the minority being represented in situations where people vote generally on ethnic or religious lines and one group is in a clear minority throughout all electoral districts. Where such a situation exists in a specific region of a country—as it does in Northern Ireland—the Commission cannot find that the application of a system more favourable to the minority in this part of the country is not in line with the condition that the people should be able to express its opinion freely. Rather, on the contrary, a system taking into account the specific situation as to majority and minority in Northern Ireland must be seen as making it easier for the people to express its opinion freely."[9]

The rules and procedures for drawing Assembly constituencies are set out in the 1978 Act. By virtue of section 2, the 81 seats awarded to the United Kingdom are allocated in the following way: to England 66, to Scotland eight, to Wales four, and to Northern Ireland, to be elected by proportional representation, three. This allocation follows the recommendations of the House of Commons Select Committee which investigated the problems of implementing a system of direct elections to the Assembly.[10] The basis of this allocation is that it is proportionate to population, but with some allowance being made for Scotland, Wales and Northern Ireland, having regard to the large size of certain areas and the scattered nature of their populations.[11] In fact the treatment of England and Wales is, as near as makes no difference, equal. A request by the Welsh Boundary Commission for an extra seat on the basis of difficulties caused by uneven population distributions, geographical factors and the diversity of interests to be represented, was rejected.[12] This is hardly surprising since, in contrast to the situation with parliamentary constituencies, the number of

[9] App. No. 8364/78, *Lindsay and Others* v. *U.K.*, 15 D. & R. 247.
[10] (1975–76) H.C. 515.
[11] *Ibid.* paras. 11–13.
[12] Boundary Commission for Wales Report, European Assembly Constituencies, Cmnd. 7362, para. 4.

United Kingdom seats for the European Assembly is fixed at 81, and an additional seat for Wales would have required another region to give up a seat.

Scotland and Northern Ireland, on the other hand, enjoy a measure of over-representation, in both cases by one seat if strict proportionality were to be observed between the parts of the United Kingdom. In the Northern Irish case, the decision to introduce a system of proportional representation, which requires the transfer of votes between candidates, necessitated the allocation of a minimum of three seats to the province. For Scotland, as has already been mentioned in the context of Parliamentary constituencies, population distributions in particular necessitate a rather more generous ratio of seats to voters if the constituencies are not to be impossibly large.

Each part of the United Kingdom having received its seat allocation, the Boundary Commissions in Great Britain are required to delineate constituency boundaries. The rules of division are set out in Schedule 2, paras. 9 and 10, to the 1978 Act:

Division of Great Britain into Assembly Constituencies

9. In Great Britain—
   (a) each Assembly constituency shall consist of an area that includes two or more parliamentary constituencies; and
   (b) no parliamentary constituency shall be included partly in one Assembly constituency and partly in another.
10. The electorate of any Assembly constituency in Great Britain shall be as near the electoral quota as is reasonably practicable having regard, where appropriate, to special geographical considerations.

It will be seen that the rules require the use of parliamentary constituencies as "building bricks" in the creation of Assembly constituencies. Since the electoral quota (calculated by dividing the electorate for each part of the United Kingdom by the number of Assembly seats allocated to it) produces an average electorate of around 500,000 voters, a typical Assembly constituency will contain between six and nine parliamentary constituencies.

The Act is silent as to what considerations are relevant in putting these parliamentary constituencies together to form Assembly constituencies. Respect for major local government boundaries, initially attempted in England, could not be achieved. The English Commission endeavoured instead

> "to reflect the broad common interests and local loyalties of an area as a whole and to take account of the pattern of communications which served the various parts in the constituencies finally selected for our provisional recommendations."[13]

Paragraph 10 of Schedule 2 allows for departure from observance "as near . . . as is reasonably practicable" of the electoral quota where "special geographical considerations" render this appropriate. This is equivalent to rule 6 of the parliamentary constituency boundary rules, save that that rule effectively empowers the creation of seats additional to those which would be required by strict attachment to the electoral quota. Here, since the number of Assembly seats is fixed, "special geographical considerations" authorise instead the creation of seats (within a region's total) having markedly fewer electors. Not surprisingly, the Scottish Commission has had recourse to this rule in creating the Assembly constituency of Highlands and Islands, whose total electorate, on creation of the constituency in 1978, was nearly 40 per cent. below the electoral quota for Scotland (which was already generous).[14] Neither the English nor Welsh Commissions have made use of the rule in paragraph 10, although the Welsh Commission would doubtless have done so in respect of North and Mid-Wales had its request for an additional seat been successful.

A feature of the drawing of European Assembly constituencies has been the use by the English Boundary Commission of computers. Paradoxically, it is the relative simplicity of drawing Assembly constituencies, particularly the limited number of possible solutions compared with the delineation of parliamentary constituencies, that has enabled computing techniques to be used.[15] This raises interesting questions as to how quickly a proportional representation system of elections could be introduced into this country, were it decided that this was appropriate. If the Boundary Commissions were required to create constituencies afresh, according to criteria which inevitably would need to be in rather general terms, this would be a

---

[13] Boundary Commission for England Report, European Assembly Constituencies, Cmnd. 7348, para. 8.
[14] Boundary Commission for Scotland Report, European Assembly Constituencies, Cmnd. 7336, para. 11.
[15] (1986–87) H.C. 97–I, p. 24. And see Barnes (1987).

lengthy process, as many different possible sets of boundaries would need to be considered. Conversely, the use of the existing parliamentary constituencies as "building bricks" for new multi-member constituencies would greatly simplify matters. The process of dividing England into 66 Assembly constituencies was achieved over a period of 12 months in 1977 and 1978.

The use of computing was not the sole reason for that expeditious procedure. Under the 1978 Act, Boundary Commissions were exempted, in respect of the 1978 review only, from the obligations to hold local inquiries into objections and to publicise revised recommendations.[16] This was done in order that the Commissions would be able to meet the timetable for elections laid down by the Council of Ministers.[17] The procedures to be followed in subsequent reviews now mirror those applicable to parliamentary constituency reviews—provisional recommendations, local objections, local inquiries, revised recommendations, further local inquiries unless considered by the Commission unjustified, and final recommendations.[18] These procedures have already been discussed. Final recommendations are implemented by way of Order in Council, provided both Houses of Parliament have voted in favour of a draft of the Order.[19]

Reviews of Assembly constituencies are conducted immediately following reviews of parliamentary constituencies, between every 10 and 15 years.[20] This provision is essential, since Assembly constituencies are created on the basis of existing parliamentary constituencies under Sched. 2, para. 9 of the 1978 Act. It is, however, to be noted that the "enumeration date" for electors on the electoral roll is different to that applicable to the review of parliamentary constituency boundaries. It is that date on which a Commission gives notice of its intention to undertake a review of Assembly constituencies.[21] The effect of this can be seen in the review which followed the 1983 redistribution of parliamentary seats. The review of parliamentary seats proceeded on the basis of 1976 electoral rolls. The review of Assembly constituencies began immediately

---

[16] European Assembly Elections Act 1978, Sched. 2, paras. 1 and 4(1)(*b*).
[17] See (1975–76) H.C. 515, paras. 21–2.
[18] European Assembly Elections Act 1981, s.1(1), 1(4)(*b*); Parliamentary Constituencies Act 1986, Sched. 3, para. 5.
[19] Parliamentary Constituencies Act 1986, Sched. 3, para. 5(4).
[20] European Assembly Elections Act 1981, s.1(1).
[21] European Assembly Elections Act 1978, Sched. 2, para. 12.

following the implementation of the Commissions' recommendations on parliamentary boundaries, and its "enumeration date" was April 25, 1983. As we have seen, in the intervening seven years from March 1976, the electorate had expanded by one-and-a-half million voters. Thus the Commissions were required in 1983 to recommend constituencies "as near the electoral quota as is reasonably practicable," but were using building bricks (parliamentary constituencies) whose boundaries were based on quotas markedly different from those applicable in 1983. It is hardly surprising, therefore, that the recommendations in 1983 did sometimes propose constituencies departing significantly from the 1983 quota for Assembly constituencies.[22]

Having said that, it is true to say that the redistribution of Assembly constituencies has occasioned far less controversy than has the redistribution of parliamentary seats. One reason for this is obviously that the European Assembly itself has not been regarded by the political parties as a particularly important institution. It is submitted, however, that the provisions in Schedule 2 to the 1978 Act, requiring the use of parliamentary constituencies as building bricks, have themselves taken much heat out of the process of redistribution, by significantly limiting the number of options available to the Commissions. Controversy in the past has been engendered by apparently surprising Commission decisions on parliamentary constituency boundaries. The scope for surprising decisions in respect of European Assembly constituencies is far smaller. Those who advocate the introduction of proportional representation into this country might do well to bear this experience in mind when suggesting how multi-member constituencies might initially be defined.

(5) CONCLUSION

The arrangements which we have outlined in this Part have been developed in an attempt to reconcile the competing (Radical) demands for equal constituencies with more traditional arguments for the retention of community representation in territorially-defined electoral units. As we saw particularly in the context of the redistribution of parliamentary seats, reconciliation is virtually impossible, and priority has to be given to

---

[22] See, for example, Cheshire East (electorate 499,418) and Essex North East (573,681). The electoral quota for this review was 539,155. See generally, the English Commission's Report, Cmnd. 9208.

one principle of representation in preference to the other. The allocation of such preferences will inevitably be politically controversial, and that controversy will be only partially mitigated by the appointment of apparently neutral redistributing agencies, such as the Boundary Commissions, to perform the redistributing function. The existence of controversy is not, of itself, a matter of concern, in our view. Rather, it may be evidence of the vitality of the political process. Nevertheless, there are aspects of the constituency delineation process that merit further investigation. Is it right, for example, that local inquiries should be conducted without any statutory rules of procedure? Ought Assistant Commissioners to be more fully acquainted with regional and local issues, perhaps as members of an expanded agency incorporating both Local Government and parliamentary Boundary Commissions, and concerning themselves full-time with these issues? Is there greater scope for computerisation of the redistribution process? The debate about the merits of proportional representation has in our view understandably but unfortunately deflected critical attention from the mechanics of the present system, and we would hope to see greater attention paid to such issues in the future. As we said earlier, the proper delineation of electoral units is a crucial determinant of the fair working of the electoral system. Our view is that insufficient attention has been paid to this in recent years, and that the rules and procedures laid down by statute are demonstrably inadequate in certain respects. The legitimacy of the electoral system is to this extent undermined.

Part Two

THE PARTICIPANTS: VOTERS, CANDIDATES AND PARTIES

3. THE ELECTORATE

"Voting rights lie at the root of parliamentary democracy. Indeed many would regard them as a basic human right. Nevertheless they are not like the air we breathe. They do not just happen. They have to be conferred, or at least defined and the categories of citizen who enjoy them have also to be defined."[1]

(1) EVOLUTION OF THE FRANCHISE

(a) Towards Popular Representation in Parliament

Although Radical arguments for universal male suffrage had been advanced for nearly 200 years before the passage of the Great Reform Act of 1832 (Birch (1964), pp. 32 *et seq.*), that Act initiated only a very limited extension of the franchise, by constructing a complex web of property qualifications for membership of the electorate. Indeed, by removing existing qualifications not based upon property rights, the Act ensured a reduction in the number of working-class men entitled to vote, in favour of the property-owning middle class (Seymour (1915), p. 88). The property qualifications were thought to show sufficient evidence of an individual's responsibility to warrant the privilege of a vote.

The importance of the 1832 Act lies therefore not so much in what it achieved as what it implied. According to Hanham,

> "Once the Reform Bill had passed, the theory of the British system of government had clearly to be changed. Overnight, as it were, the constitution had ceased to be based on the principle of prescription, and had come to be based on the principle of representation."

(Hanham (1971), pp. 7–8)

Debates after 1832 were concerned with identifying those who were entitled to be represented. Birch tells us that Radical ideas as to the extent of the franchise became more widely accepted in

---

[1] Sir John Donaldson M.R., *Hipperson* v. *Newbury Electoral Registration Officer*, [1985] Q.B. 1060, 1067.

the second half of the nineteenth century (Birch (1964), p. 60). Gladstone's famous *dictum*, that "every man who is not presumably incapacitated by some consideration of personal unfitness or of political danger is morally entitled to come within the pale of the Constitution," reflects that view. But each new decision as to the scope of the franchise was resolved more as a result of political assessments reached according to the interests of the Liberal or Conservative parties than by a commitment to any particular version of democratic theory (see, for example, Vincent (1976), p. xlix; Blake (1985), pp. 98–111). On each occasion these political decisions were effected by manipulating the property qualifications required of individual electors.

The 1832 Act introduced a system of registration of electors. The complexity of the property qualifications was such that much time was occupied in Registration Courts contesting the entitlement of individuals to vote. Many appear to have had neither the time nor enthusiasm to find their way around the complexities of the law, and failed to register. Equally inevitably, political parties recognised the scope for winning elections by ensuring that their own supporters who were qualified were identified and registered, and that opposing supporters were struck off the register (Seymour (1915), p. 370). It is difficult to estimate the numerical consequences of each successive widening of the franchise, for the numbers are masked by failures to register, but it has been estimated that in 1833 one in five adult males were eligible, by 1869 this had risen to one in three, and after 1884 this doubled to two in three (Hanham (1971), p. 35). Yet only some 60 per cent. of adult males were on the parliamentary register before 1914 (Pugh (1978), p. 1).

The complex property qualifications were swept away by the Representation of the People Act 1918 (R.P.A. 1918), which finally established the notion of a universal male, adult, franchise as well as introducing a limited parliamentary franchise for women (see generally, Pugh (1978)). The 1918 Act set out three qualifications for men to vote in parliamentary elections:

(a) The residence qualification: a man was deemed eligible to vote if he had been resident in the constituency on the last day of the qualifying period, and had lived in the constituency or within an adjoining constituency for six months immediately preceding that date.

(b) The business qualification: eligibility was achieved through occupation of business premises in the constituency on the last day of the qualifying period and for the immediately preceding six months, providing the premises had a yearly value of not less than £10.

(c) The university qualification: a man could be registered to vote in a university constituency if he had received a degree from a qualifying university.

The changes this brought about did little to expand the potential male electorate (as distinct from those actually registered to vote). The 1918 Act's importance lies in the simplified system it created. After 1918 the franchise was clearly seen to be primarily dependent upon residence in the electoral area, rather than upon property rights, so that every adult male in principle qualified for a vote somewhere in the United Kingdom.

The 1918 Act was also notable in that the right to vote in parliamentary elections was at last conferred upon certain classes of women. Women had been entitled to vote in some local elections for nearly 50 years, but this was the breakthrough into the parliamentary franchise. Coke had stated that at common law women were not entitled to vote.[2] Furthermore the rights conferred by the 1832 Reform Act were expressly accorded only to "males." The passage of Lord Brougham's Act of 1850 rendered the position less certain, however. That Act stated that "words importing the masculine gender shall be deemed to include females unless the contrary is expressly provided." Relying upon Lord Brougham's Act many suitably qualified women claimed to be entered upon the electoral register, and some Registration Courts upheld such applications. The issue came to a head in a series of cases in the Court of Common Pleas arising from the 1867 electoral register, including the leading case of *Chorlton* v. *Lings*.[3] The court held that in the case of the franchise, "man" does not include "woman." The view was taken that women had never been entitled to vote at common law, and that it would require a clear statute to reverse this position.

Women had therefore to wait until 1918 for the parliamentary franchise, and then it was restricted to certain categories of women over the age of 30. The 30-year age limit was imposed so as to keep women in a minority within the electorate. Some eight-and-a-half million women voters were enfranchised, but a further five million between the ages of 21 and 30 continued to be excluded. The categories of women enfranchised were those

---

[2] Institutes, Vol. 4, p. 5. But see Wallis Chapman and Wallis Chapman (1909), pp. 20–28.

[3] (1868–9) 4 L.R.C.P. 374.

over 30 who were entitled to be registered as local government electors either because they were in occupation of (rather than resident in) a dwelling-house or were in occupation of land or premises other than a dwelling-house of not less than £5 yearly value; or were wives of husbands who were themselves entitled to be registered as local government electors. These provisions served to continue to disenfranchise single women who could not meet the stricter property requirement of occupation rather than residence. Thus, for example, adult women, unmarried and living with their parents or in lodgings, did not qualify. Women were finally placed on the same footing as men for parliamentary elections by the Representation of the People (Equal Franchise) Act of 1928. Under that Act women received all the entitlements conferred on men in the 1918 Act, and in addition the spouse of someone entitled to a business vote became entitled to vote in that constituency.

The 1918 Act also introduced a new qualification to vote. Recognising that most of the servicemen engaged in the war would not be entitled to register as they were not resident in the United Kingdom, Parliament made special provision in section 5 of the 1918 Act to entitle them to register at the address where they would have been entitled to register, but for their absence in service. Once this was conferred on adult males, the anomaly of allowing only soldiers over 21 to vote was apparent. Accordingly, section 5 conferred this service vote on any serviceman attaining 19 years of age. And, as the soldiers were gradually demobbed, so in 1920 this right was extended to ex-servicemen who had reached their 19th birthday whilst in the services and therefore become entitled to the servicemen's vote. The legislation conferred this franchise not just on servicemen, but also on Red Cross personnel, St. John's helpers, and those serving in any other job recognised as being of "national importance." Special provisions for servicemen have continued through subsequent Acts, although the special age privilege was removed in 1948.

The Representation of the People Act 1948 (R.P.A. 1948) completed the simplification process by removing the University franchise and the business franchise, thereby establishing a system of "one person one vote." Henceforth the sole qualification to vote in a Parliamentary election was to be residence in the electoral area on the qualifying date. As a result, all adult citizens are now in principle eligible to register somewhere in the United Kingdom. The requirement for a period of residence was removed, but for Northern Ireland a three-month residence qualification was reimposed in 1949.

Only three changes have been made since 1948. First, the minimum age for voting was lowered from 21 to 18 by the Representation of the People Act 1969. The Act also removed the requirement that a person must have reached the qualifying age at the qualifying date. That requirement had meant that many people were aged 22 before being entitled to vote. Since 1969 a person may be entered on the register as long as he or she reaches 18 years during the period of the register. Such "attainers" can then vote as soon as they reach 18. Secondly, the same Act brought merchant seamen into the special category of people who can register as if they were resident at a home address, or a seaman's hostel.

Finally, the Representation of the People Act 1985 introduced the principle of overseas voting. Hitherto, the only people absent from home who were entitled to register and vote had been service personnel and merchant seamen. This provision has now been extended to any British citizen residing overseas, providing they resided at an address within the United Kingdom within the preceding five years. This is further discussed below.

(b) The Local Government Franchise

The Municipal Corporations Act of 1835 conferred a new municipal franchise on every male of full age who had occupied premises in the borough for two years preceding registration and had actually lived either within the borough or within seven miles, subject to their being ratepayers who were up to date with their rate payments and who had not received parochial relief in the preceding 12 months. The Municipal Corporations Act 1869 shortened the required period of occupation to one year; but far more importantly, it afforded the municipal franchise to women on the same property and ratepayer terms as men. When the county councils were established in 1888, women similarly became entitled to vote for them. In each case the franchise was lost if the woman married,[4] but this restriction was abolished by section 43 of the Local Government Act 1894, and married women retained their vote provided that a husband and wife did not claim to be qualified in respect of the same property.

[4] R. v. *Harrald* (1871–2) 7 L.R.Q.B. 361.

Throughout this period voting qualifications depended upon occupation of property, as of course did the parliamentary franchise; but when, in 1918, the parliamentary franchise for men was reconstituted in terms of "residence," the occupation qualification for local government voters was retained. It was not until 1949 that residence was adopted as the primary qualification. Even then, occupation as owner or tenant of any land or premises with a yearly value of at least £10 also entitled individuals to a vote. This implied the retention of the "business" vote, but the occupation qualification also applied to people who owned premises which they rented out as furnished, providing they intended to occupy them within nine weeks of the end of the tenancy. The extent to which this vote was a relic of the 1835 Act can be seen from the continued retention of the £10 value qualification, which had long since been devalued. Its removal in the 1969 Act brought the local franchise into line with the parliamentary franchise by making residence the sole criterion for the franchise.

Since 1969 the local franchise has differed from the parliamentary franchise only in the most minor respects. Peers of the realm are entitled to register and vote in local elections, whereas the overseas voter franchise introduced in 1985 for parliamentary and European elections does not so extend. Service voters and those voluntarily resident in mental hospitals are required to make special declarations in order to be entered upon the parliamentary register. There is no provision permitting the making of such declarations in respect of local elections, but once such individuals are entered on the parliamentary register, they can vote in local elections. In all other respects the parliamentary and local government franchises are now identical, and the ensuing discussion will consider the modern position solely in terms of the parliamentary franchise.

(c) European Assembly Franchise

The franchise for the European Assembly elections is based upon identical requirements to the parliamentary and local government franchise. It extends to anyone qualified to vote in either parliamentary or local government elections, to overseas voters eligible for a parliamentary vote, and to those who would be qualified to vote as overseas voters but for a peerage. A wider European franchise, giving the vote to all Community nationals resident within a member-state of Europe has been discussed by the Council of Ministers, but as yet no agreement has been reached.

(2) THE PARLIAMENTARY FRANCHISE TODAY

Section 1 of the Representation of the People Act 1983 provides:

"1. (1) A person entitled to vote as an elector at a parliamentary election in any constituency is one who—
    (a) is resident there on the qualifying date...; and
    (b) on that date and on the date of the poll—
        (i) is not subject to any legal incapacity to vote (age apart); and
        (ii) is either a Commonwealth citizen or a citizen of the Republic of Ireland; and
    (c) is of voting age (that is, 18 years or over) on the date of the poll.
(2) ...
(3) A person is not entitled to vote as an elector in any constituency unless registered there in the register of parliamentary electors to be used at the election."

The section therefore establishes a number of tests which have to be met by an intending voter. He or she must establish: residence, an appropriate citizenship, the requisite age, inclusion on the register, and must show that the narrow categories of legal incapacity to vote do not apply to him or her. We discuss each of these in turn, save that questions of voting age are conveniently considered in the context of registration. One preliminary point should be made. Until 1948, questions as to the scope of the franchise excited considerable controversy between the parties. With the achievement of "one person one vote" these disputes seem to have disappeared, but it would be wrong to believe that questions of voting entitlement are now exclusively a matter of administration rather than the subject of political contention. Like other governments before it, the Conservative government has since 1979 introduced legislation on the scope of the franchise which is designed to enhance its own party interests, and it has promoted other policies which, intentionally or not, may operate to reduce the voting strength of the Labour Party. We shall refer to these below.

(a) Residence

Since 1918 the residence qualification has been the primary determinant of the right to be entered on the electoral register. If entitlement to vote is now regarded as a necessary incident of membership of the political community, the test of "residence" is an administrative device, in an electoral system based upon geographically-defined constituencies, to determine *where* particular citizens may exercise that entitlement. It also accords with our traditional conceptions of community representation that electors be required to exhibit some degree of commitment to a given community by residing within it. In reality the degree of commitment required is minimal. The 1948 Act envisaged the taking of a snapshot on a given qualifying date, and registering electors wherever they happened to reside on that date. That principle has been retained, save in respect of Northern Ireland, where three months' residence is required. Were this not so, large numbers of Irish citizens could cross the border purely to establish voting entitlements for Northern Irish elections.

Despite these simplifications, the residence requirement still causes problems and effectively disenfranchises some voters. People can only vote in the electoral area for which they are registered. With an increasingly mobile population as much as 20 per cent. of the electorate may have moved from their address in the electoral area by the end of the period for which that qualifying date applies. It was hoped that a liberalisation of the postal voting regulations in 1987 would alleviate this problem, but the timetable and the complexities of this procedure have limited its use.

The 1983 Act provides, by section 5(1):

"... any question as to a person's residence on the qualifying date for an election—
   (a) shall be determined in accordance with the general principles formerly applied in determining questions as to a person's residence on a particular day of the qualifying period within the meaning of the Representation of the People Act 1918; and
   (b) in particular regard shall be had to the purpose and other circumstances, as well as to the fact, of his presence at or absence from the address in question."

Since the abolition of the continuity of residence requirement in 1948, there have been few cases in which this test has fallen to be applied. The leading English case is *Fox* v. *Stirk*,[5] which was concerned with whether students could be held to be "resident" at their term-time address. This is a matter of considerable practical importance, especially in seats like Glasgow Hillhead, which is amongst the 50 seats with the highest student electorate in the country, and where the M.P. prior to 1987 had a majority of just 2·8 per cent. The issue of student voting emerged as a result of the reduction of the voting age to 18 in 1969. Whereas in the past only a small number of students had registered, large numbers of students registered in October 1969, intent on taking part in the election due the following year. *Fox* v. *Stirk* was treated as a test case in respect of these registrations.

Section 5(1)(*a*) requires the Electoral Registration Officer (E.R.O.) to have regard to the general principles applied in determining residence questions under the 1918 Act. There is only one reported case on the interpretation of the 1918 Act,[6] and that was not cited to the Court of Appeal. Instead the Court went back to first principles, Lord Denning relying upon the O.E.D. definition, "to dwell permanently or for a considerable time, to have one's settled or usual abode, to live in or at a particular place." From this he derived three principles by which to judge residence:

> "The first principle is that a man can have two residences. He can have a flat in London and a house in the country. He is resident at both. The second principle is that temporary presence at an address does not make a man resident there. A guest who comes for the weekend is not resident. A short-stay visitor is not resident. The third principle is that temporary absence does not deprive a person of his residence. If he happens to be away for a holiday or away for the weekend or in hospital, he does not lose his residence on that account."[7]

Taken overall he expressed this test in the phrase "a considerable degree of permanence."[8] On this basis the Court held that the students were indeed "resident" within the meaning of the legislation, and it is nowadays regularly the practice to include on the register students in an equivalent position.

---

[5] [1970] 2 Q.B. 463, C.A.
[6] *Ferris* v. *Wallace* 1936 S.C. 561.
[7] [1970] 2 Q.B. 463, 475.
[8] *Ibid.*

As Lord Denning made clear in *Fox* v. *Stirk*, it is entirely possible for an individual to have two residences, and to be registered in both. In some areas, second-home owners form a large percentage of the potential electorate. Although the properties may only be occupied for a few weeks each year, the owners may qualify as resident at that address. Contested registration disputes on this have seldom come to court in England, but in Scotland the matter has been raised on a number of occasions.[9] In *Ferris* v. *Wallace*,[10] (the Scottish case ignored by the Court of Appeal in *Fox* v. *Stirk*), a resident of Glasgow spent every weekend between April and September in a "wooden hut" in a Scottish rural constituency. He also lived in this hut throughout the months of July and August. He was refused inclusion in the register of electors in the rural constituency, and his appeal against this decision was dismissed, the Registration Appeals Court holding that his holiday home was merely incidental to his primary residence in Glasgow. Similarly, in *Scott* v. *Phillip*,[11] the question was whether staying at a holiday cottage for three-and-a-half months each year could amount to "residence." The Registration Appeal Court accepted that this use had been going on for many years, and did show the considerable degree of permanence referred to by Lord Denning, but the Court felt that *Fox* v. *Stirk* had placed insufficient weight on the nature and quality of the residence. The latter was particularly important where a person had two residences. The Court adopted the approach in *Ferris* v. *Wallace* of asking, "Is the residence at Marlyrig a substantive residence or merely a residence which is incidental to the residence at Inveresk?" The Court took the view that a holiday home for leisure and relaxation was incidental to the main home. The Court did not go so far as to state that *Fox* v. *Stirk* was wrong, but did suggest that "the dicta in that case ignore some of the general principles which should be applicable."

Whereas in *Scott* v. *Phillip*, three-and-a-half months' stay each year was not deemed sufficient for "residence," in *Dumble* v. *Electoral Registration Officer for Borders*[12] residence confined to weekends was found sufficient. The court distinguished between the two cases by reference to the purpose of residence rather than length of stay. Indeed the court said that the cases

---

[9] See Stewart (1975) and Stewart (1980).
[10] n. 6, above.
[11] [1974] S.L.T. 32.
[12] [1980] S.L.T. 60.

bore no more than a superficial similarity. In *Scott* the house was owned by the family, and used for leisure and relaxation. In *Dumble* it was rented, but used as the political base for the Conservative candidate in the constituency. Applying the "incidental purpose" approach, the second home in *Dumble's* case was not merely incidental to a main home in the city, but was one of two substantive residences.

Notwithstanding this, the Scottish courts have clearly shown less sympathy to registration by second-home owners than the English Court of Appeal, in *Fox* v. *Stirk*, showed itself to have.[13] As a matter of principle, this more rigorous Scottish approach has much to commend it. The 1983 Act prohibits double voting in Parliamentary and local government elections,[14] but dual registration is, as we have seen, quite permissible. The select groups who are able to take advantage of this are thereby given an opportunity to choose where to vote in any particular election, and thus enabled to maximise the influence of their votes in a way which is not open to other electors. A proposal from the 1973 Speaker's Conference on Electoral Reform,[15] that multiple registration should be prohibited, was ignored by the then Conservative government. In 1984 the present government also rejected the proposal of the Home Affairs Select Committee that those with two or more residences should be obliged to select one of them as their "electoral residence" for registration purposes.[16] With the continuing growth in the number of second homes, it is unlikely that this will be the last to be heard of the matter.

The Court of Appeal has most recently had occasion to consider the "residence" qualification in the very different circumstances of the Greenham Common case, *Hipperson* v. *Newbury Electoral Registration Officer*.[17] A number of women established a camp outside the United States Air Force base at Greenham Common, protesting about the introduction of Cruise missiles into the United Kingdom. They slept in tents, vehicles or in the open air. Mail was regularly delivered there, and many of the women spent substantial periods at the camp, whether or not they had additional homes elsewhere. On this basis the Court of Appeal held that the E.R.O. had been entitled

---

[13] See Stewart (1975).
[14] R.P.A. 1983, ss.1(4), 2(3); see also, s.61(2)–(7).
[15] Cmnd. 5363.
[16] Cmnd. 9140, paras. 4.1–4.7.
[17] [1985] Q.B. 1060, C.A.

to regard the women as "resident" for registration purposes. Residence did not depend upon bricks and mortar, and the quality of the accommodation enjoyed was irrelevant for registration purposes. The test was one of permanence, and the purpose of the residence. As Sir John Donaldson M.R. pointed out, "Permanence, like most aspects of residence, is a question of fact and degree,"[18] which is ultimately to be determined by the tribunal of fact, in this case the E.R.O. In the light of the marked degree of continuity of the camp, it was not surprising that the E.R.O. had found the camp's inhabitants "resident" there, especially as, being self-proclaimed "peace workers," they could claim to be living "over the shop." Furthermore, the Court of Appeal considered the question of the lawfulness of the "residence" irrelevant. "Residence" could not be tied to the niceties of property law and the right to occupy, or this would reimport all the complexities of registration which the 1918 Act had sought to eradicate:

> "We do not consider that Parliament could have intended to cast on an electoral registration officer the duty of deciding which residential breaches of the criminal law should disqualify an aspiring voter and which should not. Accordingly we reject the submission that the franchise is affected by the fact that the qualifying residence is illegal or, *a fortiori*, unlawful."[19]

There is one further practical problem to mention. Although it is residence on a particular date rather than continual residence which matters, the more unstable the residence, the more significance the length of residence may have. Someone who has purchased a property and moved in will probably not need to show anything more than residence on the qualifying date. Someone staying in a boarding house on that same date may well find that the Registration Officer will want to know how long his stay is likely to be before he is deemed resident. The extent to which the duration of stay affects questions of residence may cause serious problems for those young people subject to the recently introduced DHSS board and lodgings regulations. People under 26 who are in receipt of supplementary benefit may receive a board and lodging allowance for a maximum of eight weeks at any one address. This period is reduced to two weeks if the address is at a holiday resort.

[18] At 1073.
[19] At 1075.

Thereafter the person must move on, or lose benefit. It will be difficult to establish the "considerable degree of permanence" spoken of by Lord Denning in *Fox* v. *Stirk* if the maximum duration of lodging is only two weeks. It might be argued that a claimant may nevertheless be registrable at his or her parental address. Yet many are in lodging because of a specific decision to leave home, and therefore could not be said to reside at their parental address. Furthermore, for some 25-year-olds, there may no longer be a parental home at which to register. It is likely that many of these people will effectively be disenfranchised, probably to the disadvantage of the Labour Party, which might reasonably expect to secure a high proportion of their votes. Even if they are permitted to register, the problems of obtaining a postal vote are likely to result in a very low turnout. It is a serious breach in the principle of a universal franchise to disqualify people in this way.

(b) Citizenship

The relationship between citizenship and entitlement to vote raises two issues. First, should "residence" be regarded as a sufficient indication of commitment to the United Kingdom to entitle an individual to vote, or should we limit the franchise by additional reference to citizenship (and, if so, which countries' citizens, resident here, should nevertheless be held ineligible)? Secondly, what of non-residents? Are we to allow British citizens (or some wider category?) who are resident abroad still to be entitled to vote in the United Kingdom?

First we consider the position of those resident in the United Kingdom. Under section 1(1)(b)(ii) of the R.P.A. 1983, to be eligible to vote a person must be either a Commonwealth citizen or a citizen of the Republic of Ireland. Historically, aliens were excluded from voting by parliamentary resolution.[20] Under the 1918 Act, when residence first became of central importance in determining the scope of the franchise, section 9(3) provided that registration could be afforded only to British subjects, that is to say any person who owed allegiance to the Crown, regardless of the Crown territory in which he or she was born. Subsequently, the achievement of independence by a number of Imperial territories necessitated the creation of new citizenship rules. The British Nationality Act 1948 (B.N.A. 1948), by section

[20] 12 Commons Journals 367 (1698). For a curious example of this bar, see *Re Stepney Election Petition, Isaacson* v. *Durant* (1886) 17 Q.B.D. 54. See also, British Nationality and Status of Aliens Act 1914, s.17(2).

1(2), created a category of Commonwealth citizen for certain purposes, this category being co-extensive with the former class of "British subjects." The 1948 Act did not affect the scope of the franchise, and the Representation of the People Act of 1949 continued to define the franchise in terms of "British subjects." However, in 1981 the British Nationality Act, Part IV, gave the phrase "British subject" a new (and highly restrictive) meaning. Accordingly, the R.P.A. 1983 now refers to the franchise in terms of Commonwealth citizenship, using that phrase in the broad sense envisaged by the B.N.A. 1948 to encompass all categories of British citizenship, the special category of British subject (without citizenship), and all citizens of the 45 Commonwealth countries specified in Schedule 3 to the 1981 Act.

Why should citizens of independent countries, albeit members of the Commonwealth, continue to be able to vote in the United Kingdom, even if they are resident here? The answer to this must be that if we were constructing the franchise *ab initio*, such people would in all likelihood be excluded; but the practical problems involved in excluding Commonwealth citizens from the register now render any such restriction virtually impossible. This is particularly the case in respect of residents of New Commonwealth and Pakistan origin. Many Indian citizens resident in Britain have refused to take out British citizenship because this would lead automatically to loss of their Indian citizenship. Such people would lose their voting entitlement if the franchise were restricted to British citizens. However, the children of such long-term residents may well have acquired British citizenship, and these would retain their voting entitlements. The complexities of British citizenship being what they are, to impose upon Electoral Registration Officers a duty to investigate the citizenship status of possibly large numbers of individuals in such circumstances would be quite impractical.[21]

The same argument holds in respect of the otherwise anomalous inclusion of Irish citizens as potential voters. From 1936 the precise position of Ireland within the Commonwealth was uncertain. The British Nationality Act 1948 resolved the citizenship aspects of this issue by establishing that Irish citizens were no longer to be British subjects (that is, under section 1(2) of the 1948 Act, Commonwealth citizens) but were nevertheless to be treated for all purposes as if they were. When Ireland formally cut its last links with the Commonwealth in 1949, it was

---

[21] For examples of this, see (1982–3) H.C. 32–II, Appendix 25, paras. 5–8. See also, Appendices 15, 20, 24.

decided by the British government that this should not affect the position of Irish citizens within the United Kingdom. Parliament accordingly passed the Ireland Act 1949, which *inter alia* declares that citizens of the Republic are not aliens. On this basis Irish citizens retained their voting entitlements, a fact which is now explicitly recognised in section 1(1)(*b*)(ii) of the R.P.A. 1983. Evidence presented to the Home Affairs Select Committee demonstrated that E.R.O.s would have the greatest difficulty in distinguishing those people of Irish origin holding British citizenship:

" . . . within that group there are people who are of Irish ancestry but only British citizens and there are people who are of Irish ancestry who are both British citizens and Irish citizens, and there are those who are of Irish ancestry and who are only Irish citizens."[22]

Furthermore, (and this argument applies with equal force to those of New Commonwealth origin), the disenfranchisement of non-British citizens could well be taken as an expression of hostility towards the disenfranchised, which would be disadvantageous both for community relations within the United Kingdom and for foreign relationships with Commonwealth countries and with Ireland.[23]

The Home Affairs Committee therefore firmly rejected disenfranchisement of non-British Commonwealth citizens and Irish citizens and the government has accepted that.[24] But a further question follows. If certain categories of non-British citizens are to be regarded as eligible for registration, provided that they can establish residence, why should not all those resident in the United Kingdom, regardless of citizenship, be so regarded? There are no practical problems here. Indeed, rather the reverse is true, because at registration no inquiry is usually made into the citizenship of individuals seeking to register, with the result that aliens are frequently registered anyway.[25] An amendment to the law repealing any reference at all to citizenship would reflect this administrative reality. Nevertheless, the Home Affairs Committee was not prepared to make a recommendation "conferring new rights on those who have never been regarded as

---

[22] (1982–3) H.C. 32–II, p. 191, para. 763.
[23] (1982–3) H.C. 32–I, p. xiii.
[24] Cmnd. 9140, p. 7, para. 2.1.
[25] (1982–3) H.C. 32–II, p. 73, paras. 290–292.

British subjects." Perhaps this is justifiable in that the residence qualification, on which all would then depend, is now more easily satisfied than when, before 1948, it implied a period of settled habitation in the country. Opening the register to all "residents," regardless of citizenship, might lead to an excessive foreign influence over an electoral system which must in the last resort be a predominantly British concern.

We now turn to the other side of the residence/citizenship coin. What of the voting entitlements of British citizens resident abroad? In a polity based upon a theory of community representation, there is no case for the enfranchisement of those resident abroad. But once it is accepted that every person not peculiarly incapacitated is "morally entitled to come within the pale of the Constitution," in other words that enfranchisement is a necessary incident of citizenship, citizens resident abroad have a stronger claim. The 1918 Act demonstrated acceptance of the Radical theory of representation by establishing registration qualifications which in principle enabled all adult males to qualify. Further, it followed the logic of that position by providing for machinery to enable a certain class of British adult males not resident in the United Kingdom also to qualify. Once it was accepted that some individuals who were not in fact resident should be entitled to vote, the door was opened for other groups of foreign residents to argue their case.[26] The problem then comes down to this: which groups' claims (if any) should be recognised, and by what criteria?

A simple extension of voting rights to all those resident abroad who would qualify if resident in the United Kingdom— Commonwealth citizens and Irish citizens—would clearly be nonsensical, since several hundreds of millions would be enfranchised. The Home Affairs Committee therefore had to devise criteria legitimately restricting the classes of individuals. A number of options was canvassed—restricting the franchise to Commonwealth citizens resident within the EEC; restricting it to those whose work necessitated their living abroad; requiring proof of an "intention to return"; requiring evidence of previous residence within the United Kingdom; laying down a time limit on the number of years' absence from the United Kingdom.[27]

---

[26] See X v. *U.K.* Appl. 7730/76, 15 D. & R. 137 (employee of the European Community, resident in Brussels); X v. *U.K.* Appl. 7566/76, 9 D. & R. 121 (resident of Paris). No breaches of Prot. 1, Art. 3 found—conditions of residence as a qualification to vote neither arbitrary nor interfering with the free expression of the people's opinion.

[27] (1982–3) H.C. 32–I, pp. xiv–xix.

The Home Office preferred what they considered the simplest test, that of residence at an address within the United Kingdom within the previous seven years. The idea of such a limit was to ensure that voters had not lost touch with this country. This also had the merit of avoiding a further problem normally resolved by the residence requirements. If all these extra people were to be entitled to vote, *where* were they to vote? Should a new "overseas constituency" be created? The Home Office solution was that they should vote in the constituency for which they were last registered,[28] and that view is now reflected in the legislation.

Sections 1–4 of the R.P.A 1985 provide that an individual may be registered as an overseas elector if he or she is a British citizen[29] (as distinct from a British Dependent Territories citizen, British Overseas citizen or British subject, or a Commonwealth or Irish citizen); is not resident in the United Kingdom; but within the last five years (rather than seven, as originally proposed) was resident at a United Kingdom address and was included on the register of parliamentary electors in respect of that address. Registration will only ensue if an overseas elector's declaration is completed in due form,[30] and this declaration must state that the declarant does not intend to reside permanently outside the United Kingdom. Unlike the service declaration procedure on which these administrative arrangements are modelled, the overseas voter's declaration must be renewed annually.[31] Registration is possible only in respect of parliamentary and European Assembly elections, and in any event is not available to residents abroad who have just attained the age of 18, since they will not already have been entered within the preceding five years on a constituency register within the United Kingdom.

Thus in the overseas voters' case the qualification to vote is citizenship rather than residence in a particular electoral area, although the five-year residential tie maintains the notion of representation of constituencies. At the 1987 General Election, when these arrangements first operated, 12,207 overseas electors had registered and made themselves eligible to vote.[32] This was many fewer than had been anticipated when the issue was extensively discussed by the Home Affairs Committee, and it

[28] (1982–3) H.C. 32–II, p. 6, paras. 11–14.
[29] See R.P.A. 1985 s.2(3)(*b*).
[30] *Ibid.* s.2.
[31] *Ibid.* s.2(2); *cf.* R.P.A. 1983, s.15(2).
[32] Hansard, Vol. 114, col. 532 (Written Answers), April 22, 1987.

remains to be seen whether the tightly-drawn qualifications will in future be relaxed in order that more overseas electors will be able to register. It seems reasonable to assume that members of this group will be predominantly Conservative Party supporters, and the Conservative Party has pressed strongly for their enfranchisement. The Conservative government may well wish further to assist them in the future.

(c) Registration

Residence at an address is not sufficient to qualify a person to vote in a particular election. Individuals must also be registered to vote in respect of that address. In some other countries the register is but one way of proving an entitlement to vote. In New Zealand, for example, entry on the register is conclusive evidence of residence, but a person can vote even if not entered on the register if he or she can establish an entitlement by some other evidence to the satisfaction of the presiding officer at the poll. In Britain registration is a precondition to being able to vote.

The 1918 Act transferred the obligation first imposed by the 1832 Act to compile and maintain a register from the overseer of the poor to the clerk of the county or borough. This represented a considerable advance upon the earlier position, imposing for the first time a clear obligation upon a public official to initiate enquiries in order to obtain an accurate register. Initially two registers per year were to be prepared, but a single annual register was introduced in the 1930's, as an economy measure. Although the double register was reintroduced in 1948 with qualifying dates on November 20 and June 15, it only survived briefly to be finally abolished in 1953. A second administrative development has been the merging of the registers, so that separate registers do not have to be maintained for different electoral purposes. Until 1949 it was necessary to compile up to five registers, but thereafter the E.R.O. was required "so far as practicable" to combine the parliamentary and local register, putting a mark against any people only qualified on the local register. With the alteration of the local franchise in 1969, the process is even simpler. There is one register for an area, which contains the names of all electors, with the names of overseas, service and some voluntary mental patient voters at the end.

In Great Britain, registration is carried out by local authority staff under the direction of the E.R.O., who is normally the Chief Executive of the relevant authority. In Northern Ireland there is a single registration officer for the whole province. The E.R.O.'s duty is to prepare, annually, a register of all electors. To achieve this he must "take reasonable steps to obtain information required by him," and in particular must make "a house to house or other sufficient enquiry."[33] The E.R.O. is not obliged to send out registration forms to each household, but in practice most do so to avoid having to canvass those households which return the completed form. If such a form is sent out to any householder or person owning or occupying any premises, it is an offence for the person to fail to complete it.[34] There is no required format for the form, although one is suggested in the Regulations.

Registration Officers adopt widely different practices because the Act allows "other sufficient inquiry." The scope for local initiative thus created has enabled successful special campaigns to be run at a local level to increase the registration of ethnic minorities, young voters and the mobile, but it also gives rise to a lack of national consistency. A recent survey has shown substantial differences in approach between different areas (Pinto-Duschinsky and Pinto-Duschinsky (1987)). In some, no door-to-door canvass is carried out, in others there is virtually no monitoring of results to see where the local system could be improved, (see also, Le Lohe (1987)). The researchers concluded that the Home Office Circular of Guidance to E.R.O.'s is largely ignored, and that unless major improvements are made in some areas it may become necessary for the Home Office to consider using its compulsory powers under the Act[35] to require Officers to carry out specified procedures, a power never known to be used in the past.

From the data derived from the canvass or inquiry the E.R.O. then draws up a draft register. If in doubt about an individual's eligibility, he can require a person to complete a declaration as to their age or nationality. In practice this rarely happens,[36] and consequently some aliens do appear on the register. How many vote in the belief that they are entitled to do so is unknown, but it is likely that many more people are inadvertently omitted from the register than are erroneously included upon it.

The draft register must be published by November 28. Members of the public are then supposed to go to the local council office or library to check. In practice very few do,[37] it being left

[33] See now, R.P.A. 1983, s.10(*a*).
[34] Representation of the People Regulations S.I. 1986 No. 1081, reg. 29.
[35] R.P.A. 1983, s.52(1), as amended by R.P.A. 1985, Sched. 4, para. 12.
[36] (1982–83) H.C. 32–II, p. 73 paras. 290–292.
[37] See O.P.C.S. (1982), pp. 15–16.

mainly to the political parties to take whatever action they deem appropriate to ensure that their supporters are not omitted from the register (see, for example, Le Lohe (1987), p. 15). This represents the last relic of what was in the nineteenth century the primary responsibility of local political parties, "attending to the register." Even today the Liberal Party retains as one of the principal duties of its local organisations "to see to the register of its supporters," and the model rules set out by the National Union of Conservative and Unionist Associations for local associations include as an association object, "To watch the revision of the constituency register in the interests of the Party and to take steps to ensure that all supporters who are qualified are in a position to record their votes." All claims for additions, or objections to inclusions must be made by December 16, and the ensuing two months are then available to adjudicate upon claims and objections. This period was once essential, but even with local party activity it is now little used. In 47 per cent. of registration areas there are fewer than five claims for additions per 10,000 electors, and there are no objections entered in 71 per cent. of areas.[38] One might be tempted to shorten the period before the register comes into effect, but there are dangers, as substantial numbers of challenges are occasionally made. The 1986/1987 draft register in Dulwich attracted over 1,000 objections by local Conservative Party activists, and large numbers of registration objections are made annually in North Cornwall, where there are many disputed questions of "residence" relating to holiday homes.[39]

After December 16, the E.R.O. has to process claims and objections, and on giving five days' notice can add to or delete from the register. If he intends to reject a claim, or uphold an objection, he must give at least three days' notice to the individuals involved of his intention to have a hearing of the issue, at which the claimant or objector and person affected can give evidence.[40] From that hearing an appeal can be lodged with the County Court and from there to the Court of Appeal,[41] although it is rare for matters even to get as far as the initial hearing.

The register, once in force, is conclusive of the question whether a person was or was not resident on the qualifying date, and conclusive of the date at which any person registered

---

[38] *Ibid.*

[39] (1982–83) H.C. 32–II, p. 115, paras. 518–519.

[40] Representation of the People Regulations 1986, S.I. 1986 No. 1081, regs. 38–43.

[41] R.P.A. 1983, s.56(1), (2); in Scotland, appeals go to a special Registration Appeals Court—see s.57.

reaches voting age.[42] Once individuals are registered the presiding officer cannot prevent them voting even if they are not qualified by reason of age, nationality or incapacity, although to vote, knowing that one is not qualified, is in itself an offence[43] and the vote can be rejected on scrutiny. The conclusive quality of the register ensures certainty during the period of the poll as to who can and cannot vote. Disputes in the hotly-political atmosphere of an election as to individuals' voting entitlements are thereby sought to be avoided.

Although the register is conclusive of individuals' rights to vote, recent research has demonstrated that it may be markedly inaccurate. In 1981 it was estimated that, nationally, about 6·7 per cent. of eligible electors were not on the electoral register. In Inner London the estimated proportion was substantially higher (14 per cent.). Those figures have remained substantially unchanged.[44] This amounts to a serious degree of disfranchisement. Those particularly liable to be omitted from the register included members of ethnic minorities, "attainers" (those attaining the age of 18 during the currency of the register), and those living in bed-sitters and lodging-houses.[45] Given its voter-base, the Labour Party is likely disproportionately to suffer from the inability of these people to vote.

One source of error in the register is that some individuals appear consciously to avoid inclusion. A survey of registration in five northern towns found that 16·9 per cent. of potentially-eligible individuals had been omitted. Of these, approximately one-third exhibited antagonism or apathy towards the political process and did not wish to register (Le Lohe (1987)). That attitude was disproportionately apparent among black (Afro-Caribbean) individuals. The "avoidance problem" is likely to be exacerbated by the introduction of the Community Charge ("poll tax") as an important source of local government finance in England and Wales. It will be necessary to create a new Community Charges Register, which will contain the names of all those deemed liable to pay the Community Charge. The Community Charges Register will be formally separate from the Electoral Register, but the latter will be the most convenient (if not the only) source of names for the former. Individuals who

[42] R.P.A. 1983, s.49.
[43] *Ibid.* s.61(*a*), as amended by R.P.A. 1985, Sched. 2, Part I, para. 2(*a*).
[44] (1982–83) H.C. 32–I, p. vi; O.P.C.S. 1987.
[45] *Ibid.* Pinto-Duschinsky and Pinto-Duschinsky have cast doubt on the proposition that there is a special problem of under-registration among ethnic minorities—see pp. 18–22. But see Le Lohe (1987).

are ambivalent about participation in the political process may well attempt to avoid inclusion on the Electoral Register in the hope of avoiding liability for the Community Charge. As Le Lohe says, "The loss of the right to vote is a small price to pay for saving several hundreds of pounds per year." (Le Lohe (1987), p. 37).

These proposals amount to the re-introduction of the "no representation without taxation" principle which was manifested in the Victorian ratepayer qualifications for the franchise. They will serve disproportionately to penalise the Labour Party in the inner city areas from where it draws its greatest strength, and where avoidance may be expected to be greatest (if only because the scale of Community Charge in such areas is likely to be very high).

A second source of error on the register is the administrative failings noted by Pinto-Duschinsky and Pinto-Duschinsky. There is clearly need for some mechanism for rectification of the register where such failings would otherwise lead to a loss of voting rights. Until recently there was no provision in statute for correcting mistakes. The only remedy was to seek an order for mandamus. Even in obvious cases like *Vine's* case,[46] where the elector's name had been accidentally omitted during printing, the only remedy was through the courts. This may have deterred some individuals from seeking to amend the register. Some improvement in the position came about in 1969, when the E.R.O. was empowered to correct the register, but this was limited to the situation where the register did not carry out the intentions of the E.R.O. to include a name, to state an age or to give effect to his decision on a claim or objection.[47] This provision allowed for sorting out administrative errors but offered no remedy to people whom the E.R.O. had not intended to register, for example those whose application forms were lost in the post. Such persons had to continue to rely upon the High Court, which could order the Registration Officer to include people whom it was satisfied were qualified but had not claimed before December 16.

This *lacuna* was filled in 1980,[48] and the relevant statutory provision was reformulated in 1985. Since then, if

"(a) a claim is duly made that any person whose name is not included in a register of electors as published is entitled to be registered in that register, and

---

[46] (1968) 112 Sol.Jo. 398.
[47] See now, R.P.A. 1983, s.11(1).
[48] R.P.A. 1980, s.2(4), re-enacted as R.P.A. 1983, s.11(2).

(b) having duly disposed of the claim, the registration officer is satisfied that the person in respect of whom the claim is made is entitled to be so registered,"[49]

the appropriate addition must be made. The procedures have been devised so that it is possible for someone who notes an error as late as February 19 still to be registered in time for the May local government elections. When a claim to be included is made, it is immediately entered on a list of claims. The Registration Officer publishes a monthly list of proposed alterations, a copy of which is supplied to the major political parties. Objections to the proposed additions can be made within the remainder of that calendar month. The claim is then determined by the Registration Officer under the same procedure as is used to determine claims made prior to December 16.

There may still be occasions when the High Court jurisdiction will have to be invoked. In R. v. *Electoral Registration Officer for the Borough of Luton ex p. Luton Borough Council*,[50] an administrative error had caused individuals to have been entered on the register in the wrong polling district; but this was not correctable by the E.R.O., whose amending powers are limited to the corrections of omissions. Here, the individuals were on the register, albeit in the wrong place. The court took the view that it had jurisdiction to order the E.R.O. to correct the register. Forbes J. held that the Act specifies the circumstances in which Registration Officers themselves can decide to alter the register. In the absence of clear words to the contrary, that did not affect the powers vested in the High Court to order the alteration of the register.

Although these provisions represent a marked improvement in our registration procedures, they are subject to two important limitations. First, they are very far from meeting the demand for a "rolling register."[51] The provisions operate only to permit individuals to show that they were "resident" on the previous qualifying date (normally October 10). With a rolling register there would be no qualifying date as such and the register would be amendable at any date in the year after residence had been established. In this way, many of the effective disenfranchisements which ensue from moving residence from one constituency to another would be prevented. In 1984 the government rejected the possibility of a "rolling register" on grounds both of cost and because

---

[49] R.P.A. 1985, Sched. 4, para. 2.
[50] Unreported.
[51] See, for example, (1982–3) H.C. 32–II, p. 104; but *cf. ibid.* p. 204.

"under a system of this kind the primary responsibility for ensuring that a person's home is on the register would have to be given to the individual concerned. This could well produce a less accurate register."[52]

Yet the introduction of the Community Charge system of local government finance necessitates exactly this degree of individual responsibility. Indeed, under the arrangements already in place in Scotland, individuals are obliged, on penalty of a surcharge, to inform the Community Charges Registration Officer of their liability for a Community Charge, a liability which depends upon residence in a local authority's area.[53] This represents a degree of personal responsibility far beyond that envisaged by proponents of the "rolling register," who advocate only that individuals should have the opportunity, at any time during the year, of having their names entered on the electoral register. No question of penalty for failing to take advantage of this could arise. To ensure accuracy, an annual check could still be made to identify those who had not notified the E.R.O. of their movement into a constituency.

The second failing in the present arrangements for rectifying the electoral register is that in most cases the error only comes to light during an election campaign.[54] No correction, whether by the Registration Officer or as a result of a court order, can be made after the close of nominations for an election. Before the R.P.A. 1980, the Court could order names to be added at any time, and indeed in the past had done so up until polling week itself.[55] However, even the High Court is now precluded from ordering the addition of names after the close of nominations, as the Act specifies that no changes can be made after that date.[56] Obviously there must be concern to avoid the late addition to the register of spurious names in an attempt to influence the result, but it is unlikely that the High Court could be misled to this effect. Registration Officers would equally be entitled to reject any claim for inclusion about which they felt suspicious. In these circumstances, the ban on additions to the register after

---

[52] Cmnd. 9140, para. 1.3.

[53] Abolition of Domestic Rates Etc. (Scotland) Act 1987, s.18.

[54] See, for example, *R.* v. *Calderwood ex p. Manchester Corporation, The Times,* February 27, 1974.

[55] *Calderwood,* n. 54 above; *R.* v. *Hammond ex p. Nottingham City Council, The Times,* October 10, 1974.

[56] Compare R.P.A. 1983, s.11(3), relating to Registration Officers' rectifications of the register, with R.P.A. 1985, Sched. 4, para. 2, referring to *any* rectification.

close of nominations seems both unnecessary and likely to deprive even this limited reform of much effect.

Generally, individuals will be seeking to have themselves *included* on the register, but the question has arisen of whether a person can refuse to be entered on the register, or seek to have an entry which relates to him or her deleted. In one rather exceptional case,[57] a Scotsman objected to his name being included on the register. He said he had never voted, did not wish to, and objected to the publicity afforded to his residence by his inclusion on the register. The Court was adamant that he could not be removed. The aim of the register is to serve as a record of all those entitled to vote. Whether they choose to exercise that entitlement is for the individual, not for the Registration Officer.

This issue arose in an acute form in the circumstances of the Scottish Devolution referendum in 1978. To take effect, the Scotland Act required the positive support of 40 per cent. of those entitled to vote in a referendum—that is, 40 per cent. of those names contained on the register. In one instance[58] a pro-devolution elector established that he was entered on the register twice, and sought the removal of one entry. Whilst normally the second entry would be useless, on this occasion it was positively harmful to his cause, for a failure by any person named on the register to vote in favour of devolution effectively counted as a vote against the proposition. Nevertheless, in the absence of any procedure to remove entries from the register, nothing could be done. Anti-devolutionists in the devolution referendum also sought to use registration as a means of affecting the outcome. The President of the Conservative Students at St Andrew's University was convicted of making false claims to include unqualified people on the register, and including people at their term time address who did not wish to have double registration.[59] The Court held that it was an offence to make a claim on individuals' behalf without their consent. Once the register was compiled and the names included, there they had to remain, however.

(d) Disqualification and Incapacity

An aspect of the gradual widening of the franchise over the last century has been the removal of various categories of incapacity

---

[57] *Davis* v. *Argyll E.R.O.* (1974) unreported (see Stewart (1980), pp. 252–253).
[58] See Stewart (1980), p. 253.
[59] *Brown* v. *Swayne* (1979) unreported (see Stewart (1980), p. 255).

to vote. Reference has already been made to the enfranchisement of women, once subject to such incapacity, by the 1918 and 1928 Acts. The 1918 Act also removed the rule that those who had received parochial relief within the period of 12 months preceding the date of registration were disqualified from registering, and earlier legislation had already abandoned the "ratepayers' default" provisions whereby individuals in borough constituencies had to demonstrate that they had paid rates up to the date of registration in order to qualify to be registered.

Nevertheless, our electoral law still contains a limited number of provisions rendering individuals incapable of voting even where they meet the requirements for the franchise in all other respects. These provisions are not necessarily incompatible with the requirements of Article 3 of the First Protocol to the European Convention on Human Rights. That Protocol incorporates no guarantee of universal suffrage. Provided that the electoral system in a signatory state permits the "free expression of the opinion of the people," it is permissible to disqualify specific groups of individuals on criteria which can be rationally justified and which are not improperly discriminatory.

Peers of the realm have been deemed incapable of voting in parliamentary elections since at least 1699, when the House of Commons passed a resolution to that effect.[60] A peer is however entitled to register, and to vote, in local government elections and in elections to the European Assembly.[61] The formal position in respect of Lords Spiritual is less certain. It has been generally thought that bishops could not vote, but in 1983 the Archbishop of Canterbury did so, contending that the spiritual title did not affect his secular voting capacity. The matter was, in practice if not in law, resolved later in 1983, when the Bishop of Derby informed the House of Lords that the Bishopry had agreed not to vote in future (Hughes and Palmer (1983)).

Offenders of various kinds render themselves legally incapable of voting.[62] Convicts used to be subject to a complex set of

---

[60] 13 Commons Journal 64 (1699). See *Earl Beauchamp* v. *Madresfield Overseers* (1872–3) 8 L.R.C.P. 245.

[61] R.P.A. 1983, s.15(5); European Assembly Elections Act 1978, Sched. 1, para. 2(1)(*b*).

[62] For Human Right Commission cases disputing such prohibitions on voting, see Appl. 530/59, Yearbook of the E.C.H.R. 1960, p. 184; Appl. 1065/61, Yearbook 1961, p. 260; Appl. 2728/66, Yearbook 1967, p. 336; Appl. 6573/74, 1 D. & R. 87; Appl. 8701/79, 18 D. & R. 250. In no case has a breach of Protocol 1, Article 3 been found.

restrictions laid down by the common law. The incapacity is now to be found in section 3 of the R.P.A. 1983, as amended by the R.P.A. 1985, Sched. 4, para. 1. This provides that a convicted person is legally incapable of voting during the currency of a sentence of imprisonment (whether or not he or she is actually detained). The incapacity does not extend to those held on remand, nor to those given non-custodial sentences, nor indeed to those imprisoned for contempt of court. However, it is one thing for a person still to be entitled to vote and quite another matter to be able to exercise this right. Voting in person will only be possible if a prisoner can obtain temporary release, since there is no power to site polling stations within prisons.[63] The relaxation on the rules for obtaining postal votes should enable remand prisoners more easily to obtain these,[64] but this assumes that individuals are entered on the electoral register. One problem here will be the question of residence. Section 5(3) of the 1983 Act specifies that someone held in lawful custody cannot use the place of custody to establish residence. In the case of a long period of custody he or she may lose the right to claim residence in any other place.

Quite apart from the difficulties of those held in custody, individuals who personally have committed specified offences against election law must be excluded from the electoral register for a period of five years. If the offence constitutes a corrupt practice the offender is excluded from any electoral register in the United Kingdom, whereas if the offence constitutes an illegal practice the offender is excluded from the register in the constituency or local government area in which the offence was committed.[65] As will be seen in our discussion of electoral practices, these incapacities are now of minimal importance because it is extremely rare for corrupt or illegal practices to be found.

Of greater practical importance is the way that the law handles those with a mental handicap or mental illness. Under section 4(3) of the R.P.A. 1949, patients in hospitals primarily concerned with mental illness were precluded from establishing residence there. In *Wild* v. *Warrington Electoral Registration Officer* (see Gostin (1977)) a refusal to register five residents of a mental hospital was successfully challenged when it was demonstrated that the five were no longer patients but continued to reside in

---

[63] See *McCartney's* case, *The Guardian,* June 13, 1984.
[64] R.P.A. 1985, s.7. *Cf. Strathclyde E.R.O.* v. *Boylan* 1980 S.C. 266.
[65] R.P.A. 1983, s.160(4), (5); but see s.174.

the hospital because they had no home to go to. In the light of this, and in view of an earlier recommendation from the Speaker's Conference on Electoral Reform, that patients in mental hospitals should be placed on the same footing as those in general hospitals,[66] amendments were made to the legislation by section 62 of the Mental Health (Amendment) Act 1982. These amendments are now incorporated into the 1983 Act, s.7.

The amended legislation now requires a distinction to be drawn between voluntary and non-voluntary patients in mental hospitals. Non-voluntary patients are still deemed non-resident and therefore cannot qualify to be registered.[67] Voluntary patients are not disentitled, but must use an address other than the hospital as their residence, and must complete a declaration before being entitled to be registered, thereby demonstrating their fitness to vote.[68] The requirement to establish a "home" residence appears to be based upon a fear that elections in constituencies with several mental hospitals within their boundaries could be unduly influenced by large numbers of patients.[69] In fact, in very few constituencies would these patients exceed one per cent. of the electorate, were they all to register. The consequence of the "home" residence requirement is that if residence is established, the only means of voting is by way of postal vote.

These provisions apply only to voluntary mental patients in a hospital used wholly or mainly for those requiring mental treatment. They do not therefore apply to any voluntary patient in the psychiatric or geriatric ward of a general hospital, nor indeed to any person living at home and receiving daycare. This is important because of the acceleration of the "care in the community" policy which encourages voluntary patients to leave hospitals.[70] Those people with mental handicaps or mental illnesses who live in the community can be registered. There is no official mechanism for checking whether an individual is of sufficient understanding to be able to vote, and presiding officers are given no advice as to how to decide whether a person is of sufficient understanding to be able to

---

[66] Cmnd. 5469.
[67] R.P.A. 1983, s.7(1).
[68] R.P.A. 1983, s.7(3)–(9).
[69] See *The Independent*, July 29, 1987, and compare the treatment of students in halls of residence.
[70] D.H.S.S. (1981); and see the report on this policy by the House of Commons Select Committee on Social Services (1984–5) H.C. 13.

vote. The ability to vote therefore depends upon whether an individual understands the registration paper, or whether some other person filling in the return registers him or her. Research suggests that many carers do not realise that their patients can vote, and accordingly they may fail to register them. A survey carried out in the South West of England indicated that practice in group schemes and hostels varies greatly. In some, almost all residents are registered, in others few are registered. In general, local authority establishments seem more willing to register these residents than health authority establishments. But in both cases, a significant number of people are not being registered who would be capable of voting (Ward (1987)).

(3) ABSENT VOTING

The assumption underlying our rules on voting is that votes will be cast in a secret ballot by voters in person at their local polling stations. Nevertheless, provision has been made since 1918 for absent voting, either by post or by proxy, for certain categories of voters. Since the easy availability of postal votes, in particular, might go some way to ameliorating the difficulties of those who would otherwise be disenfranchised because (for example) of the "static" nature of the register or because of the intricacies of the "residence" requirement, it is worth mentioning here the circumstances in which such votes are now permitted.

The 1918 Act permitted individuals to be entered on an Absent Voters List if it could be demonstrated to the E.R.O.'s satisfaction.

> "that there is a probability that the claimant, by reason of the nature of his occupation, service or employment, may be debarred from voting at a poll at parliamentary elections held during the time the register is in force...".[71]

Absent voters so listed were then entitled to a postal vote, save that those serving abroad or civilians working at sea could appoint a proxy to vote in their place. Section 2 of the R.P.A. 1920 reformulated the rules as to proxies, permitting them to any absent voter who could bona fide state that there was a probability that he would be at sea or out of the United Kingdom at the time of a parliamentary election; further, proxy voting was to be the only mechanism available to overseas voters, since

[71] R.P.A. 1918, Sched. 1, para. 16.

henceforward no ballot paper was to be sent by post to any address outside the United Kingdom. This in essence remains the position today in respect of postal votes.[72]

The 1948 Act substantially expanded the categories of civilians to whom absent votes were permitted. Among those newly permitted a postal vote were persons who were no longer resident at their qualifying address and had moved out of the area.[73] Those suffering blindness or other physical incapacity rendering attendance at the polling station impossible were also now permitted to apply for a postal vote.[74] Proxy votes continued to be available to those serving abroad or who were likely to be abroad on the date of the poll because of the general nature of their occupation, service or employment. The 1948 Act also drew a distinction between those wishing to be entered upon the Absent Voters List indefinitely (for example, because of continuing physical incapacity) and those who sought only to be so listed in respect of a particular election.[75] Finally, absent voting became permissible for most local government elections.[76]

This structure of law was retained until 1985. The method of listing the categories of those entitled to claim absent votes produced obvious anomalies. A person who was frequently away in the general nature of his employment could obtain an absent vote even if not absent on polling day, whereas a person away on business on polling day who did not normally travel in the course of employment could not. Those away visiting the sick, taking examinations or on holiday were not eligible. This last was a particularly important exclusion if elections were called in (say) June, as they were in 1970, 1983 and 1987. In the light of these considerations and following the Home Affairs Select Committee's investigation of the matter,[77] the absent voting provisions were substantially reformed by the 1985 Act.

The new provisions retain the distinction between indefinite and temporary inclusion in the Absent Voters List. The categories of those eligible permanently to be registered as absent voters include service voters, the new overseas voters

---

[72] See R.P.A. 1985, s.6(6) cf. R.P.A. 1945, s.25, making temporary provision for servicemen overseas to vote by post in the exceptional circumstances of the 1945 General Election.

[73] R.P.A. 1948, s.8(1)(e), s.8(4)(b), s.8(7).

[74] *Ibid.* s.8(1)(c).

[75] *Ibid.* s.9.

[76] *Ibid.* s.25(4), (7).

[77] See (1982–3) H.C. 32–I, pp. xix–xxiv, and also Cmnd. 9140, pp. 11–18.

(British citizens resident abroad), those suffering blindness or other physical incapacity, and those whose attendance at the polling station cannot reasonably be expected in view of the general nature of their occupation, service or employment.[78] This represents in practice a minimal change from the pre-1985 position, given that, as we have seen, the number of overseas voters who have registered is unexpectedly small.[79] Far more important is the amendment made in respect of applications for temporary inclusion for particular elections in the Absent Voters list. Now these applications must be acceded to if the E.R.O.

> "is satisfied that the applicant's circumstances on the date of the poll will be or are likely to be such that he cannot reasonably be expected to vote in person at the polling station allotted or likely to be allotted to him under the appropriate rules...."[80]

Thus, all the various categories of those temporarily entitled to absent votes are swept away, and the elector must simply show (the burden being upon him) that his circumstances effectively preclude his presence at the polling station on polling day. This principle applies to all types of election, whether parliamentary, local government[81] or for the European Assembly.

Although this does not amount to the absent voting on demand which was opposed by both the Labour and Conservative parties in their evidence to the Select Committee,[82] it could permit an increase in the numbers of absent votes which will become available.[83] The conventional wisdom is that the Conservative Party, with its superior constituency organisation, benefits disproportionately from the postal vote,[84] and it is certainly the case that that party pressed strongly for the

---

[78] R.P.A. 1985, s.6(2). In respect of the last category, *cf.* Cmnd. 9140, para. 3.6. See also, Home Office Circular R.P.A. 303, paras. 8–9.

[79] The deletion of the provision (R.P.A. 1949, s.13(2)(*d*)) that those no longer resident at their qualifying addresses should be entitled to indefinite listing as Absent Voters is of minimal significance, since such listing was "indefinite" only so long as they continued to be regarded as "resident" at that address. Normally this would be at most for one year after departure.

[80] R.P.A. 1985, s.7(1)(*a*).

[81] The prohibition on postal voting in parish or community councils in England and Wales (R.P.A. 1983, s.32(8)) is repealed by R.P.A. 1985, Sched. 5.

[82] (1982–83) H.C. 32–II, p. 77 (Labour Party), and *ibid.* p. 91 (Conservative Party); but see *ibid.* p. 119, para. 539 (Liberal Party).

[83] These have not normally exceeded 3 per cent. of votes cast—see H.C. 32–II, p. 236, and Cmnd. 9140, para. 3.16.

[84] Butler (1963), pp. 210–211, and see also (1982–83) H.C. 32–II, p. 213, para. 894.

inclusion of holidaymakers within the categories of those entitled to absent votes; furthermore, it is a Conservative government, going beyond the Select Committee's report, which has remodelled the temporary absent voting provisions.

How will these changes affect specific groups of voters previously discussed? Those who have moved residence during the currency of a register have been entitled as of right to a postal vote (provided they have left the electoral area) since 1948. Such voters will now have to show not only that they have moved, but that their removal is to such a place that they "cannot reasonably be expected to vote in person." This seems unlikely to make any significant difference. Similarly, students registered at their college addresses have previously been able to obtain postal votes for elections during vacations.[85] The new provisions are likely simply to confirm that (and perhaps make this possibility more widely known). Second-home owners who have secured registration in respect of their holiday residences will now find it possible to obtain absent votes in their holiday home constituencies, should they wish to exercise their voting rights there. This exacerbates the unfairness of allowing multiple registration by making the possibility of choice in voting places real rather than the theoretical one which it might have been for those whose principal residence was far away from their holiday residence. The Government's rejection in 1984 of a ban on multiple registration, previously referred to, should be seen in the light of its simultaneous expansion of absent voting facilities.

The position so far as overseas voters, (that is, British citizens resident abroad) and overseas holiday-makers is concerned is affected by retention of the rule that ballot papers will only be sent to an address within the United Kingdom (although this need not be the voter's address as entered on the register. Any address nominated by the voter will suffice).[86] Therefore, overseas voters will almost inevitably have to vote by proxy. Overseas holiday-makers will be able to vote by post if still within the United Kingdom when the ballot-paper arrives. This would normally be about one week before polling day. Those who have already left for their holiday will have to vote by proxy. Holiday-makers within the United Kingdom can have their ballot-papers sent to their holiday addresses. Alternatively, because the 1985 Act for the first time permits all absent

[85] *Maccorquodale* v. *Bovack* [1984] S.L.T. 328.
[86] R.P.A. 1985, s.6(6).

voters, whether or not abroad, to vote either by post or by proxy, holiday-makers within the United Kingdom can choose to vote by proxy.

The principal problem with postal voting is the opportunities which it offers for electoral misconduct:

"All postal voting is more open to abuse than personal attendance at the polling station, where the secrecy of the ballot can be vigorously maintained. Personation, undue influence and other forms of malpractice are much harder to prevent when an elector votes by post, and the issue of postal ballot papers to a permanent list of electors who may not need or want them provides dangerous and unnecessary opportunities for abuse."[87]

In *Phillips*[88] the appellant, canvassing on behalf of the Conservative Party, visited an elderly voter and with his agreement arranged a postal vote for him. Unbeknown to the voter, she had the ballot paper sent to her address. She duly voted for the Conservative candidate, completed the declaration of identity and signed the voter's name. The appellant also obtained the ballot paper of a neighbour who had recently died, and she again voted, and completed and signed the necessary forms in the name of the deceased. Her appeal against sentence of two months' imprisonment and disqualification from the register of electors for five years was dismissed. Notwithstanding her previous good character, the court felt bound to take a serious view of such a matter, and considered that it would normally be the case that such conduct should be punished by a substantial custodial sentence.

The procedures for obtaining and exercising postal votes are intended to prevent such abuses occurring. Applications to be entered indefinitely on the Absent Voters List must be accompanied by the appropriate attestations by medically-qualified personnel in the case of physical incapacity or blindness and by employers where the application is based upon the applicant's occupation, service or employment.[89] Applications for temporary listing must explain what are the circumstances which mean that the voter cannot reasonably be expected to vote in person. Such applications must be signed and attested by an adult who knows the applicant but is not related to him and who "has not

---

[87] Cmnd. 9140. para. 3.6.
[88] R. v. *Phillips* (1984) 6 Cr.App.Rep.(S) 293.
[89] S.I. 1986 No. 1081, regs. 64, 65.

attested under this paragraph any other application in respect of the election of which the application he attests is made.'[90] The effect of this could be rather unfortunate. For example residents of an old people's home who suffer from physical incapacity can apply for indefinite listing, and their applications can all be attested by a single attendant or matron. On the other hand, voluntary patients in a mental hospital, entered on the register for their home residence, are not entitled to indefinite listing. They must apply for absent votes at each election, and these applications can only be attested by someone who has not attested some other application in respect of that election. Failure to satisfy this attestation requirement will lead to loss of voting rights.

If the applicant has actually succeeded in obtaining a postal vote, the ballot-paper, once completed, must be returned together with the voter's declaration of identity. Omission to include this disqualifies the vote, but as the *Phillips* case demonstrates, it is all too easy to circumvent this obligation.

(4) CONCLUSION

The procedures for registration of voters are intended to take questions of voting entitlement out of the immediate political arena, just as are the procedures for boundary redistribution previously discussed. In this they have been largely successful. Peel's declaration in 1837, that "The battle of the Constitution will be fought in the registration court,"[91] reflects hardly at all the reality of modern problems of voting entitlement. Nevertheless, primarily tactical questions as to the scope of the franchise still divide the parties, as the recent overseas voter and multiple registration issues demonstrate, and it would be a mistake to regard these matters as islands of technical or administrative dispute floating in a sea of political conflict. They remain part of that conflict, albeit removed from the immediate site of battle and fought with different weapons out of the public eye.

---

[90] *Ibid* reg. 66(3)(d).
[91] Quoted in Seymour (1915), p. 125.

4. CANDIDATES AND PARTIES

(1) INTRODUCTION

In this chapter we are concerned with the processes of selection and nomination of candidates. We follow Ranney in our understanding of those terms:

> "Like most other Western democracies except the United States, Great Britain makes a distinction between *nomination* and *candidate* selection. Nomination is the legal process by which election authorities certify a person as a qualified candidate for an elective public office and print his or her name on the ballot. Candidate selection is the extralegal process by which a political party decides which of the persons legally eligible to hold the office will be designated on the ballot and in campaign communications as its recommended and supported candidate."
>
> (Ranney (1979), p. 12)

We shall consider the nomination process before party selection procedure because *all* candidates, in order to stand for election, are required properly to be nominated, whereas there is still some scope, especially in local government elections, for serious candidates to present themselves without having gone through any party selection procedure. As a preliminary to our analysis of nomination we first look at the legal limitations on individual candidacy.

(2) THE RIGHT TO BE A CANDIDATE

In its jurisprudence the European Commission on Human Rights has concluded that Article Three of the First Protocol to the Convention incorporates an individual right to candidacy for election to bodies possessing a substantial portion of the legislative power of the state:

> " . . . the Commission concludes that Article 3 guarantees in principle . . . the right to stand for election to the legislature. This right, however, is neither absolute nor without

limitations... states may impose certain restrictions on the... right to stand, provided that they are not arbitrary and do not interfere with the free expression of the people's opinion. It is for the Commission to decide, in each particular instance, whether or not this negative condition is fulfilled."[1]

The nature of this right was considered in *M. v. U.K.*, a case brought by Mr. Seamus Mallon against the United Kingdom following his disqualification from membership of the Northern Ireland Assembly[2]:

"The Commission observes that the applicant was not prevented from standing for election to the Northern Ireland Assembly. The Commission considers, however, that it is not enough that an individual has the right to stand for election, he must also have a right to sit as a member once he has been elected by the people. To take the opposite view would render the right to stand for election meaningless."[3]

This is an important conclusion because, with one exception later to be discussed, our electoral law provides no restraints on individuals presenting themselves as candidates for Parliamentary election. There are, however, numerous qualifications which must be satisfied by individuals before they are allowed to sit as members of the various elected bodies. In respect of local government bodies, these requirements must be satisfied on the date of nomination as well as on the assumption of membership. This is apparently not the case in respect of parliamentary candidatures—satisfaction of the requirements on assumption of membership of the House of Commons is all that is required. However that may be, the question in the context of the Human Rights Convention will be whether any ground of disqualification from membership is arbitrary and an interference with the free expression of the people's opinion.

(a) General Provisions

In order to sit as members of the House of Commons or local government bodies, individuals are required to be "not alien"; in other words they must be Commonwealth citizens (which

---

[1] *W, X Y and Z v. Belgium*, Appls. 6745/74 and 6746/74 2 D. & R. 110, 116.
[2] For discussion of the case leading to this disqualification, see Chap. 9 below.
[3] *M. v. U.K.* Appl. 10316/83, 37 D. & R. 129, 133.

includes the various categories of British citizenship) or Irish citizens.[4] Further, all member-states of the Community appear to operate on the assumption that only its nationals may be elected to the European Parliament. The citizenship qualification for membership of elected bodies in the United Kingdom is obviously of very limited significance, especially since Commonwealth citizens are permitted to serve. There is, however, a further qualification to be satisfied in respect of local government bodies. This is the requirement that the elected member have some form of local connection with the authority on which he or she sits. A distinctive feature of our parliamentary candidacy law (such as it is) is that individuals need not satisfy any residence or similar qualification in respect of the constituency in which they are standing (although it may be politically advantageous to indicate an intention to establish residence within the constituency if elected).[5] Local government elections law provides a contrast in stipulating that candidates demonstrate beforehand a sufficient connection with the authority's area, if not necessarily for the specific electoral area in which they are standing. This requirement is satisfied by showing either that the candidate is a local government elector for the authority on election day and remains one throughout the term of office; or that in the preceding 12 months the candidate has been the owner or tenant of land or premises in the authority's area, has had his or her principal place of work within the authority's area, or has lived within the authority's area. In addition, in a parish or community council election candidates are eligible for nomination and election if they can show residence in the parish or community, or within three miles of it, for the preceding 12 months.[6]

This complicated mixture of residence, work, and property qualifications appears to represent the last vestige of nineteenth-century qualifications for the franchise. It excludes as potential candidates people from wholly outside the area or those who have only recently moved into the area and have not yet been entered on the electoral register. There would seem to be little justification for the retention of these requirements as a matter

---

[4] Erskine May (20th ed., 1983), p. 39; Local Government Act 1972, s.79(1).
[5] *Cf.* the American constitutional requirement (Article 1) that a member of the House of Representatives be "an Inhabitant of that State in which he shall be chosen." An electoral system based on a traditional theory of community representation might place considerable importance on such a provision.
[6] Local Government Act 1972, s.79(1); and see *Herbert* v. *Pauley* (1964) 62 L.G.R. 647 on the equivalent provision in the Local Government Act 1933.

of law. If relevant at all, they should go to the issue of the candidate's "electability" in the eyes of the electorate, rather than to his or her entitlement to stand. (This conclusion, of course, follows only if one accepts the Radical theory of representation, that it is *people* who are to be represented, and that they should be free to choose whoever they like to represent them. Theories of community representation would obviously attach considerable importance to close identification by the representative with the life of the community).

Turning from citizenship and residence qualifications, the next general requirement is that the candidate must be 21 years old on assumption of membership (and at time of nomination in respect of local government elections).[7] The reduction in the age of majority to 18 years by the Family Law Reform Act 1969 did not affect this.[8] A Speaker's Conference on Electoral Law in 1973 recommended in favour of equating voting and candidacy ages at 18 years,[9] but nothing has come of this despite some pressure, both Parliamentary and extra-Parliamentary (Norton (1980)). The European Commission of Human Rights has held that the minimum age of 25 years required for candidacy for the Belgian House of Representatives is "obviously not (to) be regarded as an unreasonable or arbitrary condition, or one likely to interfere with the free expression of the opinion of the people in the choice of the legislature"[10] and so would be hardly likely to take objection to the United Kingdom's age stipulation of 21 years. In practice the impact of the provision is likely to be restricted to local government elections and even then to be of minimal significance.

Two other matters may briefly be mentioned. First, peers continue to be ineligible for membership of the House of Commons, although they can serve as members both of local authorities and of the European Parliament.[11] Secondly, women are now eligible for membership of all elected bodies. In 1889 Lord Esher M.R. said: "I take it that by neither the common law nor the constitution of this country from the beginning of the common law until now can a woman be entitled to exercise any public function"[12] and in 1899 Wright J. gave as examples of "a mere abuse of the right of nomination" a purported nomination

---

[7] Erskine May (20th ed.) p. 39; Local Government Act 1972, s.79(1).
[8] Family Law Reform Act 1969, Sched. 2, cl. 2.
[9] Cmnd. 5363.
[10] Appl. 6745/74, n. 1 above at 117.
[11] European Assembly Elections Act 1978, Sched. 1. cl. 5(3)(*a*).
[12] *Beresford-Hope* v. *Lady Sandhurst* (1889) 23 Q.B. 79, 95.

of "a woman or a deceased sovereign."[13] In fact, women had been eligible to serve as Poor Law Guardians since 1834 and to sit on Education Boards since 1870. In 1894 the Local Government Act provided for the possibility of female membership of the District Councils therein created and in 1907 this entitlement was extended to membership of county and borough councils.[14] Finally, the Parliament (Qualification of Women) Act 1918 rendered women eligible for membership of the House of Commons. No doubt has ever arisen as to their eligibility for membership of the European Parliament.

(b) Specific Exclusions

Individuals otherwise eligible for membership of elected bodies may nevertheless find themselves excluded by virtue of a large number of specific provisions. These broadly speaking fall into two categories: exclusion based upon employment or calling, and exclusion based upon previous conduct. The former category is in constitutional (if not necessarily in practical numerical) terms of far greater importance. The bulk of those excluded in this first category fall foul of what may be called the public service disqualification.[15] This applies in various forms to membership of Parliament, of local authorities, and of the European Assembly.

So far as Parliament is concerned, the House of Commons Disqualification Act 1975 lays down categories of office, the holding of which renders an individual ineligible for membership of the House of Commons. The Act is regularly updated by statutory instrument.[16] The criteria applied[17] in determining whether the holder of an office should be disqualified are these:

(a) whether the office is one the holder of which is required to be, or to be seen to be, politically impartial. This criterion serves, for example, to exclude civil servants (whether full-time or part-time, in established or non-established posts),[18] and the holders of judicial office other than part-time recorderships or the magistracy[19];

---

[13] *Harford* v. *Linskey* [1899] 1 Q.B. 852, 862.

[14] Qualification of Women (County and Borough Councils) Act 1907.

[15] Exclusion based on employment or calling also applies, so far as the House of Commons is concerned, to the clergy of the Church of England. See Erskine May (20th ed.) pp. 44–45, and *Re Macmanaway* [1951] A.C. 161.

[16] See, for example, S.I. 1985 No. 1212, S.I. 1986 No. 2219.

[17] For discussion, see Hansard, Vol. 83, cols. 798–806 (July 22, 1985).

[18] House of Commons Disqualification Act 1975, s.1(1)(*b*).

[19] *Ibid.* s.1(1)(*a*) and Sched. 1, Part 1.

(b) whether the office is a paid office in the gift of the Crown or Ministers at or above a particular salary level (which is raised periodically in accordance with salary movements generally);

(c) certain positions of control in companies in receipt of Government grants and funds to which Ministers usually, though not necessarily, make nominations. This criterion and the preceding one together serve to disqualify from House of Commons membership those holding a vast range of offices, such as members of boards of nationalised industries, directors of companies in which the State has an interest, members of quangos (why should a member of the Eggs Authority or the Sugar Board not be eligible for membership of the House of Commons?) and so on.[20]

(d) offices imposing duties which, with regard to time or place, would prevent their holders fulfilling their Parliamentary duties satisfactorily. The offices referred to are of course public offices. There is no disqualification if the M.P. is self-employed or works full-time for a private concern, but an equivalent position in a public enterprise may serve to debar him or her. The Act specifically disqualifies from membership of the House of Commons someone who is a member of the legislature of any country or territory outside the Commonwealth.[21] In *M.* v. *U.K.*, Mr. Seamus Mallon contended that the same provision in the Northern Ireland Assembly Disqualification Act 1975 constituted a breach of Article 3 to Protocol 1 of the European Convention when applied to disqualify him from membership of the Assembly. Prior to his election, Mr. Mallon had been appointed to membership of the Senate of the Republic of Ireland. The Commission dismissed his application as manifestly ill-founded. The disqualification provision in respect of the Northern Ireland Assembly was reconcilable with the rights afforded by Article 3. Furthermore, the discrimination between someone who was a member of a non-Commonwealth legislature and someone who was a member of a Commonwealth legislature (only the former being disqualified from membership of the

---

[20] *Ibid.* Sched. 1 Part II, Sched. 2.
[21] *Ibid.* s.1(1)(e).

House of Commons or the Northern Ireland Assembly) could be justified "in the special historical tradition and special ties that are shared by members of the British Commonwealth of which Ireland does not form part."[22] This conclusion is particularly ironic in view of the earlier discussion on the voting entitlements in the United Kingdom of Irish citizens, which are historically justified on the ground of the close links between Britain and Ireland!

The equivalent public service disqualification for membership of elected local authorities is to be found in section 80(1)(a) of the Local Government Act 1972. This disqualifies from election to, or membership of, a local authority any individual who holds paid office or employment, appointment to which may be made or confirmed by that authority. Thus, a teacher may not be a member of a county council in the county where he teaches, since he or she will be employed by that council. There is, however, no restriction on membership of some other local authority, perhaps a district council within the same area,[23] and the Widdicombe Committee found in 1986 that about 10 per cent. of all councillors were employed by other local authorities.[24] This "twin-tracking" has been the subject of adverse comment, but the Committee was not prepared to recommend a general ban on the practice, since this would deprive some three million local government employees of the right to be councillors.[25] The Committee did, however, recommend that senior local authority officers be prohibited, either by their standard terms of employment or by legislation, from standing for and holding any public elected office. In this, the position of such officers would then be equated with the position of civil servants in central government.[26]

Public service disqualifications from membership of the European Parliament are derived both from domestic law and from Community sources. The exclusions from domestic law cover all those disqualified from membership of the House of Commons save where the disqualification is related to some constitutional feature peculiar to the British Parliament. Thus,

---

[22] *M. v. U.K.*, Appl. 10316/83, 37 D. & R. 129, 135.
[23] See, for example, *Re Berwick Election Petition* (1946) 44 L.G.R. 134.
[24] "The Conduct of Local Authority Business," Cmnd. 9797, para. 6.29. See also, *Zetland County Council v. Thomson* [1974] S.L.T.(S) 67.
[25] *Ibid.* paras. 6.29–6.35.
[26] *Ibid.* paras. 6.205–6.217.

peers and Church of England clergymen are eligible for election.[27] Provision was made in the European Assembly Elections Act authorising delegated legislation to permit individuals who would otherwise be debarred from membership of the European Parliament to be allowed to be members, even though they hold offices mentioned in Parts II and III of Schedule 1 to the House of Commons Disqualification Act 1975 (and would therefore be debarred from membership of the House of Commons).[28] No such orders have been made. Even if it is accepted that a member of the Eggs Authority should not be a member of the House of Commons, why should such a person not be a member of the European Parliament? In addition to the restrictions created by domestic law, a Decision of the Council of Ministers has identified a list of offices in Community institutions, the holding of which is deemed to be incompatible with membership of the European Parliament.[29] The same Decision affirms that there is no incompatibility between membership of national legislatures and of the European Parliament.[30] It is thus left to the various political parties to decide whether they wish to encourage or discourage dual membership.

The second category of specific exclusions from membership of elected bodies is based upon individual conduct or circumstance. Those convicted of offences which constitute corrupt or illegal practices in electoral law are precluded from being elected for some years subsequently, depending upon the nature of the offence and their personal culpability.[31] Local government councillors are liable to exclusion from membership of a local authority for five years after having been surcharged for more that £2,000 for loss incurred or deficiency caused by "wilful misconduct."[32] They are further precluded from election to or membership of an authority if they have within the previous five years been convicted of any offence and sentenced to at least three months' imprisonment without the option of a fine.[33] There is no equivalent for either of these in respect of membership of the House of Commons or of the European Parliament.

---

[27] European Assembly Elections Act 1978, Sched. 1, para. 5(3).
[28] *Ibid*. para. 5(3)(*d*).
[29] Decision of the Council of the European Communities, Cmnd. 6623, Article 6.
[30] *Ibid*. Article 5.
[31] R.P.A. 1983, ss.159–160.
[32] Local Government Finance Act 1982, s.20(4); and see *Lloyd* v. *MacMahon* [1987] 2 W.L.R. 821.
[33] Local Government Act 1972, s.80(1)(*d*).

Section 1 of the R.P.A. 1981 makes special provision, in respect of election to the House of Commons or to the European Parliament, for those convicted of any offence and sentenced to be imprisoned either indefinitely or for more than one year. Such persons are disqualified from membership of the House of Commons during the period of their sentence. Further, and uniquely in respect of Parliamentary candidacies, any nomination of such a person is deemed to be void.[34] These provisions were introduced in response to the election of members of the Irish Republican Army while imprisoned in Northern Ireland. The effective prohibition on nomination of such individuals as candidates is intended to deny them the propaganda benefits which candidacy, and possible election and subsequent disqualification, may bring. As has been pointed out, this is a somewhat dangerous path to tread, in that it forecloses one constitutionally-permissible avenue to express political dissent and perhaps encourages violence instead. Further, it is questionable whether the inability of a prisoner-candidate to perform an M.P.'s duties if elected should be relevant to his ability to stand.[35] This issue should go to the candidate's "electability" in the eyes of the electorate, rather than to the validity of his candidacy. It is highly unlikely, however, that this limitation would constitute a breach of Protocol One, Article Three, since non-prisoner candidates may still be put up in support of the same views and the opinion of the people may therefore be freely expressed (Walker (1982)).

The effect of a holding that an election winner is disqualified is that the election is void. A new election will be ordered save where the electors who have voted for the disqualified candidate must be taken deliberately to have thrown their votes away. In such circumstances the runner-up may be declared the winner.[36] Challenges to the eligibility of a candidate are made by way of election petition, discussed in Chapter 9. The 1975 Act imposes no penalty for sitting and voting while disqualified, and the only statute now imposing any punishment in such circumstances is the House of Commons (Clergy Disqualification) Act 1801, the effect of which can be negated by legislation to deal with the individual case as it arises.[37] The Local Government Act 1972 specifically provides that any acts performed by a holder of elected office who is found to have been

[34] R.P.A. 1981, ss.1, 2(1).
[35] See Walker (1982), pp. 391–392.
[36] *Re Bristol South-East Election Petition* [1964] 2 Q.B. 257.
[37] See, for example, Macmanaway's Indemnity Act 1951.

disqualified shall nevertheless "be as valid and effectual as if he had been qualified."[38]

(3) THE NOMINATION PROCEDURE

"The whole purpose of a nomination procedure in our electoral system is to prevent a plethora of unknown candidates presenting themselves as candidates for election to office... the purpose is to identify clearly for the voter who it is who is offering himself as a candidate for election..."[39]

The details of nomination procedures for candidates in elections to Parliament, local authorities or to the European Parliament, are laid down in the relevant election rules.[40] The procedures follow a common pattern—nomination of a candidate by a specified number of supporters, with the provision of some (minimal) information about the candidate; and the candidate's indication of consent to be nominated. In addition, in parliamentary and European elections, a deposit has to be paid by each candidate.

In parliamentary and European elections the process of nomination is elevated into a ritual out of all proportion to its modern significance. In an era in which elections frequently were uncontested, the nomination procedure was important as effectively constituting the election, but today a valid nomination is merely sufficient to get one's name on the ballot paper. Nevertheless, for parliamentary and European elections the nomination paper must be presented to the Returning Officer between 10.00 a.m. and 4.00 p.m. on one of a number of specified days, and can only be presented by the candidate, agent, proposer or seconder. These, plus the candidate's spouse, are the only people permitted to be present at the formal delivery of the papers. In contrast, for local elections a nomination paper can be handed in by anyone, or sent by post.

A candidate stands nominated on satisfactory completion of two forms, the nomination paper and the consent paper. The nomination paper must show the candidate's name (which may be the name by which he is generally known, even if it is not

---

[38] Local Government Act 1972, s.82.
[39] O'Connor J., in *Greenway-Stanley* v. *Paterson* [1977] 2 All E.R. 663 at 666.
[40] Parliamentary Elections Rules (Sched. 1 to R.P.A. 1983), Rules 6–17; Local Elections (Principal Areas) Rules, S.I. 1986 No. 2214, rules 4–12; European Assembly Elections Regulations, S.I. 1986 No. 2209, Sched. 1.

strictly accurate)[41]; home address[42]; and, if desired, a description which must not exceed six words in length "and need not refer to his rank, profession or calling so long as, with the candidate's other particulars, it is sufficient to identify him."[43] The paper must be subscribed by two electors as proposer and seconder, and by eight other electors as assenting to the nomination, save in the case of European elections where nominees must provide 28 assentors in support. This requirement appears to be designed to show that the candidate has sufficient local support to merit inclusion on the ballot paper. It is a minimal qualification (which has not been changed since the Ballot Act 1872, when the electorate was much smaller) but in the case of parliamentary and European Assembly elections is supplemented by the requirement of a deposit. The legitimacy of this requirement is considered below, but here it may be noted that the deposit must usually be tendered in cash or banker's draft, rather than by cheque or credit card.[44]

The candidate's consent to nomination must be witnessed by one person. The requirement obviously serves to prevent individuals from being nominated without their consent, but the consent form also imposes upon candidates an obligation to confirm that they are qualified to serve if elected to office. In the case of parliamentary and European elections this is simply a witnessed statement that they are aware of the relevant disqualification rules and believe themselves not to be disqualified, but for local elections an individual must also state on what basis—as elector, by occupation of property, or through employment in the area—he claims to be entitled to seek election. This may be important, for if a candidate claims only to be qualified on one ground, he or she cannot later claim to have been qualified in other categories. Claims based upon electoral status are dependent upon that status being maintained.[45] Thus, if an individual on the consent form claims to be qualified to be a member of a local authority solely on grounds of electoral status and subsequently loses that status (by ceasing to reside in the authority's area, for example), disqualification will ensue,

---

[41] *Greenway-Stanley's* case, n. 39, above.

[42] *R. v. Election Court, ex p. Sheppard* [1975] 1 W.L.R. 1319 (D.C.). See (1982–83) H.C. 32–II, p. 99, para. 460 on the security aspects of this requirement, and the Government's response, Cmnd. 9140, para. 6.9.

[43] Parliamentary Elections Rules, s.6(3).

[44] *Ibid.* r. 9(2), and see (1982–83) H.C. 32–II pp. 75–76, paras. 314–6 and pp. 231–232, paras. 982–5.

[45] Local Government Act 1972, s.79(1)(*a*).

even though at the date of election that individual had in fact satisfied other criteria for membership of the authority.

The Returning Officer's obligation, on receipt of the completed nomination and consent papers, is to see that, on their face, they are in due form. Not only is he not obliged to investigate the accuracy of the information therein provided, he appears to be under a positive duty not to engage in any enquiries.[46] A nomination paper may be rejected only if the particulars of the candidate or supporters are not as required by law; that it has been improperly subscribed; or, in respect of parliamentary or European Parliament elections, that the candidate is disqualified for nomination as a prisoner serving sentence of more than one year.[47] The Returning Officer acts in an administrative rather than an adjudicative capacity. He is there to receive the forms and then to organise an election in respect of those candidates he declares to have been validly nominated. The rules do not envisage that he will adjudicate between candidates in respect of contested nominations. In practice this may cause difficulties.

Suppose, for example, that a candidate presents himself for nomination alleging that he has the same name as another, no doubt more eminent, candidate? In the Glasgow Hillhead by-election of 1982, one of the candidates was Mr. Roy Jenkins, the then leader of the S.D.P. However,

> "A second 'Roy Jenkins' ... also entered the contest as the Social Democratic Party candidate. This other Mr. Jenkins had changed his name in time to compete against the S.D.P. in the Warrington by-election in 1981. The Returning Officer in Warrington was not convinced that he had the right to use the name 'Roy Jenkins' and was not impressed with his claim to have founded a previous Social Democratic Party months before the S.D.P. broke away from Labour. In Strathclyde, however, the Returning Officer thought nine months of using the same name was sufficient and allowed the other Roy Jenkins to stand. He received no objection to his decision within the time allowed: the real Roy Jenkins turned up with his objection five minutes too late."[48]

It is not at all clear that the Returning Officer at Hillhead could legitimately have excluded the imposter, since he presented his

---

[46] *Greenway-Stanley* v. *Paterson* [1977] 2 All E.R. 663, 670d.
[47] Parliamentary Elections Rules, r. 12(2).
[48] Edinburgh University Politics Group 1982(b) p. 255.

papers in due form and the name was one which he had used widely.[49] Suppose, however, that the Returning Officer *had* excluded the imposter. Would any remedy have been available to him?

This was the issue in the *Finchley* case in 1983.[50] The appellant, a man, changed his name by deed poll to Margaret Thatcher and declared the address of his flat henceforth to be Downing Street Mansions. A colleague likewise changed his name to Ronald Regan and his address to Whitehouse Mansions. "Thatcher" then presented his nomination papers, claiming to represent the Conservationist Party, and designated "Regan" as his agent. Following an objection by the real Mrs. Thatcher's agent, the Returning Officer rejected the nomination on the grounds:

"1. That it is an abuse of the right of nomination;
2. That it is an obvious unreality;
3. That the form of consent of candidate to nomination was not duly attested;
4. That the particulars of the candidate provided in the statutory documents are not as required by law."

"Thatcher" then sought judicial review of the Returning Officer's decision, and an order of mandamus requiring that his nomination papers be accepted and his name entered on the ballot paper. The application failed both at first instance and on appeal, although the Court of Appeal accepted that an application for judicial review was an appropriate proceeding in such a case. The appellant argued that the Returning Officer had exceeded his powers, in that the first two grounds for rejection of the nomination were not available to him in the light of rule 12 of the Parliamentary Election Rules. This is probably correct. The grounds are derived from a dictum of Wright J. in *Harford* v. *Linskey*,[51] but that case proceeded under election rules affording Returning Officers rather greater discretion than does rule 12 now, and at a time when candidacy rules precluded women from standing in most elections. The abolition of the latter provision makes it far less easy now to identify nominations which are "an obvious unreality." Be that as it may, the Court of Appeal was able to dismiss the appeal on the ground that the appellant's motives (as he had admitted) were malign—he was

[49] *Cf. Greenway-Stanley's* case, n. 39 above.
[50] *R.* v. *Barnet and Finchley Returning Officer ex p. Bennett*, June 3, 1983 (unreported).
[51] [1899] 1 Q.B. 852, 862.

seeking merely to confuse the Finchley electorate, and the court exercised its remedial discretion against him without having to decide on the merits of his case.

The Glasgow Hillhead instance and the *Finchley* case involved the adoption of other candidates' names, but they were also concerned with possibly false descriptions. The assumption of other parties' titles presents difficulties for Returning Officers. Political parties in the United Kingdom are not state-registered entities, and do not seem to have any exclusive entitlement to the use of the names which they have adopted. In *Kean* v. *McGivan*[52] an attempt was made to use the tort of passing-off to restrain a newly-formed party's assumption of an existing party's name. A political party called the Social Democratic Party was founded in July 1979. Another party, calling itself by the same name, was formed in March 1981 by former leading members of the Labour Party. The "first" S.D.P. sought to restrain the second S.D.P. from using "its" name. The attempt failed (and the fact of failure no doubt led to a member of the "first" S.D.P. assuming Mr. Roy Jenkins' name to fight the Warrington and Hillhead seats). The Court of Appeal held it to be well-settled that, apart from specific statutory provision to the contrary, there is no property in a name. Anyone could, in the absence of some malicious motive, assume any name he or she liked. The tort of passing-off provided a possible remedy in the commercial field by protecting the goodwill of a business (as distinct from its name), but the tort could not be committed against a non-trader, such as a political party:

> "The situation is simply that a non-commercial activity—a political party—is seeking to use the same name, the same initials, as a very small other such party with . . . somewhat similar values and ideals. It does not provide a situation, in my judgment, in which there is any basis for contending that a tort has occurred."[53]

The importance of this is obvious. Suppose that that faction of the (real) S.D.P. which opposes merger with the Liberal party decides in the future to put up its own candidates, describing them as S.D.P. candidates. There seems to be no basis in law to restrain them from doing this. Electoral law seems to offer the Returning Officer no control over the description which the candidate asserts to himself, beyond the requirement that this

---

[52] (1982) 8 F.S.R. 119.
[53] At 121 (Ackner L.J.).

does not exceed six words and is "with the candidate's other particulars ... sufficient to identify him." Could it be argued that "sufficient to identify him" means "sufficient to distinguish him from other candidates"? If so, the adoption of another candidate's party label might properly be rejected by the Returning Officer, but it is not clear that the statutory rules can be so interpreted. In any case, if the S.D.P., on merging with the Liberals, abandons its distinctive title, the anti-merger faction could properly argue that no confusion would arise by *its* candidates using the S.D.P. label on the ballot paper. What is clear is that Returning Officers can be placed in a very difficult position by nominations or descriptions of this kind, and if "the purpose (of nomination) is to identify clearly for the voter who it is who is offering himself as a candidate,"[54] some explicit powers might need to be given to Returning Officers to reject deliberately confusing nominations or descriptions. This would require that Returning Officers take a rather more positive role than the present conception of them as passive recipients of nomination papers permits.

As the *Finchley* case shows, a Returning Officer's rejection of nomination papers may be made the subject of judicial review. In the converse case of acceptance of nomination papers, rules 12(5) and (6) of the Parliamentary Election Rules[55] provide:

> "5. The returning officer's decision that a nomination paper is valid shall be final and shall not be questioned in any proceeding whatsoever.
>
> 6. Subject to paragraph (5) above, nothing in this rule prevents the validity of a nomination being questioned on an election petition."

In *R. v. Election Court, ex p. Sheppard*,[56] a candidate's nomination paper was accepted as valid and he was subsequently elected. A defeated candidate brought an election petition on the ground that the winner's nomination paper contained a false statement as to his home address. This petition was upheld and the winner unseated. The winner in turn sought certiorari to quash the Election Court's finding, arguing that the Returning Officer's acceptance of his nomination paper was conclusive as to its validity and that the Election Court had had no power to investigate the allegation. He failed. Lord Widgery C.J. said:

---

[54] *Greenway-Stanley's* case, n. 39 above, at 666.
[55] See in the same terms for local elections S.I. 1986 No. 2214, r. 7(6), (7).
[56] [1975] 1 W.L.R. 1319 (D.C.)

" . . . if the returning officer makes a pronouncement on the form of the nomination paper and pronounces it to be valid as to form . . . then his decision is final and cannot be questioned. But if and in so far as the nomination paper is to be attacked on grounds other than form . . . then subrule (6) allows such a matter of complaint to be raised. Here the defect complained of . . . was not apparent on the form. . . . Accordingly . . . the returning officer's approval of that paper does not exclude the possibility of its validity being attacked for the substantial complaint."[57]

(4) THE DEPOSIT

The most controversial element in the nomination process for parliamentary and European Parliament candidates is the requirement to make cash or cash-equivalent deposits of £500 for parliamentary candidates[58] and £750 for European Parliament candidates[59] in order that their names may appear on the ballot paper. A deposit is not recoverable if a candidate fails to obtain a specified percentage of the valid votes cast, the percentage currently being set at 5 per cent.[60] The deposit system, which has never operated in respect of local government elections, was instituted in 1918 when the state accepted full responsibility for meeting the costs of parliamentary elections. Previously these had fallen to be met collectively by the candidates. Following a number of unlikely candidacies, the deposit was introduced "as a safeguard against candidacies which added to the cost and complexity of the election whilst having no serious prospect of polling a sufficient number of votes to influence the result."[61] At that time the deposit required was set at £150, this being recoverable if the candidate obtained not less than one-eighth of the votes cast. This remained the position until 1985, when the deposit was raised to its current figure, but the fraction of votes required to save the deposit was set at one-twentieth. European Parliament candidates were in 1979 required to deposit £600, and this was increased to its present figure in 1986.

As a matter of principle, the deposit system is surely wrong. It cannot be correct to tie an individual's ability to stand as a

[57] At 1324–1325.
[58] R.P.A. 1985, s.13(*a*).
[59] S.I. 1986 No. 2209, Sched. 1.
[60] R.P.A. 1985, s.13(*b*).
[61] H.C. 32–II, p. 14 (Home Office memorandum).

candidate to the size of his or her financial resources. As the Ecology (now the Green) Party put it in its Memorandum of Evidence to the Home Affairs Select Committee, "There is no guarantee that ideas backed by money are necessarily better than those without vested financial interests,"[62] and candidates ought in principle to be allowed to put their ideas forward to the electorate regardless of financial tests. As will be seen later, the proposition that money shall not be entitled disproportionately to be heard lies behind much of our campaign law (however inadequately this is carried through in practice), and the same principle would seem to be appropriate here. Why then is the deposit system retained?

If it is accepted that frivolous candidates must be discouraged, what mechanisms other than a financial test are available to achieve this? One possibility might be to empower the Returning Officer to disallow such candidacies. This is a prospect not worth contemplating further. It would be wholly incompatible with our understanding of democracy to allow a state official to decide who could offer themselves for election. The remaining alternative would then appear to be to require a potential candidate to demonstrate a "lack of frivolity" by exhibiting some evidence of local support for his candidacy. As we have seen, there is already a minimal requirement to this effect in the stipulation for nominators, seconders and assentors to signify their support. Requirements that prospective candidacies be backed by large numbers of signatures in order to be valid are common in other countries, and the European Commission of Human Rights (which has never considered the deposit system) has found such stipulations to be wholly compatible with Protocol One, Article Three:

> "It is neither unreasonable nor arbitrary, having regard to the principles of a democratic society, that the procedural rights related to the exercise of the right to stand as a candidate or to propose candidates reflect the character of the elections as a public political process, and that these rights are accordingly circumscribed in such a way that they cannot be exercised by an individual acting alone, but only with the support of a certain minimum number of persons holding the same views."[63]

---

[62] *Ibid.* p. 272.
[63] *X. v. Federal Republic of Germany*, Appl. No. 8227/78, 16 D. & R. 179, 180–181. See also Appl. 6850/74, 5 D. & R. 90, and 7008/75, 6 D. & R. 120.

It must be doubted, however, whether such a system could be introduced in a workable form in this country. The principal objection is one of practicability.[64] In the time available, it would simply not be possible for the Returning Officer to check large numbers of electors' signatures in support of several different candidates. Were parliamentary elections to take place at set times, the nomination date might be set sufficiently early beforehand to enable such checking to be done. As matters are now, when "snap" elections can be called, there is no checking even of the limited numbers of signatures presently required. This has enabled at least one candidate to be held validly nominated on the basis of allegedly-forged signatures.[65] There would be little point in instituting a new obligation for a greatly increased number of signatures in support of a candidacy without a checking mechanism, and there seems no possibility within the current timetable for parliamentary elections of instituting one.

Thus we are left with the deposit as the only available regulator of frivolous candidacies. Experience since the raising of the parliamentary deposit to £500 does not indicate that such candidates have been unduly dissuaded from standing, whereas fledgling parties seeking to operate at a national level, such as the Green Party, continue to suffer disproportionately from the deposit system. It cannot be said that the compromise reached in 1985, of raising the deposit level while reducing the percentage of votes required for it to be returned, has yet been struck at a level which penalises the frivolous and encourages the serious. This continues to be a defect in our electoral system.

(5) PARTY SELECTION PROCEDURES

The procedures which parties adopt to select their candidates are important for two reasons. First, our electoral system has become almost entirely a battleground for the political parties. No non-party candidate has ever been elected to the European Parliament from a British constituency, and no independent candidate has won a parliamentary seat in a General Election since February 1974. Local government polls continue to return independent candidates, but their numbers are decreasing. The Widdicombe Committee found in 1985 that only about 15 per cent. of councillors described themselves as independent (as

---

[64] See also, Cmnd. 9140, paras. 5(3)–(4).
[65] See *R.* v. *Tynebridge Returning Officer ex p. McGuire*, December 2, 1985 (unreported).

against 39 per cent. in 1965), and that nearly 40 per cent. of those were in fact members of political parties who nevertheless had chosen to fight as "independents."[66] Given this party dominance of the electoral system, party candidate selection procedures are obviously highly significant. Secondly, in the case of parliamentary elections at least, the number of seats changing hands between the parties is relatively small, as the 1987 General Election results illustrate. In these circumstances, party selection procedures in seats already held by the party are frequently more important for the ambitious politician than is the election itself. As Rush puts it, in such circumstances "selection is tantamount to election." (Rush (1969), p. 4).

As is commonly the position in other countries (see Ranney (1981)), selection procedures in British political parties are extralegal, in the sense that they are regulated not by the public law of the state but by the private law of the parties' constitutions or internal arrangements. Responsibility for candidate selection characteristically reposes in the constituency party or association, subject to a measure of central party control, the scale of which varies between the parties. Among the major British parties, only the S.D.P. has allocated the candidate selection power to a body other than a constituency party. The S.D.P. is organised on an area rather than a constituency basis, and the power of selection of candidates for constituencies within the area lies with party members in the area.

The first stage in candidate selection is a party decision that the seat will be fought. A local Conservative Party Association will decide this *sub silentio*, it being assumed that the party will fight all seats that become vacant. The Labour Party Constitution provides that the desirability of contesting the seat is to be considered by the local party in consultation with the National Executive Committee (N.E.C.), but again this is normally a formality. Any future arrangements for an electoral "pact" with other non-Conservative parties might change this. Ultimate power seems to repose in the N.E.C., in that a local party has to seek the N.E.C.'s authority to secure nominations for the candidature. The S.D.P. constitution likewise places the final decision in such circumstances in the hands of its National Committee, which can direct an Area Party not to contest a seat and can also recommend members to vote for candidates of another party in any seat for which there is no S.D.P. candidate.

---

[66] Cmnd. 9797, paras. 2.37–38.

This was obviously important in both the 1983 and 1987 General Elections, when the S.D.P. and the Liberal Party had to decide which party's candidate would represent the Alliance in each constituency. The decentralised power structure of the Liberal Party precluded any firm instructions being issued from party headquarters in 1983, and three Liberal Associations nominated candidates in defiance of national agreements reached with the S.D.P. (see Curtice and Steed (1983)). There was no recurrence of this in 1987, when negotiations between the parties were conducted at regional level.

Once it has been decided to fight the seat, each local party organisation will proceed to selection, following its constitution or established procedure.[67] The details vary, but it is broadly the case that while national party organisations prepare lists of candidates, it is open to local organisations to make their own selection of individual candidates, who may or may not already have been nationally listed. Inclusion on the national list has different significance among the different parties. A Conservative who is listed can be regarded as an approved potential candidate, and the party organisation requires applicants to pass tests of fitness before they will be admitted to the list. The Labour Party, in contrast, does not attribute great significance to inclusion on the national candidates' lists, and it is quite possible that the N.E.C., whose endorsement of a candidate once selected is the final stage of the selection procedure, will refuse to endorse a constituency's choice who appears on the national candidates' list (see Rush (1969), pp. 132 *et seq.*).

Differences also exist as to who within the local party organisations are empowered to select candidates. In the Conservative Party the decision is effectively made by a delegate body, the constituency executive council. Until 1987 Labour Party rules also provided for selection by a delegate body, the management committee, but rule changes have now been made to provide for selection by constituency "electoral colleges." The colleges will be composed of individual party members and of representatives of affiliated organisations (principally, trade unions), the latter having not more than 40 per cent. of the votes in an election for the constituency's candidate. In contrast, both the S.D.P. and the Liberal Party select their candidates simply

---

[67] The Conservative Party has no formal constitution. Its candidate selection procedures are set out in the National Union's Notes on Procedure for the Adoption of Conservative Parliamentary Candidates in England and Wales. See also, Conservative Central Office's Parliamentary Election Manual (15th ed., 1987), pp. 8–17.

by ballot of local party members. The S.D.P. constitution requires that all candidates be selected by a postal ballot of all members of the party within the area. This means that members outside the constituency are eligible to vote. The Liberal Party does not go so far. Provision is made for all party members within the constituency to vote, either by post or by attendance at a selection meeting, the choice being made by the local Liberal Association.

It is rare that disputes as to the operation of these selection procedures become public,[68] and even rarer that such disputes have to be resolved in court. Potential candidates are hardly likely to initiate legal action against constituency organisations that unfairly refuse to consider them because of the damage that would be done to their reputations within the wider party. There *is* potential for dispute between constituency Labour parties and the N.E.C. as to any refusal by the latter to endorse individuals as official Labour candidates, but endorsement is very rarely refused and in only one instance has it led to legal action. Following the resignation of the sitting Labour M.P., a Constituency Labour Party selected a former Labour M.P. and current member of the European Parliament to represent Labour at the forthcoming by-election. The N.E.C. resolved that this person be not endorsed, but that the local party be advised to select another named individual. This was in purported exercise of an N.E.C. power in the circumstance of by-elections to "co-operate" with the local party and, if it deemed it necessary in the interests of the (wider) Labour Party, to "advise" the local party to select the N.E.C.'s nominee. The local Labour party alleged that the N.E.C. had misused its powers and had acted in breach of natural justice and sought injunctions restraining the N.E.C. from endorsing its own nominee, as the N.E.C. had resolved to do. The injunctions were refused. Parliamentary leaders of the Labour Party had moved the writ for the by-election soon after the N.E.C. decision, and Hoffman J. declined, in this situation, to make orders which might create difficulties for the party in its by-election campaign. An appeal was dismissed.[69] Thus the N.E.C. was able to get its preferred candidate, possibly in breach of the party's constitution, by manipulating the immediate occurrence of the by-election. Whether the result would have been the same with no election pending would be

---

[68] Reselection disputes within the Labour Party may be an exception. See Young (1983).
[69] *Huckfield* v. *Tierney* October 27, 1986 (unreported).

dependent upon judicial interpretation of the constitutional relationship between the N.E.C. and the local party, although Sir John Donaldson did suggest that the N.E.C. had very considerable discretion in its decisions on endorsement.

The N.E.C. was equally able to get its way when claiming the power to suspend a candidate from her parliamentary candidacy shortly before the 1987 General Election. It is not clear that the N.E.C. has a power of suspension of parliamentary candidates, although the National Constitutional Committee, the party's disciplinary body, does have power to withdraw the party's endorsement of a candidate (which is curious, given that it is the N.E.C. rather than the N.C.C. which endorses the candidate in the first place). The exercise of that disciplinary power would have to be in accordance with the rules of natural justice. The candidate chose not to take legal action, and her constituency party felt compelled reluctantly to accept the N.E.C.'s alternative candidate. In other cases, constituency parties have defied the N.E.C. and insisted upon having their chosen candidates, and the N.E.C. has had to give way, if only to ensure that the local party will undertake an active election campaign for a candidate they support.

It has from time to time been argued that party selection procedures are defective in failing to involve the whole of the local party membership in the selection process. The Hansard Commission on Electoral Reform (Hansard Society (1976)) has recommended that legislation be enacted laying down principles to be observed in candidate selection procedures. Selection would be made by all constituency party members, voting by secret postal ballot, the costs of which would be met by public funds. Only if this procedure were followed would a candidate be permitted to use a party label as part of his or her description on the ballot paper.[70] This proposal, as the Commission recognised, is incompatible with that element in the British liberal tradition "that voluntary associations (including political parties and trade unions) should be free to choose whatever form of internal organization they prefer" (Birch (1985), p. 88). Admittedly, that tradition has been significantly undermined by legislation imposing obligations upon trade unions to select members of their principal executive committees by secret postal ballot, and by requiring them to maintain a register of members' names and addresses for election purposes,[71] and so the counter

---

[70] Hansard Society (1976), p. 19.
[71] Trade Unions Act 1984, ss.1–4.

argument based on tradition may not be as strong as when the Commission reported. It must nevertheless be doubted whether legislation is appropriate. These matters seem best left for the parties to work out for themselves; it is reasonable to assume that if they do not take sufficient steps locally to involve their members in party affairs, they will simply lose those members. As it is, the Hansard Commission's proposals on candidate selection have received minimal support.

Part Three
ELECTION CAMPAIGNS

5. THE LEGAL FRAMEWORK OF ELECTION CAMPAIGNS

(1) INTRODUCTION

The law regulating the process of electoral campaigning is now principally to be found in Part II of the R.P.A. 1983. In some respects a tight legal framework is imposed on the campaigning process, but in certain (arguably the most important) areas there are minimal legal constraints. We first examine the framework of campaigning law, identifying the assumptions behind it; we next consider the processes of national and local campaigning, seeking to assess how far these legal provisions fit with the realities of modern campaigning practice ; we then briefly refer to the funding of election campaigns, considering how the parties raise sufficient moneys to conduct their campaigns and what legal restrictions, if any, are imposed on their fund-raising efforts; and we finally discuss the conduct of the poll itself and challenges to the results once declared.

(2) CAMPAIGN LAW: THE BASIC FRAMEWORK

Legal controls on election campaigning are principally concerned with controls on expenditure. Broadly speaking, there are three types of provision: those controlling the "personal expenses" of the candidate; those designed to limit the level of expenditure permitted in a campaign; and those forbidding certain forms of expenditure altogether. These provisions are in large part a re-enactment of legislation designed to rectify the grosser abuses of Victorian electioneering. That legislation was predicated on two assumptions. First, it was assumed that the primary campaigner was the individual candidate, rather than the party. Secondly, it was assumed that campaigning law should centrally be concerned with the regulation of campaigning at the constituency, rather than at national, level. This is not surprising, in that the concept of the national campaign was in its infancy when the Corrupt and Illegal Practices Prevention Act 1883 (the source of much of our present campaign law) was passed, but it also reflects the traditional perception of the position of the House of Commons in the constitution which we discussed earlier. This perception of the House as "a geographical representation of the Kingdom"[1] or a "congress of constituencies"[2] inevitably directs attention to the regulation of constituency electioneering, whereas a system providing for "a mass poll of the citizenry"[3] might lead legislators to formulate rules dealing with the national campaigning that would inevitably ensue.

How far it is correct to see modern electoral campaigning in candidate-and-constituency rather than in party-and-national terms is open to the most serious doubt, but our present campaign law continues to operate on this basis, as is demonstrated by the *Tronoh Mines*[4] case. Between the issue of the writ for the 1951 General Election and the day of polling, the Tronoh Mines company inserted an advertisement in *The Times* excoriating the Labour Party for its proposal to introduce a scheme of company dividend restraint, and calling for

> "a new and strong government with Ministers who may be relied upon to encourage business enterprise and initiative, under the leadership of one who has, through the whole of his life, devoted himself to national and not sectional interests...".

After the election the company, its secretary, and *The Times* were all charged with committing corrupt practices in that they had incurred expenses in issuing advertisements or publications without the authority of an election agent with a view to promoting or procuring the election of the Conservative candidate in the constituency where *The Times* was printed. The judge refused to allow the matter to go to the jury and directed a not guilty verdict. He held that section 63 of the R.P.A. 1949 (now section 75 of the 1983 Act) was concerned to prohibit the incurring of expenditure to support a particular candidate in a particular constituency, save with the written authorisation of the candidate's election agent. It was not concerned with "general political propaganda, even though that general political propaganda does incidentally assist a particular candidate among others."[5] Accordingly, the electoral expenditure rules were inapplicable.

---

[1] Hansard, Vol. 69, December 10, 1984, Col. 782.
[2] Mr. Powell, Hansard, Vol. 72, January 29, 1985, Col. 197.
[3] See n. 1 above.
[4] [1952] 1 All E.R. 697.
[5] [1952] 1 All E.R. 697, 700.

This decision is an excellent illustration of the blindness of our electoral law to the realities of national election campaigning. It also lays open the way for extensive intervention by outside elements with vested interests to protect, whose only constraint is the size of their financial resources, and who can engage in advertising both before and during the campaign. The rigorously restrictive expenditure rules should be seen in the light of these "third-party expenditure" and national expenditure loopholes. The result of this is that while in a given constituency there may be a financial limit in a General Election campaign of about £5,500, the party nationally, and third-party interveners, can spend unlimited sums, subject only to their ability to raise funds. This absence of regulation poses a serious threat to any principle of financial control of campaigning.

(3) EXPENDITURE: RULES, LIMITS AND ACCOUNTING

To understand the somewhat eccentric structure of the expenditure controls, it is necessary first to consider the events which gave rise to their development (O'Leary (1961)). Seen in its historical context the content of the rules is quite understandable, but at the same time the question may be asked as to whether rules developed in very different circumstances are the most appropriate way of regulating modern electioneering.

The history of the expenditure rules is the history of the battle to eradicate pre-Reform Act election practices from the modern electoral system. Before the Ballot Act 1872, voting was carried out in public, and many electors appear to have considered their vote a saleable commodity. Concern at such practices was not new. As early as 1695 an Act was passed to prohibit treating and excessive expenditure,[6] although with little effect. The Bribery Act of 1729 had equally little impact, perhaps because it was considered perfectly reasonable to show favour to electors. Concern nonetheless was voiced by parliamentarians, even if they would privately or publicly indulge in the practices themselves; indeed, control of bribery was one articulated reason behind the Reform Act 1832. The Act did little to cut down bribery, and the practice may have increased as candidates sought to win over the new electorate.

The first step in the campaign which ultimately stamped out these practices was the 1854 Corrupt Practices Prevention Act, which defined bribery, treating and undue influence, and set up

---

[6] 7 & 8 Will. 3, c. 4.

a system of audits of returns. It was believed that if candidates had to account publicly for what they had spent, this might deter corruption. This is the origin, in a modified form, of today's election return. The administrative procedure failed, and was largely ignored. If anything it simply drove bribery underground. Penalties for bribery were also greatly increased, to no avail. In 1869, an inquiry into one constituency[7] indicated that in every election since 1832, 75 per cent. of the constituents were "hopelessly addicted to bribery." Even Bagehot, the noted writer on constitutional affairs, became embroiled in such dealings (O'Leary (1961), p. 54).

The first significant step towards the control of bribery came not from new expenditure rules, but from the ultimate success of the long campaign for the secret ballot.[8] An important argument in the debates was the ballot's likely effect on corruption. Each time one form of corruption had been prohibited, a more subtle form had emerged. The secret ballot was seen as a way around this; although the recognition of voting as an individual right probably had more influence on the passage of the Act, these practical matters were highly relevant (O'Leary (1961), pp. 58 *et seq.*). Nevertheless, while the Ballot Act can properly be hailed as a constitutional milestone, its initial effects on corruption were less apparent; petitions alleging corruption fell, but corruption continued, if less systematically.

Further evidence of corruption in the General Election campaign of 1880 led to renewed attempts at reform and the Parliamentary Elections (Corrupt and Illegal Practices) Act 1883 introduced fundamental change. First, it limited the number of people a candidate could employ as campaign helpers, and secondly it imposed a maximum ceiling on expenditure. The immediate effect on declared expenditure was dramatic. Thirdly, it created the modern system of administrative controls and placed the liability for expenditure firmly on the candidate. It also created the distinction between corrupt and illegal practices. This legislation produced a system of regulation in contrast to previous piecemeal measures and established a workable framework of campaign law. The Act was remarkably successful, in that by the turn of the century bribery was extremely rare, and the number of election petitions alleging corrupt practices declined dramatically.

[7] Bridgwater 1870 Parl. Papers XXX 5–7.
[8] Ballot Act 1872.

The structure created by the 1883 Act remains, but its rationale has changed. No longer concerned with overtly corrupt activities, its purpose is now said to be to limit the power of the wealthy to purchase seats by excessive but otherwise lawful expenditures. Yet, with the growth in national campaigning, the effects of an individual's campaign are less, and the legislation makes no attempt to control the purchasing of victory on a national scale. In many cases, we believe, the rules have the opposite effect to that desired. They limit local electioneering by the smaller parties who cannot afford massive national campaigns, and have had a significant restrictive impact on the development of election techniques at local level. The legal expenditure maxima, which are laid down from time to time by the Secretary of State, have failed to keep pace with rising costs for election materials and printing and the need to limit expenditure to meet legal requirements may be a prime factor in campaign planning. We now consider the detail of these rules.

(a) Personal Expenses of the Candidate

What expenditure counts as a "personal expense"? There is no exhaustive statutory definition but section 118 of the R.P.A. 1983 gives some guidance as to the sort of expenditure covered. It includes "the reasonable travelling expenses of the candidate, and the reasonable expenses of his living at hotels or elsewhere for the purposes of and in relation to the election." Hire expenditure for the candidate to drive (or be driven in) a car falls within this, whereas hiring an identical car to transport helpers would not.[9] Renting a house for the duration of an election is not a "personal expense," nor are the ordinary costs of meals at home, as these are primarily incurred for purposes unconnected with the election. The candidate would need somewhere to live in any event.[10]

Controls on personal expenditure are few. The candidate may incur "reasonable" personal expenditure, but there is no legislative guidance as to what is reasonable, save that if a Parliamentary candidate spends more than £600 on personal expenses, the excess, seemingly limitless, must be paid by the agent.[11] In general these "personal expenses" are less significant in local elections, as the candidate will normally live at

[9] Sankey J. in *Berwick on Tweed Case* (1923) 7 O'M. & H. 24.
[10] *Rochester Borough Case* (1892) 4 O'M. & H. 156.
[11] R.P.A. 1983, s.74 as amended by R.P.A. 1985, s.14(2).

home. While "personal expenses" do not count towards the total campaign expenses limit in Parliamentary elections (although any such expenses must be included in the agent's return of election expenses), they do count against expenses limits in both local and European Assembly elections. It is difficult to justify this exclusion from the overall limit on expenditure in the case of parliamentary elections but not others. Perhaps a reason is that a parliamentary candidate would be more likely to require hotel accommodation, or incur high travel costs, which could easily eat up the maximum. The failure to treat European elections in the same manner as parliamentary elections would seem to be an oversight.

(b) Campaign Expenditure

The main class of controls by which legislation seeks to restrain election expenditure is widely drafted to cover expenditure before, during or after the election, providing it is "on account of or in respect of the conduct or management of the election."[12] A maximum figure is set for the amount a candidate or agent can spend on the conduct or management of the election, and under ss.73–75 of the 1983 Act, almost any expenditure other than that authorised by the candidate or agent is prohibited.

(i) **What expenditure is controlled?** No attempt has been made exhaustively to define the phrase "conduct or management of an election," although it has been said to cover anything which promotes or procures the election of a candidate.[13] The latter phrase is used elsewhere in the legislation concerning expenditure.[14] Its importation into this context has two significant consequences. If the controls only apply to something which promotes or procures the election of a particular candidate, most national campaigning falls outside the controls. Similarly, general work undertaken locally or nationally, aimed at promoting the party rather than an individual, will fall outside the controls. This emphasis upon candidates rather than parties is based on the archaic notion that elections are won by the efforts of individual candidates, and that general promotional work for the party is not part of an election.

Difficult questions may arise as to whether expenditure on any particular activity should count against election expenses.

---

[12] R.P.A. 1983, s.76.
[13] *Maidstone Borough Case* (1906) 5 O'M. & H. 200, *per* Lawrence J.
[14] R.P.A. 1983, s.75.

The purpose of the activity will be highly relevant, and it is a question of fact on each occasion whether the main object of an activity is to promote the candidate, or was undertaken with some other object in view.[15] If the main aim of an event is not connected with the election, and only incidentally will the candidate gain, that is not an election expense. In the Great Yarmouth Case of 1906, Arthur Fell was selected as prospective Conservative candidate. Not being local, in February 1905 he held a giant "At Home" to get to know the community, entertaining nearly 800 people to tea in the Town Hall. Despite some disagreement between the judges, this was held not to be an election expense in respect of the election which took place in 1906. Here the length of time between the event and the election was clearly important. As the date of election approaches it must become increasingly difficult to ascribe to events any purpose other than that of electioneering.

Things deemed done to promote or procure the election of a particular candidate include the holding of public meetings or organising public displays; issuing advertisements, circulars and publications; or otherwise presenting to electors the candidate's views. It must also be noted that promoting or procuring the election of a candidate includes disparaging his rival.[16]

(ii) When do the rules come into play? The controls apply to expenditure before, during or after an election, and so the formal timetable rules do not determine whether a particular expense counts as expenditure for these rules.[17] The sole question is whether the expenditure was concerned with the conduct or management of an individual's campaign. The vagueness of this rule may occasion considerable uncertainty, and this is increasingly true now that campaigning is becoming regarded as a continuing process. By July 1985, all the major parties were warning constituencies that it was already too late to be starting work on the next general election, possibly as much as three years away. Increasingly in local government there is no break between campaigns. The issue of local party newsletters continues all year round, and seems mainly aimed

---

[15] *Great Yarmouth Case* (1906) 5 O'M. & H. 176. *Elgin & Nairn Case* (1895) 5 O'M. & H. 1.

[16] *D.P.P.* v. *Luft* [1977] A.C. 962.

[17] *Dorsetshire, East Division Case* (1910) 6 O'M. & H. 22 expressly rejected the notion that expenses cannot start until the notice of election. *Cf. Walsall Case* (1892) 4 0'M. & H. 123.

at winning elections. Yet nobody suggests that the cost of these issued between elections counts towards election expenses, and so at what point do the expenses rules begin to apply?

There are several stages which could provide an adequate dividing line: when the election is first mentioned ("Don't forget next May's elections"); when a candidate is first mentioned ("Remember, in the May elections, vote Smith"); or as late as when the writ is issued or notice of election published. This simple problem arises in almost every election, but the legislation provides no direct answer, save that the expenditure must be "by the candidate or agent in respect of the conduct or management of the election." This provides a partial solution to the problem: for expenditure to fall within the controls there must be a candidate, or an agent. Section 118 of the 1983 Act provides:

"candidate" —

(a) in relation to a parliamentary election, means a person who is elected to serve in Parliament at the election or a person who is nominated as a candidate at the election, or is declared by himself or by others to be a candidate on or after the day of the issue of the writ for the election, or after the dissolution or vacancy in consequence of which the writ was issued;

(b) in relation to an election under the local government Act, means a person elected or having been nominated or having declared himself a candidate for election, to the office to be filled at the election;

The process of obtaining and announcing a party candidature has two stages, selection and adoption. For parliamentary elections, and increasingly in other elections, candidate selection takes place long before the election. The result of the selection process is that someone is chosen who will be adopted as the candidate when the election is reached. The second stage is the formal adoption meeting, which normally takes place just prior to submission of the nomination paper. Selection does not of itself start election expenses running, although the selected person can do other acts which start expenses running. On the other hand, if expenses have not already started to run, the formal motion to adopt the candidate will start expenses running.

To avoid setting expenses running before formal adoption, a practice has developed in the case of parliamentary elections of calling selected but unadopted candidates "Prospective Parliamentary Candidates," or "PPCs." The word "prospective" probably has no legal significance *per se*,[18] as the law is concerned with substance rather than form, but it may be useful as an indicator of the intention of the person involved, and thereby evidence that he has not yet declared himself a candidate and fully entered the battle. In any event, the legal value of this term is unlikely ever to be challenged, for the general public are not aware of such matters, and other parties need the protection of the phrase. If someone were successfully to challenge the practice in an Election Court, all parties would be severely handicapped in campaigning prior to an election. Consequently, it appears to be accepted that expenditure undertaken by a "PPC" will not normally be considered as counting towards election expenses, at least if undertaken before the dissolution of Parliament (or issue of the writ in a by-election). In local government elections there is no such understanding and so the phrase "prospective candidate" will not prevent expenses running; in any event, in local elections, words like "campaign organiser" or "local spokesperson" are equally effective in achieving publicity for a candidate without the risk of setting expenses running.

Expenses can also be set running indirectly, if, without declaring oneself to be a candidate, a person nonetheless appoints an agent,[19] or employs election staff.[20] In general this is not a problem, as a candidate either uses existing professional party agents and staff, or obtains voluntary help. In either case, the person will probably already have declared himself a candidate before making such an appointment. But it may be that even the use of voluntary workers can set expenses running if they are doing what is obviously electoral work. As Cave J. said:

> "In some cases canvassers are set to work and committees are formed long before the dissolution or the issue of the writ. If those expenses are not to be returned as election expenses the words of the Act as to the maximum amount of expenditure are set at naught."[21]

---

[18] "I take the view that there is no difference whatever between candidature, and prospective candidature, but there is a great difference between campaign and battle. When the time of battle comes all expenditure must be returned as election expenditure under the Act." Grantham J., *Cornwall, Bodmin Division Case* (1906) 5 O'M. & H. 225.

[19] *Rochester Case* (1892) 4 O'M. & H. 156.

[20] *Stepney Case* (1886) 4 O'M. & H. 38.

[21] *Rochester Case*, n. 19, above.

A number of cases illustrate the difficulty of deciding when expenses start to run. In one extreme case expenditure 30 months before the election was held to be an expense. The Guest family had traditionally held a particular seat for the Liberals, but a Conservative had been elected in 1904. In 1908 Ivor Guest reached an agreement with the Conservative M.P. that the Conservative would get an Edinburgh seat, and Guest would stand, unhindered, as a Liberal. Expenses for the 1910 election were held to run from the date of that arrangement.[22] Equally unequivocally, in Shoreditch, in the winter of 1894–5, a year before the election, the Unionist candidate distributed food tokens to the poor, and placed an advertisement in the paper to tell people of his generosity, describing himself as "the Unionist candidate." Expenses immediately began to run.[23] Today a person could avoid this by using the title "PPC."

The *Richmond* case provides a modern illustration of these rules.[24] In the 1981 elections for the Greater London Council, the Liberal candidate won a seat previously held for the Conservative Party. The Conservatives subsequently issued an election petition on a number of grounds, one of which was that expenditures had been incurred but omitted from the Liberal candidate's return of expenses. The question arose as to whether expenses had begun to run at the time at which the particular expenditures were undertaken. Four possible events could have set expenses running for the May election: general Liberal Party posters in March; a leaflet distributed 12 months before the election describing Slade as "the prospective GLC candidate"; a newspaper advertisement for his adoption meeting on April 1; the adoption meeting itself. In this particular case the court held that expenses started with the formal adoption of Slade. Whilst it may be simpler to avoid examination of events a year or more earlier when petitions are presented, if the *Richmond* case represents a trend towards holding that expenses start very late, it deserves at most a cautious welcome. The later expenses start to run, the greater the scope for wealthy candidates to influence matters—precisely what the law aims to prevent.

(iii) Expenditure maxima. A maximum figure is laid down for expenditure on the local campaign in each constituency, and it is

[22] *Dorsetshire Eastern Case* (1910) 6 O'M. & H. 22.
[23] *Shoreditch Haggerston Case* P.P. 1896, lxvii. 436.
[24] Unreported, but see Williams (1982).

an offence to incur any expenditure in excess of that figure, even
if at the time the liability was incurred the person did not realise
it would carry the campaign over the maximum. The risk,
therefore, of inadvertent offending is substantial, and the
determination of the maximum important.

The maximum figure which may be expended is determined
by reference to the size of the electorate and the nature of the
constituency or ward. In the case of parliamentary and local
elections the maximum is altered from time to time by the
Secretary of State, where "in his opinion there has been a
change in the value of money since the last occasion on which
that sum or amount was fixed, and the variation shall be such as
in his opinion is justified by that change."[25] There is no
equivalent power in the case of European Assembly elections.
Instead amendments have to take place by variation of the
European Assembly Election Regulations, again vesting effective control in the Secretary of State. Proposals by the Secretary
of State are made by statutory instrument, laid before both
Houses of Parliament, requiring Affirmative Resolution. These
powers have not been used frequently in recent years, and any
criticism has been of a failure to use them rather than of their
excessive use. For example, between 1979 and 1985 the
maximum permitted expenditure in local elections was
increased by 40 per cent., whereas the cost of paper, a crucial
element in any election campaign, increased by 60 per cent.

The present maxima, set in May 1987,[26] illustrate the elements
which are taken into account in determining the maximum
expenditure for any one electoral unit. In the case of parliamentary elections the maximum in county constituencies is £3,370
plus 3·8p. for every entry on the electoral register as first
published, but the lesser additional sum of 2·9p. per elector is
added in borough constituencies. For local elections the maximum is £150 plus 3p. for every entry on the register as first
published. Special provision is made for elections to the Inner
London Education Authority, where the figures are £655 plus
3·9p. per elector. Finally, for European Assembly elections the
equivalent figures are £8,000 plus 3·5p. for every registered
elector.[27]

These legal maxima seem to have been determined on a
largely arbitrary basis, without reference to the actual costs of

---

[25] R.P.A. 1983, s.76A, inserted by R.P.A. 1985, s.14(4).
[26] Representation of the People (Variation of Limits of Candidates' Election
Expenses) Order: S.I. 1987 No. 903.
[27] European Assembly Elections Regulations S.I. 1986 No. 2209, Sched. 1.

the different types of campaign. The maximum for local elections seems low in relation to other elections, especially given that economies of scale to reduce printing costs are less likely to be available. Further, parliamentary elections distinguish between the type of constituency when adding an amount per elector, rightly recognising that in rural areas costs, particularly for transport, are much higher. However, this distinction is not carried through into other elections. Many European Assembly constituencies are very largely rural. It is unclear why these seats do not receive a more favourable allowance, like rural parliamentary seats.

In local elections these rules are complicated by the presence of multi-member wards, although this can also serve to alleviate the tightness of financial constraints. If two or more persons stand in a ward as joint candidates, the economies this produces are recognised by a reduction in the maximum permitted per candidate, although the total for the joint campaign is greater than for one candidate.[28] Difficulties do, however, arise in identifying joint candidates. The use of common electoral literature, a joint agent or a joint committee room go to identifying joint candidates (unless the use of common personnel or premises is of an accidental, casual, trivial or unimportant nature). However, when the S.D.P. was first formed and Liberal and S.D.P. candidates stood side by side in two member wards, the differences in campaign style led in some cases to the distribution of separate literature. Were the candidates joint candidates nevertheless, in standing for the Alliance? The matter never came to an Election Court, and so the answer is uncertain, but such candidates are now advised by their parties to use the lower maxima for joint candidates rather than for two independent candidates.

If elections for two authorities (for example District Councils and Parish Councils) coincide, a person standing for both can spend the maximum for each. Similarly, in a ward which elects two District Councillors and five Parish Councillors, if a party nominates a full slate for all seven seats, the slate can spend almost five times that available to an individual candidate.[29] This recognition of the role of parties in local electioneering is quite inconsistent with the general thrust of the rules.

---

[28] R.P.A. 1983, s.77.

[29] s. 77(1) permits three-quarters of maxima on each District Council candidate and two-thirds of maxima on each Parish Council candidate—a total of nearly five times the normal maximum.

(iv) Administrative controls: the return. Such a complex system of substantive controls having been created, there is inevitably an administrative system to ensure that the substantive controls are obeyed, or at least that any breach is documented. In this case, however, the administrative rules are so complex in their own right as sometimes to cause further offences to be committed.

Throughout the legislation, to ensure that one person is accountable, the reporting onus is placed entirely upon the agent.[30] In addition, however, the candidate can be penalised for any breach of the expenditure rules, and so he has a direct interest in ensuring compliance with the rules. The levels of expenditure are monitored through the requirement that an agent submit a return of his expenses, together with copies of all invoices and receipts. Challenges to expenditure are generally based upon this document, either on the ground that it is incorrectly completed, or that expenditure has been incurred in excess of that shown. This heavy burden of paperwork is to simplify challenges. If the paperwork is not provided for any proven expenditure, that is an offence. Without the requirement for detailed paperwork, unlawful expenditure could be concealed by vague figures.

Although the expenditure rules are central to legislative control over electioneering, the role of the Returning Officer in their enforcement is minimal; he merely acts as an administrator, to receive the return of expenses, and related declarations. In most cases he will not even bother reading them. The responsibility for scrutinising election returns, and ensuring that the rules have been obeyed, lies with other candidates and the local electorate, but their only method of challenge is through the Election Courts. It is not possible to compel an agent to complete another, correct, return: either an error must be ignored, or an election petition must be presented.

The obligation upon the agent is to authorise all expenditures undertaken as part of the campaign, and to account for all expenses incurred. The requirement that the agent's authorisation be obtained for expenditures is an important one, designed to limit uncontrolled third-party intervention in the election on behalf of individual candidates, but as the *Tronoh Mines* case demonstrates, the constituency-based nature of our electoral law allows a degree of third-party intervention at national level which significantly undermines the agent's formal position as regulator of financial participation in elections.

---

[30] R.P.A. 1983, ss.72–75.

So far as the return of expenses is concerned, the agent must assemble and complete it, in the specified form,[31] within 35 days of the day on which the results were declared. This is required for every candidate, although inevitably the winning candidate's return will be scrutinised more thoroughly and must be accurately compiled. In theory, an inadequate return from any agent can result in that candidate and agent being convicted of an election offence and possibly being disqualified for up to five years. It should simply be a matter of bookkeeping but, in the heat of an election, accounting systems are not always reliable and the forms require very careful completion. Providing the intention is honest, an agent would be unlikely to be disqualified for miscompleting the form, but a disorganised, albeit honest, return could nonetheless result in an election petition. In the *Richmond* case a conviction occurred despite the agent involved seeking advice from her Party's Chief Agent and following what was then generally accepted practice in filling out returns. Because of these complexities, parties sometimes nominate a formal agent, skilled at book-keeping and election law, and appoint a political organiser who actually runs the campaign.

The return is a public document. The Returning Officer in parliamentary and European Assembly elections has to publish, in at least two local newspapers, within 10 days from the last date for submission of the returns, information as to where it can be inspected.[32] This requirement for publicity does not exist in the case of local elections. The return and declarations must be available at all reasonable times for two years following their receipt in the case of parliamentary elections and open to inspection by anyone on payment of a prescribed fee (generally inspection is free to anyone with a bona fide interest), and copies must be provided for payment on demand.[33] After two years, the Returning Officer can destroy them or the candidate or agent can ask for them back.

(c) Prohibited Expenditures

In addition to the maximum controls on campaign expenditure, certain forms of expenditure are totally prohibited. In general

---

[31] R.P.A. 1983, s.81 and Sched. 3.

[32] R.P.A. 1983, s.88.

[33] R.P.A. 1983, s.89. Returns for expenditures on European Assembly elections need be kept only for 12 months, and those for local elections only for six months.

these prohibitions antedate the maximum expenditure rules and it is here that the law is most clearly derived from old common law offences, developed to combat ancient malpractices. Incurring a prohibited expenditure constitutes the commission either of a corrupt practice or of an illegal practice. Corrupt practices, in general, prohibit conduct which it is still important to control, but many practices designated illegal appear harmless, and could safely be rendered lawful.

(i) Treating. By section 114 of the R.P.A. 1983, it is a corrupt practice to "treat" an elector, or for an elector to receive a treat, if this is done "for the purpose of corruptly influencing" a person to vote or refrain from voting, or on account of anyone voting or not voting. "Treating" is an offence whether carried out before, during or after an election. A "treat" is defined as directly or indirectly paying the whole or part of the cost of providing any meat, drink, entertainment or other provision for a voter. The offence at once conjours up pictures of pre-Reform Act election campaigns. It is unlikely that any contemporary electors would be influenced by such activities; indeed such tactics might be counter-productive. However, the continued existence of this offence causes certain practical difficulties for political parties, for while in most of these cases it will be difficult to show a corrupt intent, this is not a matter upon which candidates would wish to take a risk.

First, many parties hold regular fundraising events, such as the ubiquitous Conservative Coffee Mornings. Parties are simply advised not to hold such events in the period immediately before, during or after an election.[34] To commit an offence a corrupt purpose would have to be shown, but the implications of an allegation of treating, even if unsubstantiated, are great. Whilst it makes sense to prohibit a special event, timed to coincide with the election, are such regular events a real problem requiring control? Surely if an elector has not been influenced by all the other coffee mornings, this one will make no difference? If the purpose of some regular event is clearly unconnected with the election, and merely happens to coincide, this will not amount to treating—so for example, a Mayor's annual civic reception

---

[34] These events have been described as "a practice dangerously akin to corrupt treating," and one which certainly would be treating if done by the candidate. *Northumberland, Hexham Division Case* (1892) 4 O'M. & H. 143.

held prior to the election has been held not to be an offence[35] — although the closer the event to the election, the harder it will be to show there is no connection. It is not treating if the refreshments are charged for at a realistic price or are merely incidental to some event.[36]

More significantly, post-election parties are also potentially "treating." Many candidates may wish to hold parties to thank their helpers and possibly celebrate the result. But such events are treating, even if held after polling day, if the (corrupt) purpose is to influence party workers to persuade others to vote for the candidate. In reality, of course, such parties are not the mischief aimed at. Rare would be the person who helps in an election campaign purely to secure an invitation to a party. National political party advice seems to be that post-election parties are legal, provided that invitations are not issued until after close of poll.[37]

Thirdly, during a campaign, particularly on polling day, party workers will spend long hours away from home, working in committee rooms; but the candidate must in theory not provide them with so much as a free cup of tea, though again the prospect of its influencing the election seems slight. There is some authority to suggest that provision of light refreshments for helpers is not treating,[38] although providing similar refreshments to non-helpers is.[39] The best advice is found in the *Wallingford* case,[40] where the court advised candidates to charge for all refreshments, but put up a sign to helpers explaining the reasons, a practice now followed by most candidates.

(ii) Bribery. Bribery is the less speculative counterpart of treating. Treating occurs when a candidate says, "Here is a treat, I hope you will now go and vote for me." In the case of bribery, a candidate is saying, "If you go and vote for me I will give you a gift." This is perhaps the most serious of election offences. In older times it was punished by Parliament itself.[41]

A person is guilty of bribery if, directly or indirectly, he "gives any money or procures any office to or for any voter in order to

---

[35] *King's Lynn Case* (1911) 6 O'M. & H. 179.
[36] *St. George's Division, Tower Hamlets Case* (1896) 5 O'M. & H. 89.
[37] *Cf. Brecon Case* (1871) 2 O'M. & H. 43.
[38] *Westminster Case* (1869) 1 O'M. & H. 89.
[39] *Bradford No. 2 case* (1869) 1 O'M. & H. 35.
[40] 1 O'M. & H. 57, at 60.
[41] *Longe's Case* (1571) 2 Doug.El.Cas. 312. The ancient common law offence remains, although in practice action is only ever taken under statute.

induce any voter to vote or refrain from voting," or corruptly does any of those things, after polling day, on account of how a person voted.[42] Indirect bribery, whereby a person makes a gift (or procures any office) to induce the recipient to seek to procure the vote of a third party—for example making a gift to a woman, to induce her to persuade her husband to support a particular candidate—is also prohibited. Even if the gift or procurement is not made for the purpose of inducing a vote, the conduct amounts to bribery if in consequence of the action a vote is procured. To ensure that just about every kind of inducement is covered, the definition of "gives any money" includes any kind of financial transaction—loans, promises to procure money and all other forms of valuable consideration; and references to "procuring any office" cover any office, place or employment.[43] The one act associated with bribery somehow omitted from this wideranging offence is a request for bribes. It is not an offence to ask for a bribe, although to give or receive one is.

(iii) Undue influence. While attempts to secure votes by exerting undue influence are not strictly connected to the incurring of prohibited expenditures, instances of the exercise of superior economic power have led to the control of undue influence being associated with the control of bribery. The offence is committed by an individual using or threatening violence, "temporal or spiritual injury, damage, harm or loss" to another on account of that other's vote or intention to vote.[44] The offence extends beyond undue influence *stricto sensu* and covers virtually any form of fraudulent device or contrivance which may affect how someone votes. To get an elector drunk so that he fails to vote is an obvious example. Many canvassers would be horrified to know that every time they pull an opponent's leaflet from a letter box, they are committing the offence of "undue influence," for they are preventing the elector exercising his vote freely, in possession of all the relevant information. In 1971 a conviction resulted from this.[45]

(iv) Illegal payments. Finally we should mention those payments which the law prohibits as "illegal." The difference between a corrupt and an illegal practice is principally one of

---

[42] R.P.A. 1983, s.113.
[43] R.P.A. 1983, s.118.
[44] R.P.A. 1983, s.115.
[45] *Roberts* v. *Hogg* [1971] S.L.T. 78.

consequence. There are five types of expenditure-related activities which are so prohibited:

    (a) inducing the withdrawal of a candidate[46];
    (b) illegally hiring committee rooms[47];
    (c) making payments for exhibition of election notices[48];
    (d) illegal employment of helpers[49];
    (e) illegally conveying voters to the polls.[50]

In each case, the severity of the penalty will depend on the exact circumstances and upon whether relief from the penalties may be granted. This is considered further in the context of election petitions.

[46] R.P.A. 1983, s.107.
[47] R.P.A. 1983, s.108.
[48] R.P.A. 1983, s.109.
[49] R.P.A. 1983, s.111.
[50] R.P.A. 1983, ss.101–102.

6. THE NATIONAL CAMPAIGN

(1) INTRODUCTION

National campaigning by political parties is principally concerned with manipulation of the persuasive powers of the mass media. Because our electoral law has no concept of national campaigning in general, or General Elections in particular—the latter are in legal terms merely situations in which a large number of constituency elections are held concurrently[1]—any discussion of the law of national campaigning will draw instead upon the general principles and legal restraints applicable to the mass media's exercise of their functions. The use of broadcasting, and of television in particular, now constitutes the single most important element in the conduct of national election campaigning, and in this chapter our attention will be focussed primarily on that. In recent years, however, campaign advertising organised at national level has come to play an increasingly important role, and the use of computer technology has facilitated the introduction of "direct-mail" campaigning on the American model.

(2) ELECTION BROADCASTING

(a) Introduction

Television now provides the most important medium for the various parties to communicate their messages to the electorate, and it is the primary source of election information for the general public, through news and current affairs coverage. It is paradoxical but characteristic that this most important medium of national electoral communication is virtually unrecognised in British electoral law.

The most obviously "electoral" broadcasting comes in the form of the Party Election Broadcasts, whose key characteristic is that the parties retain full editorial control of content and presentation. The B.B.C. and I.B.A.'s sole function is to make their broadcasting facilities available. Although these party broadcasts now constitute only a small percentage of election

[1] *Grieve* v. *Douglas-Home* 1965 S.C.315, 329.

151

coverage at times of national elections—they are of course, supplemented by news and current affairs coverage under the editorial control of the B.B.C. and I.B.A. respectively—they nevertheless are central to the phenomenon of election broadcasting in that, as a matter of deliberate policy, broadcasters provide news and current affairs attention to each party in roughly the same proportion as those parties are allocated party election broadcasts.[2]

It is therefore first necessary to consider the allocative process by which parties gain their broadcasting opportunities. This process should be considered in the light of Blumler's observation that television is a medium

> "that is suited to shaking up previously firm political loyalties . . . television has in many countries made a critical difference to the recognition-gaining chances and the persuasion opportunities open to certain minor party challenges, which are taken more seriously than they might otherwise have been, and are given lines of contact to less politically-minded people who might be more open to their appeals."[3]

The minor parties will therefore have a particular interest in the allocation of election broadcasting time. Furthermore, recent research indicates that television coverage of General Elections may have a significant influence on the overall result.[4] Finally, it should be borne in mind that while the right to impart and distribute information under Article 10 of the European Convention on Human Rights does not include a general and unfettered right to have access to broadcasting time on radio or television, the European Commission of Human Rights has pointed out that in certain circumstances the barring of a specific person or group may result in a violation of Article 10, either in combination with Article 14 (prohibition on improper discimination), or by itself.[5]

(b) The Process of Allocation

The B.B.C. and the I.B.A. companies are permitted to broadcast on matters relating to an election without infringing the prohibitions against the incurring of an unauthorised

---

[2] Gurevitch and Blumler (1982), pp. 81–82.
[3] Blumler (1977), para. 38.
[4] Gunter, Svennevig and Wober (1986).
[5] *X and Association of Z v. U.K.* App. 4515/70, (1972) 38 Coll. Dec. 86.

expenditure.[6] Both the Corporation and the I.B.A. companies profess impartiality in their political coverage. The I.B.A. is statutorily enjoined to ensure that this is achieved[7] and the B.B.C. (which operates under authorisation of Royal Charter and Licence rather than by virtue of statute) has given undertakings to like effect, although the extent to which there is a legally enforceable duty of impartiality on the Corporation is uncertain.[8] But impartiality and equality of exposure are not the same thing, and some process of allocation of broadcasting opportunities must be worked out, to meet the various parties' legitimate aspirations. There is no political advertising on either B.B.C. or I.B.A. networks—the B.B.C. of course takes no advertising of any kind and the I.B.A. is statutorily prohibited from accepting advertisments inserted by or on behalf of any body whose objects are wholly or mainly of a political nature, or any advertisement directed towards any political end.[9] The reason is obvious. In some electoral matters at least, "money shall not talk" and we avoid the dilemma of reconciling civic equality in electoral matters with unequal ability among the parties to purchase air time.[10] But if money is (very properly) not to determine broadcasting time, what allocative principle is to be used, and who is to implement it?

The body determining questions of allocation is the Committee on Political Broadcasting, which is usually chaired by the Prime Minister and composed of representatives of the major parties and senior management of the B.B.C. and the I.B.A. respectively.[11] In the best traditions of British constitutionalism, this body is unofficial in status, unknown to the general public in the details of its membership, applies uncertain and unpublished criteria of allocation, and is, within its particular field of competence, all-powerful.

At the 1945 General Election it became clear that (radio) broadcasting by national party leaders was of increasing importance in the conduct of election campaigns.[12] The alloca-

---

[6] R.P.A. 1983, s.75(1)(c) affirming the decision in *Grieve* v. *Douglas-Home*.

[7] Broadcasting Act 1981, s.4(1)(b), and s.4(1)(f). See also, s.2(2)(b) of the 1981 Act, discussed below.

[8] *Lynch* v. *B.B.C.* [1983] 6 N.I.J.B.; *R* v. *Broadcasting Complaints Commission, ex p. Owen* [1985] Q.B. 1153, 1172–3.

[9] Broadcasting Act 1981, Sched. 2, para. 8; See [1984] P.L. 177–179.

[10] J. Blumler, M. Gurevitch, J. Ives (1978), p. 16.

[11] C. Munro, "Party Politicals—who says they are legal and why?," *The Times*, February 12, 1982, p. 9.

[12] Nuffield (1945) study, 139–140, 154–155.

tion of broadcasting time, then and subsequently, was determined by the leaders of the three major parties, the B.B.C. being wholly compliant with these decisions.[13] Given the distribution of political support during the 1950's, when the Conservative and Labour parties between them were able to secure over 90 per cent. of the popular vote, these comfortable arrangements for the division of broadcasting time between the two main parties, with the Liberals also permitted a limited amount of time, were not unreasonable. Provision was also made in 1950 for one broadcast for any party with 50 or more candidates on nomination day, and the Communists qualified for such a broadcast then and at some subsequent elections. This 50-candidates threshold figure has remained a constant feature of allocation decisions since 1950. In theory it would be open to a group to nominate 50 candidates, at the cost of 50 lost deposits, in order to obtain "free" broadcasting time, but this, although threatened,[14] has never been done.

Two political developments have served to undermine these arrangements for allocating broadcasting time. When the unofficial Committee on Political Broadcasting was first constituted, the party system was both limited in numbers (two, or at best two-and-a-half parties of any significance), and nationally uniform, with minimal regional differentiation. From the 1960's onwards, each feature began to change, with the growth of new parties—the National Front, the S.D.P., the Green Party—operating at the United Kingdom level, and regional parties—the S.N.P., Plaid Cymru—playing a significant role in parts of the country. The challenge that these political developments presented to the Committee can be seen both in the reconstruction of its membership to include nationalist party and S.D.P. representatives, and in a number of legal actions which have been initiated (usually unsuccessfully) in respect of allocation decisions.

So far as the principles of allocation are concerned, these seem to have been amended over time by Committee decision, although the details are never published. In the early years of the Committee, it seems that the extent of the entitlement to broadcasting time was determined by the number of candidates any particular party was presenting to the electorate,[15] although this was not an inflexible rule and the Liberal Party's allocation

[13] Nuffield (1950) study, 124–126.
[14] Nuffield (1964) study, 157 n.
[15] Nuffield (1950) study, 125.

seemed at different times either quite ungenerous or markedly over-generous.[16] Subsequently, in *Grieve* v. *Douglas-Home*, the then Director-General of the B.B.C., Sir Hugh Greene, gave evidence to the effect that time was allocated to each of the three major parties in accordance with its strength in the House of Commons at the dissolution[17] (although the entitlement to a single broadcast based on 50 candidates nominated had been retained). Next we find the development of dual criteria, in which allocation decisions were based not only on candidate numbers but also on the total number of votes obtained and seats won in the preceding General Election.[18] More recently, it has been said that the strength of a party's votes at the previous General Election has been taken as the primary criterion.[19] The intervention of the S.D.P. in the 1983 General Election rendered that criterion arguably inappropriate, since the party had not fought the previous General Election yet clearly had attained considerable national support in the intervening period and so, it has been suggested, candidate numbers have again become important (Boyle (1986), p. 579). In 1983, for the first time ever, the Committee failed to agree on the appropriate allocations and it was left to the broadcasting authorities to make their proposals and ultimately to implement them, with the grudging acceptance of the parties,[20] a procedure which was also followed in 1987 when Labour, the Conservatives and the Alliance were all given five 10-minute broadcasts.

(c) *Challenges to Allocation Decisions*

The Communist Party, which has long complained of its allocation of broadcasting time,[21] was the first to initiate legal action when in 1964 it unsuccessfully sought to persuade the Attorney-General to initiate relator action proceedings for an injunction against the B.B.C. in respect of its broadcasting allocation for the 1964 General Election.[22] The subsequent well-

---

[16] Compare Nuffield (1950) study, 125, with the 1951 study, 61–62.
[17] 1965 S.C. 313, 326.
[18] H.A.C. (House of Commons Select Committee on Home Affairs) (1979–80) H.C. 756—ii, "The Law Relating to Public Order: Evidence and Appendices," p.292 (evidence of the National Front). See to like effect the affidavit of the editor of B.B.C. News and Current Affairs (Northern Ireland), quoted in *Lynch* v. *B.B.C.* (1983) 6 N.I.J.B.
[19] C. Munro, n. 11 above.
[20] Nuffield (1983) study, 147–148.
[21] See the Party's evidence to the Home Affairs Committee on its investigation into the Representation of the People Act, (1982–83) H.C. 32—II p. 330.
[22] Nuffield (1964) study, 158.

known case of *Grieve* v. *Douglas-Home*[23] should be seen in this context. In that case the defeated Communist candidate for Kinross and West Perthshire contended that the broadcasting authorities had, in presenting Sir Alec Douglas-Home in party political broadcasts on behalf of the Conservative Party, incurred expenditure with a view to promoting or procuring Sir Alec's election in his constituency; that this expenditure had not been authorised by the candidate or his agent, as required by section 63 of the R.P.A. 1949; and that Sir Alec, in failing to include this expenditure in his return of expenses, was guilty of a corrupt practice and his election void. This amounted to nothing less than a frontal attack on the whole system of national political broadcasting, for had the case succeeded, all political broadcasts by party leaders during a General Election would have been within the terms of section 63, and required to be covered by the constituency expenditure rules. Given the tightness of expenditure maxima and the considerable cost of making television broadcasts, the effect would have been that nearly all electoral broadcasts would have ceased. This was of course what the petitioner wanted, given his party's complaint about its very limited allocation. The Election Court held that the broadcasts had not been made with a view to promoting Sir Alec's individual candidacy (even though that might have incidentally benefited), but with the objective of informing the public on a matter of national importance. Accordingly the broadcasts fell outside section 63, and Sir Alec had not committed a corrupt practice in omitting to include the expenditure in his return. This conclusion was subsequently affirmed by statute,[24] so that the broadcasting authorities are in effect statutorily permitted to present to the electorate party figures who happen to be candidates without being accused of promoting their candidacies for the purposes of electoral law. It is this provision which ensures the continuation of party election broadcasting.

Further challenges to the allocation process have nevertheless followed. In 1970 the S.N.P. sought interdict to restrain the B.B.C. from broadcasting its Election Forum programme unless time was given to the party's leader equal to that offered to the three major parties. The action failed because the S.N.P. was unable to point to any law requiring the

[23] 1965 S.C. 313.
[24] R.P.A, 1969, s.9(4), now the R.P.A. 1983, s.75(1)(c), proviso.

B.B.C. to afford equal time to the parties.[25] Subsequently the party complained to the Parliamentary Commissioner for Administration (P.C.A.) about the arrangements for the allocation of broadcasting time. The Commissioner refused to investigate. The broadcasting authorities were (and are) outside his jurisdiction, and he declined to investigate the role of the then relevant Minister (of Posts and Telecommunications) on the ground that this would involve the consideration of essentially political matters.[26]

The first successful challenge to an allocation of broadcasting time occured in 1978, in the context of the referendum on Scottish devolution.[27] Each of the three major parties and the S.N.P. had been allocated a political broadcast and each chose to use this to express views on the wisdom or otherwise of the Scottish devolution proposals. The practical effect of this was that only one broadcast, that of the Conservatives, was planned to be an expression of opposition to the proposals, the remaining three being supportive of them. Some opponents of devolution sought interdict to restrain the I.B.A. from broadcasting the programmes, on the ground that the broadcasts would infringe the Authority's duty to preserve due impartiality in matters of political controversy under section 4(1)(*f*) of the 1981 Broadcasting Act, and also would constitute a breach of the Authority's duty to maintain "a proper balance . . . in (the) subject matter" of their programmes laid down by section 2(2)(*b*) of the Broadcasting Act 1981. So far as the latter duty is concerned, this might appear to be an instruction to the I.B.A. to broadcast programmes on a wide variety of subjects, maintaining a proper balance between such subjects. Nevertheless, it was held that section 2(2)(*b*) required a proper balance in respect of particular subject-matter (such as the devolution proposals) and this could obviously not be achieved if only one of four broadcasts would be directed to giving the opposing view.

This judgment would appear to open the way for a political party, aggrieved at the broadcasting time allocated to it, to argue that the I.B.A. was not maintaining a proper balance in the subject-matter of election broadcasts. It should be pointed out, however, that this result depends upon a controversial reading of section 2(2)(*b*) which has subsequently been criticised in

---

[25] *The Times*, May 27, 1970.
[26] Annual Report of the P.C.A. 1971 (1971–72) H.C. 116 p. 6.
[27] *Wilson* v. *I.B.A.* [1979] S.C. 351. See Dickinson, "Restraining the I.B.A." [1979] S.L.T. (News) 181, and Munro, "The I.B.A. in Court," *New Law Journal*, February 7, 1980.

another Scottish case.[28] Furthermore, even if this reading of the subsection is correct, the question of what constitutes a "proper balance" of political broadcasts between the various parties is a question very much more of judgment and degree than the assessment of the same question in the context of two opposing forces over a single issue such as devolution. It would follow that any allocation decision could only be attacked if the judgment as to what constituted a "proper balance" was wholly unreasonable. That certainly seems to have been the approach of Lord Prosser in the Court of Session in respect of the S.N.P.'s allegation in 1987 that the I.B.A., by allocating only two broadcasts to the S.N.P., had failed to maintain a proper balance between it and the major United Kingdom parties, which had received five such broadcasts.[29] The basis of the S.N.P.'s argument was that this allocation ignored the "Scottish dimension" of electoral politics, that within Scotland the S.N.P. was just as significant an electoral force as were the other United Kingdom parties, and was therefore entitled to equal treatment in respect of numbers of broadcasts made within Scotland. The I.B.A. in reply drew attention to the "United Kingdom dimension." Merely because the S.N.P. chose to confine itself to Scottish politics, that did not absolve the I.B.A. from its obligation to reflect the wider political battle. The I.B.A. therefore felt it had to reconcile the competing demands of the "Scottish Dimension" and the "United Kingdom Dimension," a view which, Lord Prosser said, was a justifiable attitude to have taken:

> " . . . the adoption of an allocation which gives extra time to the United Kingdom parties for United Kingdom transmissions must in my opinion be regarded as a tenable decision, reflecting United Kingdom dimensions as well as a Scottish dimension, and consistent with the respondents' duty to ensure a proper balance."

Two further cases merit mention here. *Lynch* v. *B.B.C.*[30] illustrates the extreme difficulties which can arise in Northern Ireland, where there are a large number of political parties, and no Committee on Political Broadcasting to make allocative decisions between them because some of the parties refuse to discuss these matters with others. It is therefore left to the

[28] See Munro, n. 27 above, discussing *Wolfe* v. *I.B.A.* (unreported); but in *Wilson* v. *I.B.A.* (1987, unreported), the earlier *Wilson* interpretation was adhered to.
[29] *Wilson* v. *I.B.A.* (1987) unreported.
[30] (1983) 6 N.I.J.B.

broadcasters to make the allocations themselves. These have been the subject of litigation.[31] In *Lynch* the plaintiff was the Chairman of the Workers' Party in Northern Ireland, which party was contesting 14 out of the 17 Northern Ireland constituencies in the 1983 General Election. The B.B.C. decided to allocate broadcasting by reference both to numbers of candidates and to previous electoral performance in the 1982 Northern Ireland Assembly Elections. On these criteria the Workers' Party was excluded from the "Election Forum" programme and a "phone-in" programme, whereas parties with fewer candidates but greater previous success were included in these programmes. The plaintiff sought an injunction restraining the B.B.C. from broadcasting these programmes without Workers' Party participation, on the ground that the B.B.C. was in breach of an implied duty of impartiality.

It was held that in fact there was no such duty of impartiality on the B.B.C. (in contrast to the statutory requirement of impartiality imposed on the I.B.A. by section 4(1)(*f*) of the 1981 Act), but in any case Hutton J. said that, even if there were such a duty, this did not require equality of treatment between parties of different sizes and popular support. If equality was not obligatory, then the B.B.C. had discretion as to how any hypothesised duty of impartiality should be satisfied, which would only be reviewable by the court if the Corporation exercised its discretion in a manner in which no responsible broadcasting authority could have reasonably exercised it. On this last point the discussion of the requirement of "impartiality" is at least as important to the I.B.A. as to the B.B.C., for the I.B.A. certainly *is* under a legal duty of impartiality, even if the B.B.C. is not. Hutton J.'s comments would seem to leave to the I.B.A. the same sort of "margin of appreciation" in satisfying its impartiality obligation as (it was submitted) is available to it in maintaining a "proper balance" under s.2(2)(*b*) of the 1981 Act. It is only if the Authority, in its allocative decision, does something which no Authority properly advised could reasonably do, that the court will quash that allocation.

One qualification to this must be entered, however. The decision as to what programmes are broadcast is ultimately a matter for the I.B.A. and B.B.C., both in Northern Ireland and on the mainland. This raises an important matter, which was in issue in the case brought by the Ecology Party (now the Green

---

[31] In addition to *Lynch's* case, see also *McAliskey* v. *B.B.C.* [1980] N.I.44 and *Kilfedder* v. *Ulster Television*, (1984) unreported.

Party) against the B.B.C. and I.B.A.[32] This case arose out of the allocation of broadcasting time for the European Assembly elections of 1984. For these elections the country is divided into 81 constituencies (78 on the mainland, three in Northern Ireland). The Ecology Party nominated 17 candidates to fight in these elections. The Committee on Political Broadcasting decided that the "threshold point" for allowing a party an election broadcast in respect of those elections should be 20 candidates. This represented a far more significant hurdle to jump than the equivalent long-standing threshold for Parliamentary elections of 50 candidates out of 650 constituencies—one in 13 as against one in four for the European Assembly elections. The Ecology Party sought leave to apply for judicial review of this decision.[33] Leave was granted but subsequently the party decided not to continue with the substantive application. The basis of the application was that the broadcasting authorities had failed to act impartially in that they had allocated broadcasts under the dictation of the Committee, who, being composed primarily of representatives of the major parties, were judges in their own cause and so in breach of the rules of natural justice. This is an important issue. It has certainly been the case in the past that the broadcasting authorities have supinely complied with the dictates of the major party representatives, although in 1983 and 1987 this did not happen because the parties could not agree among themselves as to what allocations to make. It would be a question of fact in each case whether a particular set of allocations was made by the broadcasting authorities having consulted the parties (which would be permissible) or whether it was made in compliance with the demands of the major parties (which would not).[34] Further, it might even be argued that the broadcasting authorities (or Committee) were not entitled to amend the threshold rules to the extent they did, at least without some process of consultation[35]— but this is a more difficult argument, in so far that the precise nature of the allocation rules has never been made public and so it might be difficult for a party without a representative on the Broadcasting Committee (and so informed of the rules) to show that it had relied on them.

---

[32] *Ecology Party* v. *B.B.C. and I.B.A.* [Application for leave to Apply for Judicial Review—Application granted June 8, 1984 (Taylor J.).]

[33] To challenge the decisions of public bodies by way of Judicial Review, leave to apply must first be obtained—R.S.C. Ord. 53.

[34] *Lavender* v. *Minister of Housing* [1970] 1 W.L.R. 1231.

[35] *A.G. of Hong Kong* v. *Ng Yuen Shiu* [1983] 2 A.C. 629; *C.C.S.U.* v. *Minister for Civil Service* [1985] A.C.374, 408–9 (Lord Diplock).

Before leaving the problem of allocation, one further point must be made. Even if a party succeeds in obtaining an allocation of time, the advantages of this may well be reduced by scheduling decisions. It is a common practice, for example, that parties who are entitled to one five-minute broadcast will find these scheduled for early evening viewing, when audiences are smaller and disproportionately composed of children who have no vote. These scheduling decisions are apparently left to the broadcasting authorities, and in so far that they amount to managerial decisions by the authorities, would not appear to be susceptible to judicial review.[36] The net effect is that even where a party has managed to obtain broadcasting time, the benefit of this may be rendered largely nugatory by scheduling decisions.[37] If the authority has reached agreement with a party about broadcasting times and the party relies on that, it will not be open to the authority subsequently to attempt unilaterally to require the programme to be broadcast at a less advantageous time, even at the request of the Committee on Political Broadcasting,[38] but this will be a very rare occurrence.

Enough has been said to indicate both the importance to the parties of the decisions on allocation of broadcasting time, and the somewhat mysterious and uncertain nature of the allocation process. Our electoral law, in failing to make any provision for this matter, is wholly inadequate, but the present position is highly advantageous to the major parties and is therefore unlikely to change in the near future.

(d) Technological Developments

There is one further matter to refer to in discussing election broadcasting—at present it is of little importance but it may become very significant in the future. We have thus far been concerned with broadcasts made from within the United Kingdom. Section 92 of the R.P.A. 1983 deals with the position of broadcasting from outside the United Kingdom, making it an illegal practice for anyone "to use, or aid, abet, counsel or procure the use of any television or other wireless transmitting station outside the United Kingdom for the transmission of matter having reference to the election" with the intention of influencing persons as to whether or how to vote in parliamen-

[36] *R* v. *I.R.C. ex p. National Federation of Self Employed* (1982) A.C. 617; *R* v. *I.B.A. ex p. Whitehouse, The Times,* April 4, 1985.
[37] See the Nuffield (1983) study, 149–150.
[38] See *Evans* v. *B.B.C. and I.B.A., The Times,* February 26, 1974.

tary or local government (but not European Assembly) elections. The only exception to this is where it is proposed that the matter be received and retransmitted by the B.B.C. or I.B.A. At present the section operates only to preclude, for example, the placing of advertisements or other election material on broadcasts such as those of Radio Luxembourg or "pirate" broadcasts located outside the United Kingdom territorial waters. It seems likely, however, that technological developments, particularly the introduction of Direct Broadcasting by Satellite (D.B.S.)[39] will expand the possibilities of cross-frontier television. If and when this happens, section 92 will assume a new importance, for the obligations of impartiality under which our domestic broadcasting systems operate will clearly not be capable of enforcement abroad. Whether section 92 in its present form will prove adequate to regulate these new sources of broadcasting is an entirely different question, dependent to some extent on the scale and rapidity of technological change.

(3) MANIPULATING THE MEDIA

We have already pointed out the centrality of the broadcasting media to the process of national campaigning. Quite apart from the direct access to broadcasting facilities represented by the Party Election Broadcasts, all major political parties seek further to utilise the media by either tailoring their campaign activities to media timetables and requirements, or by putting on events which would not occur without media attendance and publicity. Examples of the tailoring process are the timetabling of party leaders' "walkabouts" to facilitate film coverage on television at lunch-time and in the early evening (see, for example, Linton (1986), pp. 156–157) and the insertion of new or key statements at an early point in party leaders' evening speeches to ensure evening news coverage on television. The most obvious example of the specially created media event is the morning press conference. Since the Labour Party first successfully developed this technique in the 1959 General Election campaign[40] such press conferences have become a familiar feature of all parties' national campaigns (Linton (1986), pp. 150–153, 158–159).

These attempts to secure additional publicity by manipulation of the media are crucially dependent upon the maintenance of a "fair" level of coverage. To what extent, if at all, are the various

[39] For a brief discussion see the Report of the (Annan) Committee on the Future of Broadcasting, Cmnd. 6753, pp. 384–385.
[40] Nuffield (1959) study, 52–53.

organs of the media obliged to observe any requirement of fairness?

(a) Broadcasting

News and current affairs coverage of elections is again defined by the duty of impartiality (if and in so far that the B.B.C. has any such duty), and all that has been said about that duty in the context of Party Election Broadcasts is equally applicable here. In a situation where the ultimate decisions on coverage are taken not by the parties (as is the case with Election Broadcasts), but by the broadcasting authorities, this requirement of impartiality must be seen against the entitlement laid down by Article 10 of the European Convention that everyone has the right, *inter alia*, to receive information and ideas without interference by public authority. The I.B.A. issues guidelines to the broadcasting companies under its supervision, offering advice on the practical problems which application of the impartiality obligation might throw up, and the B.B.C. has produced material for internal use within the Corporation explaining its methods for ensuring impartiality and fair treatment.

As has already been pointed out, broadcasters seek to meet this obligation of impartiality by allocating news and current affairs coverage in approximately the same proportions as each party is allocated election broadcasts. This approach seems to have received some degree of judicial approval in *Wolfe* v. *I.B.A.*[41] where interdict was sought by office-holders of the S.N.P. to restrain the I.B.A. from broadcasting news and current affairs programmes relating to the 1979 General Election campaign unless the S.N.P. received coverage of its views and activities equal to that given to the Conservative, Labour and Liberal parties. The action failed: even if, as had been held in *Wilson* v. *I.B.A.*,[42] the requirement for a "proper balance" in programming could be applied to particular subjects (which the judge doubted), it was not clear that the rather limited treatment given to the S.N.P. in programmes transmitted throughout the United Kingdom amounted to a breach of duty, because the S.N.P. was, in the context of the whole of the United Kingdom, a relatively unimportant party. Again, it would appear that only if the coverage of a particular party's activities were so minimal (compared to its political significance) as to constitute a wholly

---

[41] Unreported—see Munro, n. 27 above.
[42] 1979 S.C. 351.

unreasonable exercise of discretion could there be judicial review.

Mention should also be made of the case brought by Dr. David Owen.[43] Strictly speaking, this did not concern electoral broadcasting as such, but was concerned with general news and current affairs coverage allocated to the S.D.P. Liberal Alliance in the ordinary course of events outside any election period. Dr. Owen felt that the coverage allocated to the Alliance parties was wholly inadequate—a contention which he sought to maintain by the citation of detailed statistics of broadcasting time—and therefore complained to the Broadcasting Complaints Commission, alleging "unjust or unfair treatment" contrary to section 54(1)(*a*) of the Broadcasting Act 1981. When the Commission refused to consider the complaint, Dr. Owen sought an order of mandamus to require it to do so. He failed, it being held that while the complaint was technically within the Commission's jurisdiction to investigate if it so wished, it was nevertheless proper for the Commission to decline to investigate a matter which could have such extensive ramifications as this one, for which the Commission's statutory procedures were quite inadequate, and in respect of which the appropriate criteria for assessing "unjust or unfair treatment" were by no means either certain or uncontroversial (see further, Boyle (1986), pp. 583–587). It is always open to an individual or a party to complain of specific individual acts of "unjust or unfair treatment" in news or current affairs coverage,[44] but the more general complaint of Dr. Owen as to the broad allocation of coverage to the Alliance parties would appear to be measurable only by use of the criterion of impartiality, with the accompanying "margin of appreciation" allowed to broadcasters.

(b) The Press

The position of the Press is very different. Having (unlike the I.B.A.) no statutory framework within which to operate, and being in private rather than public ownership, there is no equivalent to the broadcasters' impartiality obligation. Indeed, the Press Council has asserted and reaffirmed a newspaper's

---

[43] *R* v. *Broadcasting Complaints Commission ex p. Owen* [1985] Q.B. 1153.

[44] For example, the complaints by the National Front and the Dowager Lady Birdwood *vis-à-vis* coverage of by-election campaigns in Peckham and Bermondsey, referred to in the Broadcasting Complaints Commission's Annual Report for 1984, (1983–84) H.C. 523. The Commission considered investigation of these complaints "inappropriate."

"Right to be Partisan."[45] This declaration of principle was made in the context of a complaint by a Constituency Labour Party, which alleged that local Press coverage of General Election campaigns in 1964 and 1966 exhibited a marked Conservative advantage and a gross imbalance in coverage. The Press Council (a body created by the newspaper industry, designed to preserve Press freedom and the maintenance of high professional journalistic standards) decided that even if gross imbalance in political coverage were proved, that would not lead to a finding that a newspaper had failed to maintain adequate professional standards. In reaching this conclusion, the Council explicitly disavowed any equation of the position of the Press with the impartial position of the broadcasting authorities. A newspaper was entitled, if it wished, to make itself an instrument of propaganda for any cause; it might be better that it did not, but if it did, it was quite impossible to say that this attitude inevitably involved a lowering of professional standards. In a subsequent adjudication, the Press Council extended the application of this principle to national newspapers.[46]

This is not to say that allegations of factual inaccuracy may not be made in respect of a newspaper's election coverage. Such allegations have successfully been made.[47] Furthermore, *The Sun* newspaper was severely criticised by the Council in 1986 for improperly misleading readers about the mental state of Mr. Tony Benn in a way calculated to influence the outcome of the 1984 Chesterfield by-election.[48] But it is clear that the broad thrust of a newspaper's electoral coverage is editorially (or proprietorially) determined without any likelihood of Press Council interference. Parties which do not have sympathetic newspaper backing may, in the face of editorial indifference, have to create their own news in order to achieve publicity.

One particular aspect of press coverage of elections is the publication of opinion polls. The 1983 General Election, in the opinion of one commentator, produced "saturation polling" by the media, and the results of such polls were presented and interpreted in a manner consistent with the newspapers' various political preferences (Crewe (1986)). There is some evidence to show that electors' voting intentions were

[45] "The Press and the People," Annual Report of the Press Council 1968 (No. 15) pp. 109–111. See also the 1978 Annual Report (No. 25) pp. 89–91.
[46] Annual Report for 1979 (No. 26) pp. 52–53.
[47] See, for example, Annual Report for 1984 (No. 31) pp. 48–51.
[48] Adjudication of June 3, 1986.

influenced by poll results (Crewe (1986), pp. 245–249 and White-ley (1986), pp. 318–323), which produced a "bandwagon effect" encouraging further votes for the Liberal/S.D.P. Alliance, whose support appeared to be increasing. In the past, this type of cover-age has evoked considerable critical comment, and in 1968 a Speaker's Conference on Electoral Law recommended that

> "There should be no broadcast, or publication in a news-paper or other periodical, of the result of a public opinion poll or of betting odds on the likely result of a parliamentary election during the period of seventy-two hours before the close of the poll."[49]

Such provisions exist in a number of countries but the British gov-ernment of the day rejected the proposal, primarily on the ground of enforcement difficulties.[50] Quite apart from these, it should be pointed out that any such provision would in all likeli-hood be inconsistent with Article 10 of the European Convention on Human Rights, as an improper restraint on individuals' rights to receive information.

The extent to which the Press provide "fair" or "unfair" cover-age of election campaigns is not something which is measurable by any objective criteria. The Conservative Party has traditionally enjoyed greater Press support than either of the other two major parties (especially since the *Daily Herald* and the *News Chronicle*, supporters of the Labour and Liberal Parties respectively, ceased to publish). While the Royal Commission on the Press was unable to detect any significant bias against the political left in news-paper coverage,[51] its analysis pre-dates the rather more aggres-sively pro-Conservative stance adopted by much of the tabloid press since 1979 (see Harrop (1986), pp. 140–145). This, in turn, may be mitigated by the emergence of new titles which are anti-Conservative in their editorial line. However this may be, it is clear that the Press Council would not regard the adoption of a political line strongly in favour of one party as unprofessional behaviour, and the demands of a free Press are sufficiently insis-tent, in our view, to argue against any form of legal intervention.

(4) CAMPAIGN ADVERTISING

Campaign advertising through the media of press and billboards is principally organised (increasingly by advertising agencies) at

---

[49] Cmnd. 3550, para. 31.
[50] Cmnd. 3717, p. 4.
[51] Cmnd. 6810, pp. 98–99.

national or regional level. As such it operates largely outside the scope of election expenses rules, in that it is not expressed to be in support of specific candidates.[52] Additionally, in so far that the election expenses rules only apply when elections are pending, much political advertising would in any event fall outside the scope of such rules. Thus in 1978 and early 1979, the Conservative Party, knowing that a General Election was necessarily soon to be held, engaged in an extensive pre-campaign advertising exercise, as did the Labour Party in 1987 in selected marginal constituencies. In contrast, in 1983 and 1987 the Conservatives engaged in virtually no pre-campaign advertising (since this would have revealed their choice of election date), but once the General Election had been announced they expended very large sums on press and poster advertising.

Posters have long been used for campaign advertising purposes. Outdoor advertising is subject to Town and Country Planning legislation, in particular the Town and Country Planning (Control of Advertisements) Regulations, 1984.[53] Under these regulations, some advertisements may be displayed without any requirement of express consent on the part of the planning authority, and election advertisements (which are defined as "any advertisement relating specifically to a pending parliamentary, European Assembly or local government election") fall into this category, subject only to the requirement that they be removed within 14 days of the close of poll. Interestingly, "Standard Condition 1," that "All advertisements displayed . . . shall be maintained in a clean and tidy condition to the reasonable satisfaction of the local planning authority" is made specifically inapplicable to election advertisements. Perhaps this is intended to take into account opponents' tendencies to deface posters, and excludes a party's responsibility for the untidy condition of its posters under such attack.

The availability of sites for posters is obviously dependent upon advance bookings of billboards by the parties. The Outdoor Advertising Association, a self-regulatory body concerned to ensure the maintenance of proper practices and standards within the industry, has issued guidance to members advising that poster contractors maintain total impartiality as between the parties in the hire of sites, orders to be taken on a

---

[52] But see Bindman, "A gap in the plug," *The Guardian*, June 19, 1987, concerning advertisements placed by the "Committee for a Free Britain." These advertisements were on the borderline between general and local propaganda, but were held permissible on *Tronoh Mines* principles.
[53] S.I. 1984 No. 421.

"first-come, first-served" basis. There is, however, no sanction upon members who favour one party to the exclusion of others. The electoral law controls on such advertising are minimal. By virtue of section 109 of the R.P.A. 1983, it is an illegal practice knowingly to pay, or to contract to pay, an elector for the facility of displaying posters on his house, land, building or premises for the purpose of promoting or procuring the election of a candidate, unless it is the ordinary business of that elector to exhibit posters for payment and the arrangement is made in the ordinary course of that business.

Press advertising by the parties is a relative latecomer to the tactics of national campaigning. It seems to have been thought that such advertising would count against constituency expenditure limits, rather than falling outside election expenditure rules altogether.[54] However, in the February 1974 General Election the Liberal Party advertised in the national press, and subsequently the other parties followed suit, to such an extent that in 1979 the Conservatives spent nearly £500,000 on press advertising during the campaign,[55] a figure that increased to £1,725,000 in 1983[56] and to more than £3,000,000 in 1987. Provided that these advertisements are not directed towards particular constituencies or particular candidates, electoral expenditure rules are inapplicable and the only constraint is whether a particular newspaper will, as a matter of proprietorial policy, choose to reject a party's advertisements. This happened to both Conservative and Labour parties in 1987. A more cautious approach to the use of such advertising has been shown by regional or county groups, it still being common to see county-wide advertisements shown as an expense shared between all candidates in a county council election campaign. This caution is perhaps justified in light of *Meek* v. *Lothian Regional Council*, discussed below.

The use of advertising at the national level is regulated less by law than by the availability of finance. This is in sharp contrast to the position in relation to broadcasting, where, broadly speaking, financial resources are irrelevant. The content of such advertising remains largely unchecked, even by the voluntary regulatory body for the advertising industry, the Advertising Standards Authority. Its British Code of Advertising Practice is concerned with the regulation of commercial advertising, and

---

[54] Nuffield (February 1974) study, 241–242.
[55] Nuffield (1979) study, 195.
[56] Pinto-Duschinsky (1985), p. 331, and see Harrop (1986), p. 143.

imposes no restrictions with regard either to expressions of opinion or to assertions of fact in advertisements concerned with matters of political controversy. In any event, the Chairman of the Authority has indicated that advertising by political parties rarely gives offence (although the same cannot be said of pressure-group advertising on political issues)[57] and the 1985 revision of the Code of Advertising Practice seems unlikely to give the Authority any extensive new remit over campaign or other party political advertising.

Although press advertising by the parties is relatively novel, the insertion into newspapers by interest groups and others of advertisements attacking particular party policies is well established. Indeed, the *Tronoh Mines* case[58] was concerned with just this. Subsequent to that decision there have been a number of anti-nationalisation advertising campaigns at times of General Elections,[59] and it has always been assumed that outside intervention of this type will be of a predominantly pro-Conservative character, under the auspices of such free enterprise pressure groups as Aims of Industry (see Ivens (1986), pp. 179–189). More recently, it has been argued,[60] there has been some rectification of this imbalance, and that the Labour Party has received some outside support. The main source of this support has been Labour-dominated local authorities, and public sector trade unions (but see also Taylor (1986) in respect of C.N.D.'s efforts in the 1983 Election). Following the Conservative victory in the 1983 General Election, new legislation was introduced and now both local authorities and trade unions are subject to legal limitations on their advertising which do not apply to free enterprise interest groups.

So far as local authorities are concerned, the main power to expend moneys on the provision of "information" is given by section 142 of the Local Government Act 1972 for English or Welsh authorities, and by section 88 of the Local Government (Scotland) Act 1973 for Scotland. Each of these sections has been

---

[57] Press Statement, May 12, 1987.

[58] [1952] 1 All E.R. 697. In the light of this case, it may be wondered why the parties felt up to 1974 that their own "general political propaganda," in the form of press advertising, might be caught by the expenditure rules.

[59] See, for example, the Nuffield (1959) study, Appendix III, especially the typology of such advertising on p. 242. In one case it was held that a company's expenditure on anti-nationalisation advertising was money wholly and exclusively laid out for the purpose of the company's trade and was an admissible deduction from its profits for income tax purposes—see *Morgan* v. *Tate and Lyle Ltd.* (1955) A.C. 21 (the "Mr. Cube" campaign).

[60] Pinto-Duschinsky (1985), p. 339

amended by section 3 of the Local Government Act 1986, restricting the provision of information to that appertaining to local authority functions or services, rather than "on matters relating to local government" or "local government matters affecting the area," as the 1972 Act had it. Furthermore, these remaining publicity powers are subject to an overriding obligation that "A local authority shall not publish any material which, in whole or in part, appears to be designed to affect public support for a political party."[61] In this context "publication" is to be taken to mean "communication, in whatever form, addressed to the public at large or to a section of the public,"[62] and thus the 1986 Act applies not only to billboard or Press advertising but to such modern campaigning devices as badges, caps or tee-shirts which proclaim a message. The phrase "appears to be designed to affect public support" imports a test of content. The question will not be whether the local authority *intended* to affect public support for a political party, nor whether that was the *effect* of its publicity; rather, it will be whether, looking at the relevant material in context, a reasonable person would consider that by virtue of its content it appeared designed to affect public support for a political party. The context may well be important. Material which might otherwise be regarded as innocuous could be held to take on a greater significance if elections are imminent, as the draft Code of Practice on Local Authority Publicity, produced in 1987, recognises. Furthermore, clause 26 of the Local Government Bill 1987 proposes a further tightening-up of the rules introduced in 1986.

Quite apart from the provisions of the Local Government Act 1986, local authority publicity, by virtue of its local character, may be caught by the provisions of electoral law. This is demonstrated by *Meek* v. *Lothian Regional Council.*[63] The Labour-controlled council published a journal known as the Lothian Clarion, which was distributed free to local residents. An edition of the journal was prepared for distribution in April 1982, just before elections were due for the Regional Council. This particular edition explained the then Council's budgetary policy, and included statements from council officials as to the disadvantageous consequences which could have ensued had the Conservative budget proposals been adopted. Conservative Councillors sought interdict to restrain the publication and

---

[61] Local Government Act 1986, s.2(1).
[62] *Ibid.* s.6(4).
[63] [1983] S.L.T. 494.

distribution of the journal. They succeeded. The proposed publication, it was held, fell foul of electoral law, in that the council had, without authorisation, incurred expenditure with a view to promoting the election of Labour candidates contrary to what is now section 75(1) of the R.P.A. 1983. The journal, by referring to the disadvantageous consequences of the Conservative budget proposals, was disparaging of Conservative candidates, and the explanations of the Council's policy were presented in such a way as to be laudatory of the majority Labour party candidates. It was true that no Conservative candidates were by name disparaged, nor specific Labour candidates praised. Nevertheless the journal could not be regarded as "general political propaganda" as that phrase was understood in the *Tronoh Mines* case, because it was insufficiently "general":

> "What is about to take place here is a regional election; the Lothian Clarion is to be delivered to substantially all homes within Lothian region; the article complained of relates to political decisions taken by the majority party in Lothian Region; attempts are made in the article to discredit the Tory group in Lothian Region."[64]

Accordingly, this was "local political propaganda," rather than "general political propaganda" and was caught by the expenditure rules. To publish such an article would be a corrupt practice, and interdict would issue to restrain such publication.

The contrast with the treatment of interest group national advertising is obvious. A local authority would not be able to get around this problem by conducting its advertising or propaganda in the national press because any such expenditure would not fall within section 142 (section 88 in Scotland), which envisages *local* publicity activity only in relation to an authority's "functions" or "services." As it is, local government advertising would hardly seem a counterweight equal to that which can be undertaken by interest groups seeking to influence voters in General Elections.

Trade unions also operate under legal restrictions as to election advertising which have no equivalent for interest groups. A trade union may only expend moneys for "political objects" out of its political fund, and it may only have such a political fund if the members have given balloted approval to its creation or maintenance within the last 10 years (or in the case of

---

[64] [1983] S.L.T. 494, 496.

funds set up more than nine years before March 31, 1985, within one year of that date).[65] In the absence of balloted approval, expenditure on "political objects" is forbidden. This is important in the present context because the definition of "political objects" was amended by the 1984 Trade Union Act to include expenditure

> "on the production, publication or distribution of any literature, document, film, sound recording or advertisement the main purpose of which is to persuade people to vote for a political party or candidate..."[66].

The 1983 General Election coincided with a £1 million advertising campaign launched by the National Association of Local Government Officers opposing cuts in local authority expenditure and services, which campaign was paid for out of general funds.[67] The effect of the Trade Union Act 1984 amendments is to require that such campaigns henceforth be paid for out of political funds. This effectively precludes a number of public sector unions from instituting such campaigns in the future, since they have no political funds. Nalgo itself was caught by this in 1987, when an extensive advertising campaign again coincided with a General Election. A member of the union sought a declaration that the expenditure incurred was in breach of the 1984 amendments to the 1913 Act, and an injunction to restrain the union from continuing so to act. He succeeded.[68] On examination of the advertising material, the judge concluded that its main purpose was to influence voters against the governing party. As such it should have been paid for out of political funds. In the absence of such a fund, the union could not undertake such a campaign. In the light of this conclusion it may be that the 1983 General Election was the high-water mark of trade union campaign advertising (see Minkin (1986)). If so, the field will be left open once again to the interest groups, which almost always operate in support of the Conservative Party.

(5) "DIRECT MAIL" CAMPAIGNING

In the United States, the use of "direct mail" is rapidly becoming an extremely important campaigning technique (see generally,

---

[65] Trade Union Act, 1913, s.3; Trade Union Act, 1984, s.12.
[66] Trade Union Act 1913, s.3(3)(f), as inserted by Trade Union Act 1984 s.17(1).
[67] Pinto-Duschinsky (1985), pp. 339–340.
[68] *Paul* v. *Nalgo* [1987] I.R.L.R. 413.

O'Shaughnessy and Peele (1985)). The same cannot yet be said of the United Kingdom; nevertheless, the 1987 General Election saw a marked increase in the use by all the major parties of computer technology, and it is to be expected that this development will continue. For what purposes do the parties use the new technology, and what legal issues might arise?

At the national level, the predominant campaigning use of computers, especially by the Conservative Party, has been for fundraising. Individuals receive "personalised" letters from senior party figures, inviting them to send contributions to meet the costs of national campaigns. (In some instances contributors are additionally invited to express their views about topical issues.) The success of these operations depends in large part upon the accuracy with which a party makes contact with its likely supporters, and this in turn depends upon the obtaining of specific information about individuals which the computer can store and retrieve. How is this information obtained?

A basic source of information is the aggregated constituency electoral rolls. Registration Officers are authorised to sell copies of electoral registers to members of the public for a fee computed in accordance with a statutory formula,[69] and these, when put together, constitute a complete list of the electorate (over 42 million individuals in 1987). The information held on electoral registers can be freely transferred even if held on computer, because the Data Protection Act 1984 does not apply to materials which any person (here, the E.R.O.) is required by law to make available to the public. Commercial companies ("roll-holders") are therefore able to compile lists of the electorate and sell them, in whole or in part, to any interested parties. This information is however inadequate for political parties' purposes as being far too unspecific. It therefore requires to be cross-checked with other information from other sources. One such source is provided by the companies legislation. Under section 356 of the Companies Act 1985, the register of a company's shareholders' names is to be open for inspection during each business day, and copies of the register may be obtained on payment of the appropriate charge.[70] Production of the register and provision of a copy is mandatory, irrespective of the

[69] Representation of the People Regulations 1986, S.I. 1986 No. 1081, r. 54(i).
[70] Companies Act 1985, s.356(3).

motive of the individual wishing to inspect, regardless of whether they are or are not themselves shareholders.[71] This means that commercial "roll-holders" may obtain lists of a company's shareholders and sell such lists to whomsoever they choose. The Conservative Party, in the months before the 1987 General Election, made extensive use of the shareholders' lists of companies which the Conservative government had "privatised." Letters were sent from Conservative Party Headquarters warning shareholders of the possible threat to their investment should the Labour Party be returned to power, and inviting contributions to Conservative Party funds. Press reports indicate that this was a highly effective and remunerative operation.

An alternative source of more specific information which can be cross-checked with the aggregated electoral roll is the lists compiled by commercial organisations of their customers or subscribers. If the directors of an organisation wish to assist a particular political party, the information contained in its customer lists can easily be made available. Provided that the organisation attracts customers who might be thought predominantly to favour that party, this information may well be of considerable assistance. The supplying organisation must be careful not to infringe the requirements of the 1984 Act. Under that Act, data users (in this case, the commercial organisation) are required in effect not to disclose computer-stored information about data subjects (here, its customers) to persons other than those whom it has properly designated in its registration document, nor for any purposes other than those specified in that document.[72] However, since, according to the Data Protection Registrar's Application for Registration form, it is permissible to register "Political Organisations" as a potential recipient of data, and since data may be accumulated for the purpose of "Electoral Registration" ("The preparation and maintenance of lists of current and prospective voters"),[73] it seems unlikely that a company would find it very difficult to meet its Data Protection Act obligations, provided that it took care in its registration. Furthermore, although the Act requires data-users to have registered their use by May 1986, the number of registrations has been much lower than had been anticipated, and it is possible that some companies which may have made

[71] *Davies* v. *Gas, Light and Coke Co.* [1909] 1 Ch. 248. See the Third Report of the Data Protection Registrar, (1987–88) H.C.33, pp. 4–5.
[72] Data Protection Act 1984, Sched. 1, Part 1, Principle 3, and Part II, para. 3.
[73] See the Data Protection Registrar's Form D.P.R. 1, Parts A and B and accompanying "Notes" booklet.

their customer lists available to a political party have not in fact registered their data-use at all.

As we have said, the parties' primary use of computers for direct mail operations has been for fundraising. There has been little attempt to persuade voters by way of nationally-organised direct mail. Such activities could easily be undertaken. It would, for example, be possible to identify the shareholders of a "privatised" company, and then produce a list of such shareholders in a "target" constituency, identifying the shareholder-residents of that constituency by their post-codes. At this level of specificity, however, a danger arises that the direct-mail operation might have to be counted against election expenses in the constituency campaign. In the 1987 General Election, both the Conservatives and the S.D.P. abandoned last-minute "mail-shots" in target constituencies on this ground, although the Labour Party did undertake a nationally-organised direct-mailing exercise in a large number of constituencies during the campaign, ignoring Conservative protests.[74]

One final point should be made. To date, "direct mail" campaigning in Britain has been undertaken exclusively by the political parties. This contrasts sharply with the position in the United States, where independent pressure groups and single-issue organisations have been particularly active in direct mail campaigning both for and against individuals (see Peele (1982), pp. 358 *et seq.*). The dominance of political party organisation in the electoral process in this country makes it unlikely that the scale of third-party intervention on the American model will be repeated here, but there is no reason to believe that direct mail will continue to be exclusively a political party tool. As we have seen, interest group intervention is already well-established in campaign advertising, and it is possible to envisage an expansion of interest group activity into direct mail in the future. If that were to happen, our present framework of electoral law would not be in any way adequate to regulate it, as the example of the non-regulation of third-party advertising activity demonstrates.

[74] *The Guardian*, May 20, 1987.

7. LOCAL CAMPAIGNS

(1) INTRODUCTION

A question which may immediately be asked about local campaigning is "why bother?" The conventional wisdom of political scientists has been that in General Elections local campaigning is of minimal significance in influencing election results. Rose has summarised the arguments for this conclusion. First, most seats are "safe" and so no amount of campaigning is likely significantly to influence the result. Secondly, studies have shown that voting swings between the major parties are, if not nationally uniform, then at least very similar, indicating that local campaigns are of little significance. Thirdly, party officials are unable to identify constituencies where effective local campaigning is likely to be influential. Finally, concentration of organisational activities on marginal or "key" seats has seemed not to influence the extent of swing in those seats (Rose (1974), pp. 69–70). Further, Kavanagh has drawn attention to the limited campaigning techniques of local candidates and observed in 1970 that such techniques had altered little in the previous 80 years (Kavanagh (1970), p. 12).

This conventional disparagement of local campaigning should not be accepted without qualification. First, the analysis is clearly inapplicable to parliamentary by-election campaigns. Recent studies of these have drawn attention to the important contributions made by local party workers in securing victories for their candidates (for example, Edinburgh University Politics Group (1982a)), and the development of computer-assisted campaigning techniques has added a new dimension to local campaigning. It has also been argued that campaigns for local authority elections are significant in influencing results (Bruce and Lee (1982)).

Furthermore, even at times of General Elections, it is by no means clear that the traditional analysis continues to hold true. Many of the studies on which these conclusions were reached were produced at a time when British politics was effectively a nationally-uniform two-party system. As has already been pointed out in the context of the allocation of election broadcasting, this simple picture has been complicated by the emergence of significant new national and regional parties, and this fragmentation of the national political system lays open the possibility that local campaigns are becoming of greater influence than hitherto. (In this context it should be noted that parties such as the Liberals and Plaid Cymru pay particular attention to local campaigning, not only because of a belief in its efficacy but as a matter of ideological commitment to the importance of decentralised organisation.) Recent research has claimed to establish some relationship between the amount of money spent in constituency campaigning in General Elections and election results in those constituencies (Johnston (1986(a), (b)).

If it is the case that local campaigning remains (or is becoming again) important, electoral law ought to be well-placed to regulate it, because that law assumes that campaigning is a constituency-based activity. There are a number of statutory provisions designed to facilitate local campaigning, and it is in the context of local campaigning that the expenditure rules have their greatest influence. In this section we discuss in turn the organisation of the local campaign and how it is influenced by the expenditure rules; we then examine the process of persuading the voter, and finally we consider media coverage of local campaigns, which in the case of broadcasting at least, raises special problems.

A preliminary word about compliance with the expenditure rules is appropriate. It is certainly the case that the vast majority of candidates make returns indicating campaign expenditure well within the statutory maxima (see, for example, Butler (1986), p. 6), and this has led one commentator to observe that "The legal limits on constituency expenditure appear to be substantially effective" (Turpin (1985), pp. 428–429). There is, however, another view, well expressed by Gordon and Whiteley:

> "Anyone who has been directly involved in electioneering knows that expenditures incurred and expenditures declared are only weakly related . . . the last thing which interests party activists is the question of recording the costs incurred in campaigning . . . Very often the money spent in local campaigns is so much less than the maximum that essentially campaign expenditure data is a measure of the fastidiousness of election agents, rather than election activity . . .".

(Gordon and Whiteley (1980), pp. 293–294)

This opinion led the authors seriously to doubt the validity of Johnston's research on constituency campaign activity (as measured by expenditure returns) and electoral outcomes. Be that as it may, it is as well to be warned of the possibility that expenditure returns may contain a substantial element of artificiality, and we offer some examples of this below.

(2) THE ORGANISATION OF THE LOCAL CAMPAIGN

(a) Campaign Workers

Local election campaigns have traditionally been run by a combination of voluntary and professional labour, but in recent times, primarily to cut costs and speed up response times, more work, including highly-skilled tasks, is being done by volunteers. This may raise expenditure rules problems. The person driving the campaign bus can give his time free, but what of a professional printer who prints leaflets in his spare time, or does the artwork on expensive modern machinery? Increasingly, election literature is produced by volunteers on small offset-litho printing machines. In the *Richmond* case in 1981, it was argued that a figure should be included in the return of expenses for use of volunteers' time and expertise. Had that contention been accepted, it could have seriously limited the production of literature by volunteers, but the Election Court took the view that voluntary labour involved no notional charge against expenditure maxima, although a charge had to be made for the use of equipment.[1] This is to be applauded; the contrary view could have led the parties to discourage voluntary participation in the electoral process, which would be both wrong in principle and unfairly advantageous to wealthier parties able to pay for such services (within expenditure limits, of course).

Whilst a candidate is free to use voluntary or paid helpers for almost any aspect of his campaign, it is an illegal employment under section 111 of the R.P.A. 1983 to pay or promise to pay canvassers. This has been the case since the 1883 Corrupt and Illegal Practices Prevention Act, but seems something of an anomaly now. If deliverers, drivers, printers, public relations consultants and designers can be employed (within the constraints of the expenditure rules), why not canvassers? As it is, expenses only may be paid to canvassers, and these must be mentioned in the return of expenses. An explanation of the origin of this prohibition may be found in the mid-nineteenth

---

[1] Unreported, but see Williams (1982).

century. To avoid allegations of bribery, candidates increasingly made payments to helpers on account of "employment," the employment generally being to solicit the votes of others. Hence, such payments were prohibited in the 1883 Act as an indirect form of bribery. The prohibition of paid canvassers is also closely connected to fears of undue influence. Canvassers at one time commonly were prominent or influential members of the community who went out to solicit the support of others. It would obviously be wrong to permit community leaders to be paid for their support. Neither of these reasons seems relevant to the realities of modern canvassing, and section 111 could safely be repealed, in our view.

The extensive use of employed staff would soon exceed maximum expenditure limits. Difficulties can arise where constituency parties have the benefit of a full-time paid agent, but expenditure problems may also arise when nationally-employed staff are deployed to assist constituency parties, in by-election campaigns for example. If the salaries of such staff were to be regarded as an election expense, this would severely limit other campaign expenditure. Several devices are therefore used by the various parties to circumvent the expenditure rules.

First, an agent's terms of employment may be drawn in such a way that no salary is paid during the election period. There is a risk that, where no salary at all is payable for a four-week period, an Election Court would hold that the arrangement is wholly artificial (which it is!), and that an element of salary paid at other times must be taken to have included a consideration for service with reference to the election, and so constitute an election expense. To avoid this possibility, a constituency agent's contract may in terms exclude responsibility for election campaigns, but an arrangement can then be made at each election that he or she serve as agent in return for an honorarium. This will be small, as it will count against expenditure maxima. A third possibility is that the agent be given unpaid leave by his party employers during the election period, to serve as agent without incurring any election expenditure.

The need to make use of devices like this illustrates the artificiality of the expenditure rules. If the rules are to prevent wealthy parties gaining an unfair advantage, then all salaried staff working on a campaign should have their salaries counted in full as an election expenditure. Even then, this could be circumvented by companies or unions, who support a party, loaning full time staff, paid from the company or union pay roll, but given "leave." Alternatively, it should be recognised that the rules cannot control the employment of staff, and that salaries should be excluded from the controls.

(b) Equipment and Premises

Equipment used and premises hired must be paid for as an election expense. As the expenditure maxima fail to keep pace with inflation, it becomes necessary for candidates to find ever more subtle ways of minimising returnable expenditure. As one example, the practice of "hiring" equipment for use in an election is developing rapidly. If rosettes and flagboards are purchased or made during the campaign, their entire cost is an election expense; but if a stock of them is purchased some months before an election, these can then be hired by the constituency party to the candidate for the campaign and a small hire fee included in the return. The fee must be a genuine figure, related to the cost and the number of times the material can be reused; but it will inevitably be lower than the purchase price. A similar saving on returnable expenditure can be made by buying envelopes and other consumables in advance, then purchasing them one by one from stock during the campaign. This is preferable to buying 1,000 envelopes in the campaign itself, because if only 500 are used, the full cost of 1,000 would nevertheless still have to be entered on the return.

Premises hired for the campaign must be paid for, even if they are hired from the local political association of the party. The expenditure rules require the hiring-cost figure to be included in the return, but this, in practice, will usually be a small sum in all but commercial hirings. £1 or £2 is the conventional figure for the hire of a room on polling day.[2] The sum shown in the return must be the one actually paid, but there is no control over how much the hirer must charge. Accordingly, if a palatial High Street shop and office building is hired from a supporter, this need not show in the return as costing much more than another party supporter's front room. There is an obvious advantage here for the party which has the wealthier supporters. Only by including the real value of the goods and benefits conferred could this inequality be controlled.

National party organisations frequently offer logistical support to local parties fighting parliamentary by-elections. Increasingly this involves the provision of computers for production of

[2] *Richmond* case, n. 1 above.

personalised or targeted literature. In principle the use made of such equipment should be costed and charged as an election expense. The extent to which this is done is unclear, but, as is so frequently the case with the enforcement of electoral rules, it will rarely be to the advantage of major party candidates to challenge the returns of other such candidates, since their own positions may well be equally vulnerable. It appears tacitly to be understood that the practices developed to mitigate the restraints imposed by expenditure maxima will only very rarely (as in the *Richmond* case) be challenged.

(3) PERSUADING THE VOTER

(a) Election Literature

The distribution of election literature by parliamentary candidates has played an important part in electioneering since the nineteenth century. This was recognised in electoral law in the R.P.A. 1918, s.33(*a*) of which provided that candidates at parliamentary elections were to be entitled to send, free of postal charge, one electoral communication to each elector. The present entitlement[3] extends to parliamentary election candidates and European Assembly election candidates only. Local government election candidates do not qualify, save in Northern Ireland. In common with other local campaigning methods, the significance of constituency election literature has probably declined in the face of the immense importance of the national campaign. Kavanagh in 1970 suggested that only 40 per cent. of electors claim to read election literature (Kavanagh (1970), p. 29). Nevertheless, printing and stationery costs represent a very large proportion of total constituency campaign expenditure (see Johnston (1986(a)), p. 468).

Under the R.P.A. 1985, parliamentary or European Assembly candidates are entitled to send, free of charge, either one postal communication to each elector, or one such communication, unaddressed, to each place in the constituency recognised by Post Office regulations as a delivery point. The latter option was introduced by the 1985 Act to meet complaints that some local parties with limited numbers of volunteer helpers found the burden of addressing communications to each elector excessive. In consequence of this, it may be that some of the smaller parties will find it easier to disseminate their messages than hitherto,

---

[3] R.P.A. 1983, s.91, as amended by R.P.A. 1985, Sched. 4, para. 34.

although larger parties may continue with the older practice to permit more targeted mailing.

There are a number of constraints on the operation of the free postage facility. Section 19 of the Public Order Act 1986 makes it an offence to publish or distribute written matter which is threatening, abusive or insulting either with the intent to stir up racial hatred or in circumstances whereby hatred is likely to be stirred up against any racial group in Great Britain by the matter in question. Members of the British Movement were in 1974 convicted of offences under this section's predecessor, section 6 of the Race Relations Act 1965, in respect of election communications.[4] In 1986 the Post Office refused to distribute the election address of one candidate in the Fulham by-election on the ground that it might be in breach of section 70 of the Race Relations Act 1976, which section 19 of the 1986 Act supersedes.

More important in practical terms are the limitations imposed by electoral law. The entitlement to free postage is said by section 91 of the 1983 Act to be subject to Post Office regulations (which are mainly concerned with posting arrangements and the size, shape, etc., of election literature),[5] but the section further specifies that the communication must contain "matter relating to the election only." This has been the source of some controversy. It is the Post Office's view that all the material in the literature must relate to "current electoral issues"[6] and that it is the responsibility of the Head Postmaster in the constituency to satisfy himself that this criterion has been met. In this task he is assisted by brief unpublished guidance prepared by the Post Office, and candidates are strongly advised by the Post Office to submit a specimen of the proposed communication as long before the proposed date of posting as possible, so that the appropriate assessment may be made.

It is not immediately obvious why the Post Office should have what appears to be a censoring role in respect of election literature, but some mechanism must be available to prevent abuse of the free postal facility. In the Fulham by-election of 1986 a candidate stood on behalf of the "Connoisseur Wine Party." His election address, which was distributed by the Post Office, invited voters to visit him at his place of work, the premises of a retail wine distributor, and included a map

---

[4] Nuffield (October 1974) study, p. 231 n. 17.

[5] "Regulations of the Post Office Under Section 91 of the Representation of the People Act 1983," reference P2246D.

[6] "Advice to Candidates on Postal Arrangements," issued by the Post Office, January 1978.

indicating their location. Although the address did contain material of an electoral nature, there can be little doubt that a substantial commercial advertising impact was achieved within the constituency through use of the free postal facility, at the expense only of a lost deposit of £500. A refusal by the Post Office to distribute such material as not "relating to the election only" would have been understandable.

On the other hand, this power does have the potential for excessively strict interpretation. Some inconvenience has been caused to candidates by local Head Postmasters taking objection to literature urging support for the candidate in the form of messages from a spouse or member of the family,[7] although this may not be thought to amount to political censorship. However, in June 1984 the Post Office refused a candidate for the European Assembly the use of free postal facilities in respect of the Assembly elections because in his literature he raised the issue of the admission of Cruise missiles to this country. The ground for this refusal was that the Assembly has no legal competence on that subject and that therefore this reference to Cruise missiles was not "matter relating to the election only." On a strict analysis of the powers of the European Assembly it is no doubt true that it cannot concern itself with Cruise missiles. Nevertheless, it might well have been in the interests of the electorate to know where the candidate stood on this important issue, as giving an indication of his general political stance. As it was, the candidate lost his opportunity to present any of his views through the medium of free postal deliveries.

If some limitation on the content of election literature is necessary so that, for example, commercial advertising material in the guise of election literature is not to be distributed free of charge, then a much less technical set of published guidelines should be drawn up, permitting (within the general framework of law on such matters as race relations) the inclusion of any material relevant to matters of public concern. Whether the Post Office is the right body to apply this criterion is a different question. The Home Affairs Select Committee has recommended that this responsibility be transferred to the Returning Officer for the constituency, but this suggestion has been rejected because any decision as to the acceptability of material would be politically sensitive and might be interpreted as inconsistent with the Returning Officer's neutrality.[8] It may well

---

[7] H.A.C. (1982–83) H.C.32–I, p. xxix.
[8] Cmnd. 9140, p. 24.

be that there is no suitable body other than the Post Office to perform this function, and that cricitisms could be met if the criteria applied were agreed with the parties and widely publicised.

The use of postal services for the distribution of election literature has frequently been supplemented by delivery of additional material to voters' homes. Recently, particularly in parliamentary by-elections, this has become increasingly important due to the introduction of computers which are programmed to produce "personal" letters to identified classes of voters such as the first-time voter or those whom canvassers have identified as potential supporters. The use of computers to assist more specific campaigning directed towards particular classes of voter seems likely to increase, serving as it does to relate the more "broadbrush" aspects of election campaigning to the individual voter. This development goes some way to reversing a trend whereby the individuality of constituency electoral literature has sometimes been reduced by the inclusion within it of centrally-prepared material.

So far as the content of election literature is concerned, three aspects of electoral law may be mentioned. First, section 110 of the 1983 Act requires that any document prepared for the purpose of promoting or procuring the election of a candidate must exhibit on its face the name and address of the printer and publisher.[9] This appears to serve as a check to ensure that the literature has been produced on the authorisation of the candidate or his agent and thus counts against expenditure maxima, and that liability for the leaflet is ascertainable, for example in the case of defamation. The provision does not, however, require that an electoral communication identify in terms the party or candidate in whose interest it has been distributed. In recent years there have been many allegations that one party has issued material which, by virtue of its colour or design, has appeared to have been produced by another party, and which contains material damaging to the latter. There is surely a case for extending electoral law to deal with such practices. In 1987 an enterprising S.N.P. candidate in this position obtained interdict against his Conservative opponent who had without authorisation re-produced the S.N.P.'s registered trade mark—its logo— on literature attacking the S.N.P.'s policies.[9a]

---

[9] See *Re Berry* [1978] Crim.L.R. 357; *Cook* v. *Trist, The Times* July 15, 1983.
[9a] See *The Guardian*, June 3, 1987.

Secondly, it is an illegal practice to publish or issue anything which so closely resembles an official poll card as to be calculated to deceive an elector.[10] The object of this is to seek to separate the official process of the election from partisan electioneering. All the information contained on a poll card may be, and generally is, supplied by parties to the electors well before the issue of the official cards, but that is acceptable providing it is not done in such a way as to imply official support for one party.

Thirdly, section 106 of the 1983 Act makes it an illegal practice for any person, before or during an election, to make or publish any false statement of fact in relation to a candidate's personal character or conduct for the purpose of affecting the return of that candidate. This section is not limited to election literature but is obviously applicable to it, as the interesting case of *Fairbairn* v. *Scottish National Party*[11] shows. This arose out of the 1979 General Election campaign. The defendant party, during the course of the campaign, published a pamphlet which contained an extract from a newspaper tending to indicate that the plaintiff, the sitting Member, was inadequate in the performance of his constituency duties. The plaintiff sought interdict to restrain further publication of the pamphlet. He alleged both that it contravened section 106 and that it was defamatory at common law. The latter point is considered below. So far as section 106 was concerned, interdict was refused. It was held that a distinction had to be drawn between a false statement in relation to the personal character or conduct of the candidate, and such a statement relating to his public or official character. The section applied only in respect of the former category of statements, whereas the words complained of went to the plaintiff's public or political character, attacking his performance as a political representative. Accordingly, there was no breach of section 106. This is a hard distinction to draw in practice, but as a matter of policy it must be right to establish it, for otherwise there would be a great danger that political criticisms of opponents could be all too easily silenced.

Section 106 will normally be prayed in aid when one candidate publishes allegedly false material about another. Can it, however, be prayed in aid by a candidate alleging that an opponent has published false material about himself? In *Banks* v.

---

[10] R.P.A. 1983, s.94, as amended by R.P.A. 1985, Sched. 4, para. 36.
[11] [1980] S.L.T. 149. For another example of the use of this section, see the Nuffield (1951) study, p. 32.

Lewis[12] the Court of Appeal considered such a case on its merits, without referring to the question of whether section 106 could be so utilised. The defendant had been a Labour M.P. for many years, but for the 1983 General Election his local constituency party selected another candidate to fight the seat. The defendant nevertheless stood for election as an "Official Labour Party Candidate." The plaintiff, the constituency party's nominee, sought an injunction to restrain the defendant from so describing himself in his election speeches and literature, on the basis that the defendant's representations of himself constituted a breach of section 106. It was held that there was no breach of section 106 because the defendant's description of himself did not amount to a statement about his personal character or conduct, as distinct from his personal qualifications for election. The fact that the Court of Appeal was prepared to consider the case on its merits may indicate that if a candidate falsely represented his own previous personal history in his election literature, this might constitute a breach of section 106.

The law of defamation may also be relevant to the content of electoral literature. At common law, it appears that statements contained in the election address of one candidate concerning an opposing candidate, providing that such statements were relevant to the matters which the electorate had to consider, were entitled to the protection of qualified privilege. In other words, even if the statements were defamatory in content, they were not actionable without proof of malice. This common law rule had much to justify it. As was said in the leading case, "the task of the electors under democratic institutions could not be satisfactorily performed if such a source of relevant information *bona fide* given were to be cut off by fear of an action for libel."[13] Nevertheless, Parliament has by section 10 of the Defamation Act 1952 excluded the operation of the defence of qualified privilege in respect of defamatory statements published by or on behalf of a candidate in any election to a local government authority or to Parliament, at least in so far that the defence depends upon the materiality of the statement to a question in issue in the election.[14] So far as European Assembly elections are concerned, the common law rule presumably still holds.

---

[12] Unreported.

[13] *Braddock* v. *Bevins* [1948] 1 K.B. 580, 590.

[14] See *Plummer* v. *Charman* [1962] 1 W.L.R. 1469, raising the possibility that the defence of qualified privilege might arise on some other ground.

The effect of this statutory amendment may be seen in *Fairbairn* v. *S.N.P.*[15] The plaintiff, in addition to seeking interdict on the ground of a breach of section 106, also argued that the defendant party's pamphlet was defamatory of him. The court upheld this contention. The passage complained of clearly bore an innuendo having a defamatory implication. The defendant sought to argue that the allegations complained of were true. In English law in such circumstances, injunctions will never issue provided that the defendant indicates an intention to run the justification defence.[16] In Scots law, on the other hand, there appears to be a greater willingness, as evidenced by this case, to grant interim interdicts, and it is for the defendants to demonstrate that there is some prima facie case of justification before interdict will be refused. In the present case the defendants were unable to surmount this hurdle, and interdict accordingly issued to restrain the further publication of the S.N.P.'s pamphlet. Had, of course, the common law rule not been removed by section 10 of the 1952 Act, this electoral communication would have been protected by qualified privilege and the plaintiff would have had to establish malice in order to succeed.

Thus far we have considered literature published and distributed by the candidates or their agents. Literature published by third parties also merits discussion. At the national level, publicity expenditures in support of a particular party fall within the category of "general political propaganda" in the *Tronoh Mines* sense, and as such are not covered by election expenditure rules. Activity on behalf of a particular candidate in a particular constituency obviously would be covered. What, however, of the situation where a trade union published a special edition of its journal both listing the Labour Party candidates who were union members, and giving the names of Labour candidates (whether union members or not) standing in marginal constituencies? This was the position in *McCarthy* v. *A.P.E.X.*,[17] which was concerned with union expenditure which allegedly should have been made from the union's political fund rather than its general funds. One would have thought that, quite apart from that issue, the union's promotion of particular Labour Party candidates was sufficiently specific to fall within the expenditure rules, and that accordingly the union was guilty

---

[15] n. 11, above.
[16] *Fraser* v. *Evans* [1969] 1 Q.B. 349.
[17] [1980] I.R.L.R. 335.

of a corrupt practice under section 75(1) of the 1983 Act in incurring unauthorised expenditure on behalf of those candidates. No legal proceedings on this point seem to have ensued, however.

On its face, section 75(1) seems concerned to restrict (*inter alia*) the publication of literature by third parties *in support* of particular candidates. However, the section goes wider than this, as is demonstrated by *D.P.P.* v. *Luft*.[18] In that case the defendants circulated leaflets calling on electors not to support National Front candidates in certain constituencies. The leaflets contained no statements advocating support for any of the other candidates, of whom there were several. Expenditure on the leaflets was not authorised by any candidate or agent. The defendants were convicted of a corrupt practice under section 75(1) of the 1983 Act for incurring expenditure without an agent's authorisation with a view to promoting or procuring the election of a candidate. It was argued on their behalf that the defendants had not sought to promote or procure the election of any candidate, but had merely sought to prevent the election of a particular candidate. The House of Lords rejected this argument. To persuade electors not to vote for one candidate inevitably had the effect of promoting the chances of other candidates. *D.P.P.* v. *Luft* is another example of the consequences of a constituency-related set of expenditure rules. A national leaflet campaign which called on electors not to support National Front candidates in any constituency would be exempt, whereas Luft's more localised efforts rendered him guilty of a corrupt practice (Munro (1976)). The logic of this (let alone the justice) is not immediately obvious.

In 1987 an independent group, T(actical) V(oting) 87, campaigned on an anti-Conservative platform with the intention of persuading voters in nearly 100 selected constituencies to vote for the candidates of the party best-placed to defeat sitting Conservative M.P.s. The *Luft* decision proved a considerable handicap to this campaign, since the dissemination of anti-Conservative literature in individual constituencies would clearly have infringed expenditure rules (unless their expenditures were authorised by a non-Conservative candidate's agent. Requests for such authorisation were widely made). Accordingly, once the General Election was announced, T.V. 87 activists confined themselves primarily to advocacy of their case through local media, and to canvassing on behalf of non-

---

[18] [1977] A.C. 962.

Conservative candidates. The campaign was able to continue at national level on *Tronoh Mines* principles.

(b) Election Meetings

"The local meeting at which the candidate faces his constituents is the very heart of a British general election. It is here that candidates get to know their constituents. Here a bond is forged between the electors and the successful candidates which should subsist throughout the ensuing Parliament. Only thus can a candidate truly represent his constituency. Without this he is a mere voting unit of his party . . ."[19].

So wrote the authors of the 1945 Nuffield study, in what even then must have been a somewhat idealistic description of the role of the local meeting in electoral campaigning, given the new importance of national campaigning through (radio) broadcasting. Since 1945 attendances at public meetings have declined, to the extent that in urban areas they have become almost exclusively a rallying call for the party faithful rather than an opportunity to convert the uncommitted. Nevertheless they have continued to play an important role in rural areas, and in by-elections where there is no national campaigning.

Because of the traditional importance of local election meetings, it is not surprising to find detailed legislation relating to them. In 1918 a statutory entitlement to hold electoral meetings in public premises was introduced. This seems to have been a response to pressure from the Labour Party, which was finding difficulty in booking private halls for meetings, owing to hall proprietors' dislike of the Party's policies. But the rules related, and still only relate, to premises owned by public authorities. In some smaller communities, there is no such building, the community hall being privately owned by the church, by trustees, or by the local landowner. In such circumstances it is possible for the use of such premises to be denied to a particular political party.

All candidates are entitled to the use of school premises, or meeting rooms maintained wholly or mainly out of public funds, for the purpose of holding public meetings in furtherance of their candidatures.[20] Local authorities are required to main-

---

[19] Nuffield (1945) study, p. 154.
[20] R.P.A. 1983, ss.95–96 (as amended by R.P.A. 1985, Sched. 4 paras. 37–8) and Sched. 5.

tain lists of such rooms, and local education authorities must similarly draw up and maintain lists of suitable rooms in school premises which candidates are entitled to use. The right to hold meetings in these premises arises once the writ for a parliamentary election has been received or notice of election given for a local government election or a European Assembly election. The premises are to be provided free, but charges may be made[21] for the actual cost of preparing the room for the meeting, providing heating and lighting, and defraying the cost of any damage to the room or its fittings. Such charges are an electoral expense and must be so recorded.

The practical operation of these provisions can present difficulties for local authorities. Under the 1983 Act, a local authority has no discretion to refuse the use of a room to a properly nominated candidate, provided that the candidate wishes to use it at a reasonable time and on reasonable notice.[22] Thus, premises must not be denied to candidates on account of the local authority's antipathy to their views—to permit that would be to frustrate the very object of these provisions. Perhaps more surprisingly, even if the local authority believes on good grounds that a meeting held by the candidate may provoke a breach of the peace or the destruction of council property,[23] it is nevertheless incumbent upon the authority to make available the room which the candidate has selected from the lists held by the Registration Officer (provided, in the case of parliamentary or European Assembly elections, that this does not interfere with prior lettings, or, for any election, with the use of the premises for educational purposes). It is not open to the authority to offer suitable premises as an alternative to those selected by the candidate. In its Report on the Law Relating to Public Order the House of Commons Home Affairs Committee, while not recommending the conferment of power on local authorities (or the police) to ban election meetings on public order or any other ground, was in favour of amending the Act

> "to allow the local authority, in consultation with the Chief Officer of Police, and on the reasonable apprehension of serious public disorder or serious disruption to the normal life of the community to apply to the Home

[21] And nearly always are—see H.A.C. (1982–83) H.C.32–II, pp. 122 and 270.
[22] R.P.A. 1983, ss.95(5), 96(3).
[23] *Per* Forbes J., *Webster* v. *Southwark L.B.C.* [1983] Q.B. 698, 702.

Secretary to require a candidate...to hold his meeting elsewhere in the constituency or electoral area."[24]

The Government has, however, rejected this proposal, as constituting an improper restraint on the candidate's right to convey his message to the electorate in the area of his choice.[25] This is a curious argument, which asserts the primacy of a candidate's rights over those of electors. If electors are sufficiently irritated by a candidate's presence in their midst that serious public disorder may be reasonably apprehended, why should they be compelled to have him among them? The Southall riot of 1979,[26] when just this situation occurred, is an example of the difficulties which can arise from the existence of a candidate's indefeasable entitlement to a room of his choice, regardless of local opinion or circumstance.

A number of local authorities have adopted a policy of denying facilities to extreme right wing groups. In the face of the statutory requirement that rooms be provided to all properly nominated candidates, such councils have frequently sought to justify the denial of rooms to National Front or British National Party candidates on the ground that these parties pack their meetings with their own supporters, permitting a minimal number of the general public to attend. Accordingly they are not genuine "public meetings in furtherance of a candidature" and the local authority is not obliged to make rooms available. The Inner London Education Authority, for example, requires applicants for the use of school premises to complete a questionnaire detailing the arrangements to be made for admission to the meeting, and a failure to allow these meetings to be truly "public" will result in a refusal to permit rooms to be used.

Decisions pursuant to such local authority policies have been challenged in court by the National Front.[27] In 1978 a local authority refused to accept a booking from the National Front candidate for the Manchester, Moss Side by-election because it

---

[24] H.A.C. (1979–80) H.C. 756–I, at p. xxvi.

[25] Cmnd. 9510 at pp. 36–37.

[26] "Southall 23 April 1979. The Report of the Unofficial Committee of Enquiry," especially at pp. 22–28, 120–129.

[27] See the Evidence of the Commission for Racial Equality to the Select Committee. H.C. (1979–80) 756–II, at p. 92. It has been held that, notwithstanding the decision in O'Reilly v. Mackman [1983] 1 A.C. 237, an applicant alleging improper denial of a meeting room may challenge that decision in proceedings commenced by writ, rather than exclusively by application for judicial review—Ettridge v. Morrell, (1987) 85 L.G.R. 100.

did not believe that the planned meeting would be truly "public." A similar view was taken by the London Borough of Brent during the 1979 General Election. In each case injunctions were sought requiring the local authority to make the rooms available, but interlocutory injunctions were refused and the party considered it pointless to pursue the matter at full trial, the date of the election having long since passed.

In neither case was there any reported judgment. This is particularly unfortunate in that the concept of what constitutes a "public meeting" in this context is wholly obscure. There is no definition in the 1983 Act. Section 9 of the Public Order Act 1936 provides that for the purpose of the public order offences therein created, a "meeting" means a meeting held for the purpose of the discussion of matters of public interest or for the expression of views on such matters, and such a meeting is to be regarded as "public" if either it takes place in a public place or is a meeting which the public or any section thereof are permitted to attend whether on payment or otherwise. The fact that, under that Act, a meeting may be regarded as "public" notwithstanding that only a "section" of the general public is permitted to attend renders this definition unsuitable for the purposes of the Representation of the People Act, since it would permit meeting organisers to select attenders, and thus enable them to pack meetings with their own supporters. Since it is the purpose of statutorily-protected election meetings that members of the public should be able to go to listen to candidates, to inform themselves of candidates' views and merits and to question them on their policies, rather than to permit candidates to make exhortatory or propagandist speeches to their own supporters, the definition of "public meeting" for the purposes of the Act ought in principle to require that members of the public be entitled to be admitted on a "first-come, first-served" basis. It must be admitted, however, that this would represent a radical departure from the existing position. It is not only the National Front and similar bodies which attempt to limit or control attendance at "public" election meetings. Major parties have very frequently resorted to "ticket-only" meetings, where ticket distribution is strictly controlled. Furthermore, a "first-come, first-served" definition of a public meeting might lead to significant public order and policing problems.

As we have seen, local authorities have no power to refuse a candidate the use of a hall for a public election meeting on the ground that it may occasion a breach of the peace. It is equally the case that the police have no banning powers in respect of such meetings, since under the Public Order Acts 1936 and 1986 the power reposing in chief officers of police (or the Metropolitan Commissioner in London) to apply for bans extends only to processions which appear likely to occasion serious public disorder. Further, the power[28] to impose conditions on the conduct of public meetings extends only to those which take place in the open air. This will not apply to election meetings in schools or other premises under electoral law. Are the police able to maintain public order by preventing those whom they suspect of disruptive tendencies from attending meetings? It is reported that in some instances of National Front meetings the police have co-operated with meeting organisers by being present while stewards decide whom to admit and to whom to refuse entry, a practice which it is admitted is contrary to the spirit of the Representation of the People Acts.[29] It would additionally now appear open to an officer to prevent an individual's entry to the meeting if he honestly and reasonably formed the opinion that there would be a real risk of a breach of the peace, in close proximity both in place and time, if entry were permitted.[30] It would be a matter of judgment for the officer on the spot to decide whether any disruption was likely to go beyond mere vigorous heckling, such that breach of the peace was likely to occur.

Once the meeting has begun, a policeman may enter and remain on the premises if he has reasonable grounds to believe that a breach of the peace is imminent, and he has powers to deal with or prevent such a breach.[31] This power is wide-ranging and extends, if no lesser measures will suffice, to dispersal of the meeting.[32] An alternative to dispersal is the arrest of troublemakers, and in practical terms this is a far more likely occurrence. Police officers have a common law power of arrest in respect of both actual breaches of the peace committed in their presence and in respect of breaches of the peace which the officer has reason to believe will be committed in the immediate future if no arrest is effected.[33] The Police and Criminal Evidence Act

---

[28] Public Order Act 1986, s.14.
[29] H.A.C. (1982–83) H.C. 32–II at p. 30 (Evidence of the Police Federation).
[30] By analogy with *Moss* v. *McLachlan* [1985] I.R.L.R. 76.
[31] *Thomas* v. *Sawkins* [1935] 2 K.B. 249; Police and Criminal Evidence Act 1984, s.17(6).
[32] *O'Kelly* v. *Harvey* (1883) 15 Cox C.C. 435.
[33] *R.* v. *Howell* [1982] 2 Q.B. 416, 426.

does not impinge upon the existence of this arrest power, although any such arrest must comply with that Act's requirements for a valid arrest.[34]

Section 97 of the 1983 Act makes it an illegal practice to act, or incite others to act, in a disorderly manner for the purpose of preventing the business of the meeting being transacted. Merely attempting to make it more difficult for the speaker to argue his case, by heckling, for instance, should not engage liability. Again it will be a matter of judgment for the officer on the spot to decide if and when this line has been crossed, but in any event the officer may not take any action under the section unless and until he is requested to do so by the person chairing the meeting. Even then, once such a request has been made, the officer's only statutory power is to ask the disruptor for his name and address. It is only if this is refused, or if the officer reasonably suspects that the name and address given are false, that a power of arrest arises.[35] Given this very limited power, it is hardly surprising that the police prefer to arrest and charge disrupters with public order offences rather than the specific election meeting offence.

The obvious charge will be a breach of section 5 of the Public Order Act 1986, which makes it an offence for any person in any public or private place unreasonably to use threatening, abusive or insulting words or behaviour, or disorderly behaviour, within the hearing or sight of a person likely to be caused harassment, alarm or distress thereby. Such an offence may be committed by the candidate speaker as well as by those intent on disrupting his meeting. Thus in *Jordan* v. *Burgoyne*[36] a speaker was convicted of a breach of this section's predecessor, section 5 of the 1936 Public Order Act, when he used words which, given the composition of the audience listening to him, would inevitably have led to a breach of the peace (and did). It is true that the result in *Jordan's* case lays open the possibility of the "hostile audience veto," whereby a candidate who wishes to express views which are repugnant to a section of his audience must either refrain from doing so, or take the risk himself of being prosecuted under section 5 of the 1986 Act. This in turn relates back to the question whether parties should be allowed to restrict entry to such meetings to an audience of their choice. In 1979, at a meeting in Plymouth, the police ensured that

---

[34] Police and Criminal Evidence Act 1984, ss.25(6), 28.
[35] Police and Criminal Evidence Act 1984, s.25.
[36] [1963] 2 Q.B. 744.

members of the public were freely admitted to a National Front meeting without vetting by N.F. stewards. The result was that the audience was composed of several hundred anti-racists, and the N.F. chose to abandon the meeting.[37]

(c) Canvassing and "Getting the Vote Out"

Most politicians consider canvassing a vital part of electioneering. It is most commonly used to produce as quickly as possible a list of the party's supporters and opponents, so that further activities can be undertaken to ensure that these supporters do vote. In more sophisticated campaigns, particularly where computer facilities are available to produce "personalised" literature, canvassing may identify groups of voters to which particular attention should be directed. The efficacy of canvassing as a method of maximising a party's voting potential is a matter of dispute. Empirical work at the time of the 1979 and 1983 General Elections produced results indicating that whereas television election broadcasts did influence voters to a limited degree, the influence of canvassing was negligible (McAllister (1985)). To conclude from this, however, that canvassing is unimportant would be to miss the point that this activity is concerned less with persuasion than with mobilisation—the identification of existing supporters, and ensuring that they vote for the candidate on polling day.

Electoral law has remarkably little to say about canvassing, although there is the specific prohibition, rooted in nineteenth century campaigning practices, against the use of paid canvassers.[38] Canvassers are also of course subject to the requirements of section 106 of the R.P.A. 1983 not to make any false statement of fact in relation to a candidate's personal character or conduct for the purpose of affecting the return of that candidate, and they likewise are required not to make defamatory statements. Furthermore, things said while canvassing can start expenses running, in the unlikely event that this has not so far happened. Beyond this, the only control over canvassing is in the hands of the individual elector, who may decline to answer questions, or even revoke the canvasser's implied licence to approach his front door by a notice to that effect. Such an event is, however, quite rare. There appears to be no evidence of widespread resentment of canvassers.

---

[37] H.A.C. (1982–83) H.C. 32–II, pp. 293–294.
[38] R.P.A. 1983, s.111.

Canvassing returns will be of little assistance to a candidate unless he can be sure that his supporters have actually voted. To obtain this information it is well-established practice for the parties to nominate tellers to attend at polling stations. The tellers' function is to obtain from voters their numbers on the electoral roll. These are then compared with canvass returns, and party supporters who are revealed as not having yet voted are "knocked up" (or, more recently, telephoned) and requested to do so. There is no obligation upon individual voters to provide their numbers and many refuse to do so. So far as the activities of the tellers themselves are concerned, they are obviously subject to all the laws against corrupt practices, such as bribery or undue influence, to which we have referred. More important in practical terms is the obligation imposed upon the Presiding Officer to maintain good order at the polling station. This might require the Officer, for example, to insist that over-enthusiastic tellers cease their activities or that they remove any of their party's advertising material from the proximity of the polling station.

The transportation of party supporters to the polling station to vote has long been a matter of controversy. Before 1858 it was regular practice to pay voters' travelling expenses "and generally so to over-pay them as to make the journey a profitable business excursion" (Seymour (1915), p. 397). In 1858 this form of bribery was forbidden, but candidates were instead permitted either to provide transport or refund voters' actual disbursements.

> "As a result, it was still possible practically to purchase votes by an over-liberal payment of expenses; and enormous bills of conveyance were rendered by the electors, and cheerfully settled by the candidates."
>
> (Seymour (1915), p. 399)

To eradicate this, section 14 of the Corrupt and Illegal Practices Prevention Act 1883 made it an illegal practice for any person to "let, lend or employ for the purpose of the conveyance of electors to or from the poll any public stage or hackney carriage, or any horse . . . " In suitably modernised form, this continues to be the law.[39] In our view this restriction on the use of hired vehicles to convey electors to and from the polls is now an anachronism, and candidates could easily be left to make

[39] R.P.A. 1983, ss.101–104.

provision for transport for electors, the cost to be returnable as an election expense.

More important in practice is the candidate's freedom to employ his supporters' cars to get voters to the polls. Between the wars this was the source of considerable Labour Party complaint, on the ground that Conservatives were able to deploy many more cars on their candidates' behalf (Butler (1963), pp. 68–79), and in 1948 the Labour Government introduced a provision limiting, by reference to the number of voters on the electoral roll, the number of cars which could be used.[40] The Conservative Government in turn removed this limitation by section 1 of the Representation of the People (Amendment) Act 1958, and no limits have subsequently been reimposed. Candidates are therefore free to make use of their supporters' cars to "get the vote out" without either incurring an election expense or committing an election offence. With the extension of car ownership to most sections of the population, this freedom is unlikely in practice to bear so heavily on the Labour Party, in particular, as once it did.

(3) MEDIA COVERAGE

(a) Broadcasting

Media coverage of election campaigns in individual constituencies and electoral areas has in recent years become of very considerable importance. One reason for this is the increasing decentralisation of broadcasting structures. I.T.V. companies and B.B.C. regions now produce many programmes relating to political matters in their areas of coverage. Radio broadcasting is even more decentralised, with I.B.A. and B.B.C. local radio stations interpreting national political developments in terms of the relatively small geographical areas which they serve. It has been suggested that the national parties have not properly come to terms with this change in broadcasting structure.[41] Does our electoral law fit this new situation?

The relevant provisions are now to be found in section 93 of the R.P.A. 1983. This complex section requires extensive quotation:

"(1) In relation to a parliamentary or local government election—

---

[40] R.P.A. 1949, s.88.
[41] Blumler, Gurevitch and Ives (1978).

    (a) pending such an election it shall not be lawful for any item about the constituency or electoral area to be broadcast from a television or other wireless transmitting station in the United Kingdom if any of the persons who are for the time being candidates at the election takes part in the item and the broadcast is not made with his consent; and

    (b) where an item about a constituency or electoral area is so broadcast pending such an election there, then if the broadcast either is made before the latest time for delivery of nomination papers, or is made after that time but without the consent of any candidate remaining validly nominated, any person taking part in the item for the purpose of promoting or procuring his election shall be guilty of an illegal practice, unless the broadcast is so made without his consent."

A number of different situations appear to be covered here, and each must be discussed in turn.

First there are unlawful broadcasts under section 93(1)(*a*). Such broadcasts are unlawful if five conditions are satisfied: there must be a "pending" election, be it a General Election or a by-election; the offending broadcast is made from a transmitting station in the United Kingdom; the broadcast is about the constituency or electoral area where an election (whether as part of a General Election or not) is pending; a person who is for the time being a candidate "takes part" in the item; and the broadcast of the item is not made with his consent.[42] The operation of the subsection was illustrated in *Marshall's* case.[43]

Marshall was the Labour candidate for the Parliamentary constituency of Leicester South in the 1979 General Election. Among his opponents was a candidate standing on behalf of the National Front. The Labour Party has a policy of refusing to be represented in programmes in which the National Front participates. The B.B.C., as part of its news coverage of the General Election campaign, decided to prepare a feature item on the election in the constituency of Leicester South, and accordingly sent a camera unit to film all the candidates as they campaigned. The candidates were informed of this. Marshall objected to being filmed and when the B.B.C. announced its intention of broadcasting the item (which included film of Marshall), he sought an injunction to restrain the Corporation

---

[42] *McAliskey* v. *B.B.C.* [1980] N.I. 44, 49.
[43] *Marshall* v. *B.B.C.* [1979] 1 W.L.R. 1071.

from broadcasting it without his consent. He obtained the injunction, but the B.B.C. successfully appealed. The Court of Appeal held that the section entitles candidates to refuse their consent to a broadcast (and so prevent it from being shown) only if they have "taken part" in it—and "takes part" means "actively participates" in it. Marshall could not be said to have actively participated in the item, he had merely been filmed as he campaigned, and even if he had co-operated with the camera unit as he campaigned, this would not have constituted active participation.

The effect of this decision is to provide greater scope for the broadcasting authorities in their news and current affairs coverage of particular constituencies or electoral areas, and as such it is to be welcomed. The ambit of the subsection is then confined to the "second thoughts" situation, where candidates have the power to veto broadcasting of what they themselves have done:

> "A candidate who is being interviewed on the television may be cross-examined by the interviewer and forced into a position in which he gives answers which he afterwards regrets. It is only right that he should be protected. The programme should not be transmitted except with his consent. Furthermore all these programmes are edited. The result of the editing may be that an impression is given which is quite unfair to the person who was taking part in that way. That is the mischief at which the subsection is aimed. It is to protect a candidate who is actively participating in a programme if he thinks it shows him in a bad light."[44]

This appears unduly protective of the candidate. If broadcasting is properly to inform the public of the quality of candidates, it ought to be free to demonstrate their inadequacies as well as their capabilities under questioning. It must be remembered that broadcasting has in large part supplanted the local election meeting as the primary mechanism of informing and persuading the voter. The candidate is given no opportunity to prevent his answers to questions at such meetings receiving general publicity. Why should this facility be available to him in respect of broadcasts? It is interesting to note that the Broadcasting Complaints Commission, adjudicating on a complaint of "unjust or unfair treatment" contrary to section 54(1)(*a*) of the

---

[44] *Per* Lord Denning M.R., at 1073.

Broadcasting Act 1981, has adopted this more robust view. A complainant, Mr. Arthur Lewis M.P., alleged that he had been misled as to the true nature of a B.B.C. programme on which he was interviewed, in that he had not known of criticisms of him that other programme participants had made and so had not had a proper opportunity to respond to them. In consequence he was very unhappy with the interview and emphasised to the B.B.C. that he did not wish any part of it broadcast or quoted. The interview was nevertheless broadcast. Although upholding the complaint on other grounds, the Commission rejected the argument that Mr. Lewis should have been able to stop the interview being broadcast. As an M.P. of long experience he should have realised that anything he said in front of a television camera would go on record.[45]

The first part of section 93(1), then, covers the situation where the candidate is able to prevent the broadcasting of something in which he himself has actively participated. The second part permits of a power to veto the appearance of rival candidates, and as such raises fundamental issues of principle[46]; it may well be in breach of Article 10 of the European Convention on Human Rights, which encompasses the freedom to *receive* information as well as to impart it.[47] The explanation for the existence of this section is that, paradoxically, it was intended as a liberalising measure. As we saw earlier when discussing *Grieve* v. *Douglas-Home*, section 63 of the R.P.A. 1949 appeared to make it a corrupt practice for the I.B.A. or B.B.C. to broadcast programmes "with a view to procuring the election of a candidate," and reference was made to the difficulties for the presentation of the parties' election broadcasts which were said to ensue. However, section 63 was also taken to mean that candidates could only be shown within their constituencies when all their opponents were given equal exposure, for otherwise the programme might be taken to be presented "with a view to procuring the election" of the candidate given undue prominence. Furthermore, even if one of the candidates was not himself prepared or able to appear but was willing to allow his opponent to appear, such a broadcast was still deemed to be in breach of section 63 as procuring the election of the

---

[45] Broadcasting Complaints Commission Annual Report for 1984 (1983–84) H.C. 523, at pp. 8–11.
[46] See [1981] P.L. 150–1.
[47] *The Sunday Times Case* (1979) 2 E.H.R.R. 245.

opponent.[48] The purpose of what is now section 93(1)(*b*) of the 1983 Act was to liberalise this position, by permitting the broadcasting of items about particular constituencies with the consent of the candidates, even though not all of them might wish to participate in the broadcast.[49]

The effect of the amendment has, however, been very different. Its consequence is, under certain circumstances, to make it an illegal practice for any person to take part in a broadcast for the purpose of promoting or procuring his election. The circumstances are that there is an election pending; and, either that the programme is broadcast before the latest time for delivery of nomination papers, or it is broadcast after that time but without the consent of one of the validly nominated candidates. The "early broadcast" limitation is obviously designed to ensure that no intending candidates in the election should be disadvantaged by failing to submit their nomination papers at the first possible opportunity; provided that they submit their papers by the last available date, they are entitled to proper broadcasting exposure. This is a perfectly proper rule. The difficulty arises in respect of the second situation, whereby it becomes an illegal practice to "take part in" (in other words, actively participate in) such a broadcast save with the consent of all of one's opponents. This consent may well not be forthcoming, and so opponents can prevent a validly-nominated candidate from appearing.

There seem to be three types of situation in which consent is likely to be withheld. First, as has already been pointed out, the Labour Party has a policy of refusing to appear in programmes featuring representatives of the National Front. On a number of occasions this has led to the cancellation of programmes,[50] although broadcasters have sought to evade the difficulties by focusing on regions rather than specific constituencies and, in one case, broadcasting a contribution from the three main parties, with a National Front spokesman recorded separately.[51]

---

[48] See, for example, the 1964 General Election where Mr. Wilson, the leader of the Labour Party, was not able to appear in a programme in which his constituency opponent was to appear, but was quite willing that the programme should be broadcast nevertheless. Notwithstanding, the opponent was excluded from the programme—see the Nuffield (1964) study p. 159 n. 1.

[49] See Cmnd. 3717, p. 4.

[50] See, for an example, [1981] P.L. 150.

[51] Nuffield (October 1974) study, p. 151 and footnote.

The Labour Party's objection to National Front broadcasts may or may not be justifiable, given the nature of the Front. Be that as it may, it surely cannot be justifiable to withhold consent to a broadcast featuring one's opponent purely as a matter of election tactics. Nevertheless, this does occur. It is reported, for example, that in the 1983 General Election the Conservative candidate for Gainsborough declared that he was fighting a seat that had been Tory for 60 years, and would therefore withhold consent for a broadcast, having no reason to give others the opportunity to make their case.[52] In the same way in 1964 the Labour M.P. Roy Mason refused to participate in a broadcast (which under section 63 of the 1949 Act automatically denied his opponents their chance) on the basis that "My opponents are unknown and unknown they shall remain. This is politics, not tiddlywinks."[53] Again in 1983, the S.D.P. candidate for Hackney South, faced with a Liberal opposed to the Alliance, used section 93 to reduce the publicity impact of the split.[54] These practices are quite unacceptable, and any system of electoral law which permits them is clearly deficient. At an election the public should be able to receive as much information as possible. It should not be open to one candidate to prevent his opponents' opportunity to make their own cases on the medium most likely to reach a large number of the electorate.

The third situation where consent may be withheld is illustrated by *McAliskey* v. *B.B.C.*,[55] and arises from the peculiar position of Northern Ireland in respect of European Assembly elections. For these elections Northern Ireland is regarded as a single constituency electing three members by a system of single transferable vote. As a single constituency, the whole of the Province attracts to it the operation of section 93. In *McAliskey*, and also in the litigation initiated by Mr. James Kilfedder in 1984, minor party candidates who objected to the allocation of time permitted to them by the broadcasters refused to participate at all on the basis of the proposed allocations. The inevitable consequence of this was that had any of the other candidates appeared on the programmes, they would have been guilty of illegal practices, and injunctions would have been available at the instance of the candidates who had refused their

---

[52] Reported in Hargreaves, "Repeal this election Veto," *The Times*, March 28, 1985.
[53] Nuffield (1964) study, pp. 165–166, n.
[54] Hargreaves, n. 52 above.
[55] [1980] N.I. 44.

consent to restrain the broadcasts.[56] In *McAliskey's* case the B.B.C. gave an undertaking to the court not to proceed with the broadcast. In the *Kilfedder* litigation, the mere issue of the writ by the aggrieved candidate was sufficient to lead to the proposed programmes being abandoned. As has been said, this situation only arises because of the treatment of Northern Ireland as a single constituency for the purposes of proportional representation.

It is submitted that section 93 has the potential to operate in a wholly unsatisfactory way and requires reform. The best solution would be to delete the special rules which apply to constituency coverage and simply require the broadcasters to observe the general obligation of impartiality previously discussed. No doubt the occasional aggrieved candidate would initiate litigation alleging that in particular circumstances there had been a failure to meet that obligation.[57] That, however, is a price worth paying to prevent candidates vetoing one another's election broadcasts.

(b) Local Press Coverage

Attention has already been drawn to a newspaper's "Right to be Partisan," a right which the Press Council originally asserted in rejecting a compaint about local press coverage of election campaigns. While we would not want to dissent from the proposition that newspapers are entitled to be partisan, this may have a considerable influence on local election campaigns, because most (if not all) local newspapers have a monopoly of circulation in their areas, whereas at national level it is possible to envisage a variety of political opinions on offer. This monopoly position is one of considerable power, and in consequence local newspapers have great responsibilities to ensure reasonably fair coverage of local campaigns. It is, however, clear from what has been said before that the Press Council will not uphold any complaint against a local newspaper on the ground of general political bias alone.

---

[56] *McAliskey's* case, pp. 48 and 53.
[57] See the comments of Dr. Butler, H.A.C. (1982–83) H.C. 32–II, p. 212.

8. FINANCING ELECTION CAMPAIGNS

(1) FUNDING THE NATIONAL CAMPAIGN

Political parties fund their activities at national level primarily by securing contributions from companies, trade unions or individuals. These contributions are crucial to the conduct of national campaigns by way of advertising through press and posters in particular. The other important aspect of national campaigning, via the broadcasting media, is relatively inexpensive in so far that broadcasting time is provided free of charge, and the only costs will be those of production of special films or the like. Another important use of national political contributions is in the funding of party leaders' speaking tours around the country at times of General Election.

Political contributions from companies and trade unions raise difficult legal issues. (See generally, Ewing (1987)). So far as company contributions (made almost exclusively to the Conservative Party) are concerned, these have been generally assumed to be legal, in the sense that they are in principle compatible with the requirements of company law (Gower (1979), pp. 170–171). Many companies include in their memoranda and articles of association clauses purporting to authorise company contributions for charitable, public or benevolent objects, or for any other purpose which may be likely, directly or indirectly, to advance the company's or its members' interests. Such clauses would seem prima facie to be sufficient authorisation for contributions to political parties. The legal position is in fact by no means so simple. (Ewing (1987), pp. 25–32).

It is nowadays common for companies to include in their memoranda and articles of association an extremely extensive list of company objects, to ensure, so far as possible, that any transaction they might wish to enter into will not be *ultra vires* the company. Additionally, such memoranda frequently include clauses which, although presented in the form of separate objects, are in reality only facilitative of the substantive objects of the company—an obvious example would be an "object" to borrow money for commercial reasons. These "objects" are to be interpreted merely as powers incidental or ancillary to the true objects of the company, and as such must be exercised to attain those objects or in pursuit of them.[1] Objects clauses allowing for company contributions to public causes or purposes so as to advance the company's interests (directly or indirectly) may (but need not) be interpreted as involving the grant of incidental or ancillary power.[2] If so, such powers may be exercised only to attain or advance the company's substantive objects.

In the context of political contributions, this raises difficulties. If, as would no doubt be asserted, a company which has made a contribution to the election fund of the Conservative Party would not expect automatically to receive public contracts or public subsidies from the new Conservative government, any contribution would be *ultra vires* unless it could be shown that the election of such a government indirectly advanced the company's substantive objects by, for example, creating a more supportive climate for private industry or eradicating the threat of nationalisation. This would be by no means an impossible proposition to establish (it might well be very difficult in respect of a corporate donation to the Liberal Party), although there has sometimes been marked disagreement between the Conservative government and the Confederation of British Industry as to the correct economic policies to adopt. Would it have been self-evident, for example, that a company in the manufacturing sector would have been advancing its substantive objects by making a contribution to the Conservative Party's election fund for the 1983 General Election?

It is in theory open to a member of the company in a personal action to seek an injunction to restrain the making of a political contribution on the ground that it was *ultra vires*. In practice, however, this is highly unlikely to occur, if only for the reason that ordinary members (as distinct, say, from a company director) would be extremely unlikely to learn of the contribution until after it was made. They would, however, learn of it later, because company law requires that political contributions in excess of £200 in any financial year be mentioned in the company's Annual Report, together with a note of the recipients.[3] A contribution is to be regarded as "political" if it is either made directly to a political party or to one who is carrying on activities which can reasonably be regarded as likely to affect

---

[1] *Re Horsley and Weight Ltd.* [1982] 3 All E.R. 1045, 1050–1.
[2] See, for example, *Simmons v. Heffer* [1983] B.C.L.C. 298; Ewing (1987), pp. 29–31.
[3] Companies Act 1985, Sched. 7, paras. 3–5.

public support for such a party. The latter proviso would appear to cover contributions to such pressure groups as the Economic League and Aims of Industry, and many companies accordingly report such contributions. The purpose of this provision, which was originally introduced by a Labour Government in 1967, is to enable a shareholder to question company directors at Annual General Meetings as to the need for, or wisdom of, particular political contributions. In practice the efficacy of the Annual General Meeting as a mechanism for control of directors' activities is minimal, and the objections of individual shareholders may be easily overridden (Hadden (1977), pp. 324–326).

In the alternative a member of the company may, if believing that the contribution was *ultra vires*, bring a derivative action (in form against the company, but in reality on its behalf) to seek to have the money returned. This occurred in *Simmons* v. *Heffer*.[4] The League Against Cruel Sports, a limited company, donated £80,000 to the Labour Party for its 1979 General Election campaign when the Party committed itself to legislating against blood sports if returned to power. Mrs. Simmons, a member of the League, initiated proceedings for the return of the money, on the ground that the payments were *ultra vires* the League. The money had in fact been contributed in two payments—a sum of £30,000 to be used specifically for activities advertising the Labour Party's commitment to animal welfare, and a further £50,000 to be used for its General Election campaign. It was held that the former payment was within the powers of the League as set out in its memorandum of association; that memorandum envisaged expenditures to alleviate cruelty to animals and promote their welfare, and the payment of £30,000 was given on condition that such objectives were advanced. The payment of £50,000 was, however, *ultra vires*, because no limitation was placed upon its use, and it was entirely possible that the moneys would be expended for objectives having no connection whatever with those of the League. Accordingly the Labour Party was required to return the £50,000.

It has been argued that individual shareholders should be entitled to have a greater say in corporate decisions to make political contributions (Constitutional Reform Centre (1985)). As will be seen in respect of trade union contributions, individual union members can "contract-out" of making payments to trade

---

[4] [1983] B.C.L.C. 298. The reasoning (but not, it is submitted, the result) would probably now be slightly different, in the light of *Rolled Steel Products* v. *B.S.C.* [1986] Ch. 246.

union political funds from which such contributions must be made, and we believe that individual shareholders should also be given the opportunity to receive dividends without deduction of moneys that are contributed to political parties out of company profits. An alternative (or supplement) to this would be to require that approval be given at Annual General Meetings each year for subsequent years' contributions. This would necessitate the Board of Directors specifying exactly why such contributions were likely to be advantageous to the company, and would enable individual members to seek an injunction if convinced that such a contribution would be *ultra vires* the company. A small number of companies have already voluntarily assumed an obligation of consultation with shareholders before political donations are made.[5] As the position is at present, corporate contributions are almost wholly unregulated by law, and recent suggestions that the *ultra vires* rule be abolished would make this even more the case.

The same certainly cannot be said of trade union contributions. The position here is well-known: trade union expenditures on "political objects," as redefined in the Trade Union Act 1984, s.17, may only be made out of political funds. The "political objects" here referred to relate to activity designed to secure and maintain a candidate in elected office.[6] Following the 1984 Act, political funds may only be established and maintained after balloted approval has been obtained from the membership within the last 10 years (or, in the case of funds set up more than nine years before March 31, 1985, within one year of that date). Without such approval, no moneys may be expended on any of the "political objects." Furthermore, even where a political fund has been approved and established, it is (theoretically, if not, perhaps, always in practice) open to any individual member to "contract-out" of making contributions, and trade unions must in law afford their members this opportunity without their suffering any discrimination by way of denial of benefits or imposition of disadvantage if they choose to make use of it.[7] The contrast with company shareholders is obvious. Unless the company voluntarily assumes such a procedure, shareholders neither have the opportunity to vote on the principle of political contributions, nor to opt out of such contributions on an individual basis should the majority adopt a policy that contributions be made.

---

[5] See 356 Industrial Relations Review and Report 12–14 (November, 1985).
[6] *A.S.T.M.S.* v. *Parkin* [1983] I.R.L.R. 448, 453.
[7] Trade Union Act 1913, s.3(1)(*b*).

Trade union political contributions, in addition to funding national campaign activities, are also used to meet a proportion of the election expenses of "sponsored" Labour Party candidates in the constituencies. This represents an important source of many Constituency Labour Parties' electoral campaign funds, and at any General Election well over 100 Labour parliamentary candidates will be in receipt of union funding in this way.[8] The expenditure of such funds must be in accordance with the electoral expenditure rules, whereas expenditure of contributions at the national level, either through the medium of the Labour Party itself or as a result of independent union activity, will fall within the *Tronoh Mines*[9] category of "general political propaganda," and so be immune from electoral law restrictions.

In contrast with corporate and trade union political contributions, individuals' contributions excite virtually no controversy and minimal legal difficulty. If the party is in law an unincorporated association (as the Labour Party nationally and at constituency level has been said to be),[10] any contribution takes effect in favour of the members of the association (whether that is the constituency party or the national party) as an accretion to the funds which are the subject-matter of the contract which the members are taken to have made amongst themselves. Such a contribution may be expended only in accordance with the terms of that contract. So far as the Conservative Party is concerned, that analysis holds equally for contributions to the party's constituency associations, but contributions to Central Office funds cannot be so treated because the constitution of the party is such that these funds are not held on behalf of an unincorporated association, but are the subject-matter of a mandate which permits them to be used for the purposes of the Conservative Party as directed by the leader of the party.[11] None of this, of course, makes any difference in practice, as it is barely conceivable that a party contributor would subsequently initiate legal action alleging that his contribution had been improperly used. Individual contributions and membership subscriptions are important to the S.D.P. and Liberal parties, especially to the latter because of its highly decen-

---

[8] Bogdanor, (1982), pp. 369–370.
[9] [1952] 1 A.E.R. 697.
[10] *Lewis* v. *Heffer* [1978] 1 W.L.R. 1061, 1071.
[11] *Conservative Central Office* v. *Burrell* [1982] 2 A.E.R 1.

tralised organisational structure which places special additional burdens on the fundraising activities of constituency parties.[12]

The present financing structure of the political parties, especially the financing of their electoral campaigns, raises important issues. It is clear that party organisation is central to the Parliamentary system as it operates in Britain now. It might be inferred from this that the maintenance of strong party organisation should be ensured by the state subsidising party activities directly (rather than indirectly by such measures as the provision of free postal services at times of General Election). This was the conclusion of the Committee on Financial Aid to Political Parties, which reported in 1976.[13] The Committee recommended both that annual grants be paid from Exchequer funds to the central organisations of the parties (the amounts being determined according to the extent of each party's electoral support in the previous General Election), and that there should be partial reimbursement of parliamentary and local government election candidates' election expenses. These proposals were received with little enthusiasm, and in any event were opposed by the Conservative Party, which felt that they undermined the voluntary nature of political organisation in Britain. They also necessarily involve taxpayers' money being allocated to political parties of which such taxpayers may disapprove. No action has been taken to implement the Committee's recommendations. (For further discussion see Ewing (1987), Chap. 6).

(2) LOCAL FUNDRAISING

During the election period, candidates' campaign funding is controlled in manner, and indirectly in extent, in the sense that there is no point in raising funds during the election period beyond the maximum permitted expenditure, save for disbursements outside the expenditure rules, or for items which can be purchased in advance to save money during the campaign.

The principal direct control is that the return of expenses must include

> "a statement of all money securities and equivalent of money received by the election agent from the candidate or

---

[12] Pinto-Duschinsky, (1985), pp. 355 *et seq.*
[13] Cmnd. 6601.

any other persons for the purposes of election expenses
incurred or to be incurred, with a statement of the name of
every person from whom they have been received."[14]

This requirement seeks to ensure that the identity of the donors
behind the campaign can be ascertained, so that all moneys can
be accounted for. However, it creates two problems: first, if
literature is being sold by the candidate at public meetings, it
appears necessary to ask every purchaser their name; secondly,
if a collection is taken at a meeting (with buckets at the door, for
example) again the amount and identity of the donors should be
noted. This is totally impracticable, but parties can easily
circumvent the requirement. If a collection is taken, it can be
stated clearly that it is not for Smith's campaign, but for the
Party fighting fund. This may be left in an account entirely
distinct from the election account. All moneys are paid into it.
The fund can then make one donation to the election account,
and only the fighting fund receipt need be shown on the return.
Receipts from the literature sales can be similarly handled.
There are no controls over such fighting funds and no public
access to their contents, and so the moneys received do not have
to be accounted for and the identity of donors need not be
revealed; all of this totally circumvents the purpose of the
original requirement. If the requirement is still valid, the rules
need to be altered in scope. If not, perhaps they should be
abandoned. The present practical need for two parallel accounts
only leads to confusion and increases the chance of innocent
misaccounting.

Many associations continue to run fundraising events such as
coffee mornings or jumble sales during the election campaign,
particularly where a by-election or parliamentary election was
not expected when the event was planned. If they are held
purely by the local association for general funds there is no
difficulty, but if there is any hint that they are raising funds for
the campaign, they are subject to election controls. To enable
the organisers to say that the function is not part of the election,
the candidate must take great care not to use the occasion to
promote himself in any way, and should not make election
material available. Indeed, to avoid the possibility of constituency association activity being imputed to the election
campaign during General Elections, some associations officially
suspend their activities. Any events can then be held by

---

[14] R.P.A. 1983, s.81(3)(*d*).

individuals who chose to donate the proceeds to the election. Ongoing fundraising events can continue, but again care is needed to ensure that there is no mention of the election in the literature or at meetings.

(3) FUNDING OF EUROPEAN PARLIAMENT ELECTION CAMPAIGNS

The 1979 election campaigns for the European Parliament were financed by the parties themselves. In 1982 the general budget of the European Community for the first time included an item providing appropriations intended as a "contribution to the costs of preparations for the next European elections" in 1984, and in 1983 the Bureau of the European Parliament laid down criteria to determine the allocation of these funds between parties and political groupings. Following the elections, the French Ecologist Party, *Les Verts*, sought the annulment both of the 1982 budgetary allocation and of the 1983 decision on criteria. They succeeded.[15] The European Court of Justice held that the system of financial support which had been established had to be regarded as a scheme for the reimbursement of election campaign costs, rather than a contribution towards an information campaign intended to explain the work of the Parliament to electors on the occasion of the 1984 elections. As such it was *ultra vires* the Parliament to authorise, for in the absence of a uniform electoral procedure throughout the Community, the establishment of a scheme for the reimbursement of election campaign expenses remained within the competence of the Member States.

The implications of this decision for British political parties are considerable. The Conservative Party received nearly four million pounds as reimbursement for its campaign expenses, and the Labour Party over one million pounds (the disparity arising out of the application of the 1983 criteria, which authorised disbursement of moneys largely on the basis of representation in the previous European Parliament elected in 1979). Future European Parliament campaigns will have to be financed without Community funding assistance, and it may even be that the funds received under the 1983 scheme will have to be repaid. These additional substantial campaign costs may

---

[15] *Les Verts-Parti Ecologiste* v. *European Parliament*, E.C.J. Case 294/83, (1987) 49 C.M.L.R. 343. See also, *Group of the European Right* v. *European Parliament* (1986) 47 C.M.L.R. 462.

cause the parties to turn again to the possibility of state funding of political parties. It is noteworthy, for instance, that the Conservatives, who took such a strong line in 1976 against state funding of domestic political campaigns, were willing to accept such funding in respect of the European Parliament campaign in 1984.

9. THE POLL

(1) ADMINISTRATIVE ARRANGEMENTS

The administrative arrangements for the poll lie in the hands of the Returning Officer, whose duty it is "to do all such acts and things as may be necessary for effectually conducting the election in the manner provided"[1] by the relevant set of election rules, parliamentary, local government or European Assembly.[2] In practice, in accordance with R.P.A. 1983, s.28, the most important of the Returning Officer's functions in parliamentary elections are performed by an Acting Returning Officer, who is the Registration Officer for the relevant constituency. In local authority elections the Returning Officer is a council officer so appointed.[3] In European Assembly elections the Returning Officer is designated by statutory instrument. He or she is selected from among the Returning Officers whose parliamentary constituencies are encompassed in the European Assembly constituencies.[4]

Broadly speaking, Returning Officers' duties fall into three categories: action to be taken before the poll to ensure that it can properly take place; administration of the poll itself; and administration of the count and of the declaration of result. The provision of a sufficient number of adequately equipped polling stations is the most important pre-poll duty.[5] Electors are then informed of the location of polling-stations by delivery of official poll cards.[6]

The administration of the poll itself is assisted by the appointment of presiding officers and clerks to serve at each polling station, although these must not be selected from

---

[1] R.P.A. 1983, s.23(2).
[2] See, respectively, Parliamentary Elections Rules, R.P.A. 1983, Sched. 1; Local Elections (Principal Areas) Rules, S.I. 1986 No. 2214; European Assembly Elections Regulations S.I. 1986 No. 2209; European Assembly Elections (Northern Ireland) Regulations S.I. 1986 No. 2250.
[3] R.P.A. 1983, s.35.
[4] See, for example, the European Assembly Elections (Returning Officers) (England and Wales) Order, S.I. 1984 No. 571.
[5] Parliamentary Elections Rules, rr. 25, 29.
[6] *Ibid.* r. 28.

persons who have been employed on behalf of a candidate.[7] Such appointees must be given a formal notification of requirement of secrecy as to the polling process.[8] The function of presiding officers is to ensure that the election rules are observed and that a proper poll by secret ballot is taken. They are required to ensure that the ballot box is empty before polling starts, that proper directions are available for voters, and that those claiming the right to vote are entitled to do so. In this last responsibility they are in theory assisted by polling agents, who are appointed by candidates to detect personation. In practice, save in Northern Ireland, such agents are not now used for this purpose, but they may be appointed to attend at a group of polling stations in order to see that the arrangements for voting are satisfactory. In Northern Ireland there are special statutory rules introduced to detect personation. Voters must present to the presiding officer or clerk one of a number of prescribed documents (such as a passport, a driving licence or a D.H.S.S. benefit book) before a ballot paper can be issued. This obligation applies to parliamentary and local government elections, and may be extended to European Assembly elections by ministerial order.[9] Early experience has suggested that the new requirement does have a significant effect on the level of personation, at the cost of disenfranchising some voters who were unaware of the obligation.[10]

Finally, the presiding officer must also ensure that completed ballot papers exhibit the official mark before they are placed in the ballot box. At the close of poll, the presiding officer seals the ballot box and delivers it to the Returning Officer, together with a record of the numbers of ballot papers used, numbers spoiled and numbers returned as unused.[11]

(2) VOTING AND COUNTING

The introduction of the secret ballot[12] effected a fundamental change in voting methods. The old system was graphically described by Lord Denning in *Morgan* v. *Simpson*:

---

[7] *Ibid*. r. 26.

[8] R.P.A. 1985, Sched. 4, para. 80, and R.P.A. 1983, s.66.

[9] Elections (Northern Ireland) Act 1985; Local Elections (Northern Ireland) Order, No. 454 of 1985.

[10] Report of the Chief Electoral Officer for Northern Ireland 1985–86, (1985–86) H.C. 429.

[11] Parliamentary Elections Rules, r. 43.

[12] Ballot Act 1872.

"The common law method of election was by show of hands. But if a poll was demanded, the election was by poll . . . A poll was taken in this way: the returning officer or his clerk had a book in which he kept a record of the votes cast. Each voter went up to the clerk, gave his name, and stated his qualification. The clerk wrote down his name. The voter stated the candidate for whom he voted. The poll clerk recorded his vote. . . . Such was the method of election at common law. It was open. Not by secret ballot. Being open, it was disgraced by abuses of every kind, especially at parliamentary elections. Bribery, corruption, treating, personation were rampant."[13]

The new legislation established instead a set of rules which in substance continue to determine voting procedure today.[14]

Voters should be presented with ballot papers which exhibit an official mark. This is to prevent the introduction into the ballot box of additional forged papers, and it has recently been decided that this safeguard should be retained, notwithstanding the difficulties which ensue when the mark is inadvertently omitted.[15] Furthermore, voters are instructed to exhibit the official mark to the presiding officer before placing their completed papers in the ballot box.[16] This requirement, which dates from the 1872 Act, is intended to defeat the so-called "Tasmanian dodge." As O'Leary explains:

"The 'Tasmanian dodge' worked as follows: A voter smuggled in a piece of paper of the same size as a ballot paper, put it into the box, brought the actual ballot out of the booth and gave it to an agent, who marked it as he pleased and gave it to another voter (for a consideration). The second voter would smuggle out another ballot, and so on."

(O'Leary (1961), p. 66, n. 1).

By stipulating that the voter exhibit the official mark on the paper placed in the box, it was intended to prevent the initial deception.

---

[13] [1975] Q.B. 151, 161–162. See also, O'Leary (1961), p. 8, n. 4.

[14] Parliamentary Elections Rules, rr. 37–41; Local Elections (Principal Areas) Rules, rr. 31–35.

[15] Cmnd. 9140, para. 6.5, responding to H.A.C. (1982–83) H.C. 32–I, paras. 85–87. The difficulties are discussed below.

[16] Parliamentary Elections Rules, r. 37(2).

A vote on a ballot paper which does not exhibit the official mark is void.[17] This used to be an inflexible rule, although its effect was partly mitigated by courts holding that a paper imperfectly marked but which clearly exhibited an intention to apply the official mark could validly be used for casting a vote.[18] In *Morgan* v. *Simpson*, Lord Denning pointed out the injustice which this inflexibility was capable of producing:

> "Rarely does a voter look to see that the ballot paper is stamped with the official mark. At least I never do. Rarely does a voter go back to the presiding officer and show him the official mark on the back. At least I never do. Often enough the polling station is not suited for it. It is so furnished that the natural thing is for the voter to go straight from the compartment to the ballot box and put his paper in it ... If (such) votes are not to count, (electors) are disenfranchised without any real blame attaching to them."[19]

It has been claimed that "at a General Election many thousands of ballot papers are invalidated for this reason."[20]

Whether this rule continues to apply in its inflexible form is, in the light of the decision in *Ruffle* v. *Rogers*,[21] unclear. In a local government election, four votes were rejected for want of the official mark. Had the votes been counted, the result of the election would have been a tie, whereas the effect of their exclusion was that one candidate won by two votes. The losing candidate challenged this result by election petition. Lord Denning dealt with the point quite briefly, asserting that "those votes certainly ought to be counted whenever the result is so close that it is necessary."[22] This proposition was supported by reference to what is now section 48 of the 1983 Act:

> "No local government election shall be declared invalid by reason of any act or omission of the returning officer ... if it appears to the tribunal having cognisance of the question that the election was so conducted as to be substantially in

---

[17] *Ibid.* r. 47(1)(*a*).

[18] *Gloucester (County) Cirencester Division Case* (1893) 4 O'M. & H. 194; *Re South Newington Election Petition* [1948] 2 All E.R. 503.

[19] [1975] Q.B. 151, 160–161.

[20] Evidence of Mr. F. L. Shaw to Home Affairs Committee, reprinted as (1982–83) H.C. 32–II, Appendix 33.

[21] [1982] 1 Q.B. 1220.

[22] [1982] 1 Q.B. 1220, 1230.

accordance with the law as to elections and that the act or omission did not affect its result."

In an earlier case[23] it had been held that this section should be transformed into positive terms, that an election should be held invalid if it was not so conducted as to be substantially in accordance with the law as to elections, or that any act or omission did affect the result. Here Lord Denning felt that the omission to place the official mark on the four ballot papers *had* affected the election result, and that accordingly the election was invalid.

The difficulty with this reasoning is that the election rules state in terms that such votes "shall...be void and not counted."[24] Lord Denning, however, would appear to authorise Returning Officers to count these votes "whenever the result is so close that it is necessary." Counting practice has invariably been that doubtful votes are accepted or rejected by Returning Officers (in consultation with candidates' agents) before the final totalling process begins, and therefore in ignorance of the effect of any acceptance or rejection (Brockington (1984), p. 809). The consequence of Lord Denning's judgment appears to be that, once provisional totals have been arrived at, Returning Officers should henceforth go back to the tally of votes rejected for want of the official mark, divide them between the candidates and then check whether the result of the election would have been different if these votes had been included. If their inclusion would have produced a different result, then they should be included in each of the candidate's final total of votes. Thus the injustice arising out of the inflexible application of rule 47, and the consequent disenfranchisement of electors, is mitigated. Whether Returning Officers do in fact adopt this practice is not known, but it seems unlikely in view of the Home Office's "Memorandum for the Guidance of Acting Returning Officers in England and Wales," paragraph 26 of which says that "any ballot paper which does not bear the official mark *must not* be counted" (emphasis in original). It might well be preferable to amend the statutory provisions to permit Returning Officers discretion to accept votes (regardless of their impact on the result) where satisfied that the absence of the official mark was the result of official error (Brockington (1984)).

---

[23] *Morgan* v. *Simpson* [1975] Q.B. 151.
[24] Rule 47(1).

Whereas the scope of a Returning Officer's discretion is rather uncertain after *Ruffle* v. *Rogers* in respect of ballot papers lacking the official mark, the same case clarifies the officer's position as regards votes which are not marked in the appropriate way. Rule 47(1)(*b*) and (*d*) of the Parliamentary Elections Rules[25] provides that ballot papers on which votes are given for more than one candidate, or which are unmarked or void for uncertainty, shall not be counted. But this is subject to the proviso that the vote is to be counted if, notwithstanding the improper marking, the voter's intention that his vote shall be for one or other of the candidates clearly appears. Soon after the Ballot Act 1872 was enacted it was held that a vote expressed by writing-in the preferred candidate's name was void,[26] but in *Ruffle* v. *Rogers* Lord Denning pointed out that the 1948 Representation of the People Act had amended the 1872 Act in this respect. Under the new provisions, now to be found in both sets of election rules, a vote will be valid if, in the opinion of the Returning Officer, a clear intention has been evinced to support a particular candidate:

> "The fact that a voter has written in handwriting the name of his chosen candidate—clearly showing that he intended to vote for that candidate—on the correct ballot paper and in the correct place does not invalidate the ballot paper... when the intention is clear—as it was in this case—it seems to me entirely wrong that his vote should not be counted."[27]

Accordingly, a vote expressed by crossing out the names of two candidates and leaving a third name unmarked has been held to evince an intention to support that last candidate[28]; on the other hand, a vote enumerating the candidates in an apparently preferred order as in a proportional representation system has been held not to indicate a certain intention, and in any event may amount to an attempt to vote for more than one candidate and be invalid on that ground also.[29]

This relatively relaxed approach to improperly marked ballot papers is, however, subject to an important proviso, that the vote will not be valid, notwithstanding the clarity of the voter's

---

[25] See also, Local Elections (Principal Areas) Rules, r. 41(1)(*b*) and (*d*).

[26] *Woodward* v. *Sarsons* (1875) L.R. 10 C.P. 733. See also, the *Borough of Exeter case* (1911) 6 O'M & H. 228.

[27] [1982] 1 Q.B. 1220, 1229–1230.

[28] *Levers* v. *Morris* [1971] 3 All E.R. 1300.

[29] *Cornwell* v. *Marshall* (1977) 75 L.G.R. 676.

intention, if the identity of the voter can be ascertained from the marks which have been placed on the ballot paper.[30] The principle of the secrecy of the ballot requires that this rule be adhered to rigorously. Accordingly, it has been held that a ballot paper to which the voter appended his initials was invalid.[31] In *Ruffle* v. *Rogers* it was argued that even if a vote was not invalid by virtue of the voter's preference being expressed in handwritten form, the vote was still invalid in that the voter was capable of being identified by reference to the handwriting. On the facts the argument failed—the voter alleged to have cast the handwritten vote was proved to have voted at a quite different polling station—but if the handwriting were of a highly unusual or individualistic character, it is possible that the vote could be disallowed on the ground that the voter could be identified thereby.

Decisions as to the validity of votes are a matter for Returning Officers. Such decisions are expressed to be final,[32] but it is open to an Election Court to amend or reverse a decision as to the validity of any particular vote. In practice, although Returning Officers make the final decisions, the candidates, acting either themselves or by their nominated counting agents, will have the opportunity to express their opinions as to the validity of individual votes. Candidates, their election agents and any counting agents are entitled to attend the count, and counting agents are to be afforded such reasonable facilities for overseeing the proceedings as is consistent with the orderly conduct of the count. In particular, counting agents must be given the opportunity to satisfy themselves that the ballot papers are correctly allocated as between the candidates' piles.[33]

The count proceeds in two stages: the count of the number of votes cast, including those cast as postal votes and the count of each candidate's share of the total vote.[34] Postal votes which are delivered after close of poll are excluded from the count.[35] This places a premium on the efficiency of the Post Office. In one local election it was reported that 20 per cent. of postal votes had been delivered late, notwithstanding that they had been

---

[30] Parliamentary Elections Rules, r. 47(1)(*b*), 47(2); Local Elections (Principal Areas) Rules, r. 43(1)(*b*), 43(3).

[31] *Re South Newington Election Petition* [1948] 2 All E.R. 503.

[32] Parliamentary Elections Rules r. 30; Local Elections (Principal Areas) Rules, r. 42.

[33] P.E. Rules, r. 44; L.E. (P.A.) Rules, r. 38.

[34] P.E. Rules, r. 45(1); L.E. (P.A.) Rules, r. 39(1).

[35] P.E. Rules, r. 45(2); L.E. (P.A.) Rules, r. 39(3)

properly posted before polling day (Brockington (1984), p. 809), and the inflexible operation of this rule may serve to frustrate the liberalisation of the postal voting rules (for holidaymakers and others) to which we referred in Chapter 3. Counting is a manual process, and as such is susceptible to human error. As Lord Parker C.J. observed in one case, "Nobody expects counting in an election to be completely accurate; indeed I suppose if you go on recounting you will get in each case slightly different results."[36] While this is doubtless true, the availability of a recount serves as a necessary control mechanism. Such recounts are available at the request of the candidate or his election agent, although the Returning Officer may refuse a recount if he or she considers the request unreasonable.[37] Normally, recounts will be requested when the result is in doubt, but in parliamentary elections recounts have also been sought when an individual candidate is threatened with a lost deposit. In such circumstances it is normal only for that candidate's votes to be recounted, to see whether the requisite percentage barrier has been surmounted. In other circumstances, a full recount will normally occur. There is no legal limit to the number of requests for recounts that can be made—in one parliamentary case as many as seven full recounts were ordered where the winning margin was finally declared as three votes[38]—and ultimately it will be for the Returning Officer to decide that requests for further recounts are unreasonable.

Once the count has been completed the Returning Officer declares the result. In the event of an equality of votes between candidates the election is decided by lot.[39] The ballot papers, counted and rejected, are then packeted and sealed and, in the case of Parliamentary elections, remitted to the Clerk of the Crown, or, in the case of local elections, to the designated council officer. These, and all other relevant papers, must be retained for one year in the case of parliamentary elections or for six months in the case of local elections, and then destroyed.[40]

---

[36] *McWhirter* v. *Platten* [1970] 1 Q.B. 508, 514. See (1982–83) H.C. 32–II, paras. 897, 900, on the advantages of introducing voting machines allowing for automated counting.

[37] P.E. Rules, r. 46; L.E. (P.A.) Rules, r. 40.

[38] Peterborough, 1966 General Election.

[39] P.E. Rules, r. 49; L.E. (P.A.) Rules, r. 43.

[40] P.E. Rules, rr. 54–5, 57; L.E. (P.A.) Rules, rr. 45–6, 48.

(3) CHALLENGING RESULTS: ELECTION PETITIONS

(a) Introduction

Once an election result has been declared, the only method of challenging it is by way of election petition. Prior to 1868, the House of Commons asserted to itself an exclusive power to adjudicate on such petitions, a power that was exercised after 1770 by Parliamentary Committee (O'Leary (1961), pp. 8–26). In 1868 this power was transferred to newly-created Election Courts presided over by a High Court judge, sitting alone.[41] In 1872 equivalent arrangements were constituted for municipal elections, although here the Election Courts were to be presided over by barristers of not less than 15 years' standing, such barristers to be appointed by the judges charged with hearing parliamentary election petitions.[42] In 1879 the 1868 Act was amended to require that henceforth two High Court judges rather than one should hear parliamentary election petitions, and that no election was to be held invalid unless both judges agreed.[43]

The structure thus established largely remains, the relevant provisions being found in the R.P.A. 1983. The distinction between parliamentary and local election petitions is retained, in that Election Courts established to hear local election petitions continue to be presided over by barristers, termed commissioners for this purpose.[44] However, a petition before a local Election Court which can conveniently be stated as a special case can be transferred to the High Court for hearing.[45] It is clearly established that local Election Courts are "inferior courts," in the sense that they are amenable to judicial review of their decisions,[46] but doubts, based on the composition of such courts, have been expressed as to whether the same can be said of parliamentary Election Courts.[47] Election Courts of either type may make orders for discovery of documents.[48] In the *Richmond* case discovery led

---

[41] Election Petitions and Corrupt Practices at Elections Act 1868.
[42] Corrupt Practices at Municipal Elections Act 1872.
[43] Parliamentary Elections and Corrupt Practices Act 1879.
[44] R.P.A. 1983, s.130. For Scotland, see s.134.
[45] R.P.A. 1983, s.146. For an example, see *Re South Newington Election* [1948] 2 All E.R. 503.
[46] *R. v. Cripps, ex p. Muldoon* [1984] Q.B. 68, 88–9 (D.C.).
[47] *R. v. Election Court, ex p. Sheppard* [1975] 1 W.L.R. 1319, 1323.
[48] R.S.C. Order 24, r. 3.

to 11 further charges being added to the four made in the original election petition.[49]

The process of petitioning is laid down in the 1983 Act and in the Election Petition Rules.[50] An unusual feature of the process is that petitions, which may after all allege behaviour of a criminal or quasi-criminal nature such as corrupt or illegal practices, are fought out as private actions between petitioner and respondent, notwithstanding the constituency (or, indeed, the wider public) interest.[51] Those eligible to bring petitions are defeated candidates and voters (and, in parliamentary elections, "a person claiming to have had a right to be elected or returned at the election"),[52] while successful candidates and, if appropriate, Returning Officers are made respondents.[53] Petitioners are required to provide security for costs when presenting the petition,[54] and costs follow the event according to the usual civil litigation rules.[55] In the *Richmond* case, these costs exceeded £42,000, three-quarters of which had to be met by the respondent successful candidate, notwithstanding that 13 of the 15 allegations made against him were dismissed by the Election Court.[56]

At the conclusion of the hearing of the petition, the Election Court determines whether the respondent candidate was duly elected or whether the election was void. In the case of parliamentary elections this determination is reported to the Speaker, and it is for the House of Commons to make the final decision as to the appropriate steps to take in upholding the election or issuing a writ for a new one.[57] In fact the House by convention never departs from the Election Court's determination.[58] In the case of local government elections the Election Court reports its determination to the High Court, and a copy is then sent to the Secretary of State for the Environment.[59] In either case the report must state whether any candidate has been guilty of a corrupt or illegal practice. If such

---

[49] See Williams (1982), pp. 10–11.
[50] S.I. 1960 No. 543, as amended by S.I. 1985 No. 1278.
[51] See O'Leary (1961), pp. 38–39.
[52] R.P.A. 1983, ss.121(1), 128(1).
[53] *Ibid.* ss.121(2), 128(2).
[54] *Ibid.* s.136, as amended by R.P.A. 1985, Sched. 4, para. 48. See *Barratt* v. *Tuckman, The Times*, November 5, 1984.
[55] *R.* v. *Cripps, ex p. Muldoon* [1984] Q.B. 686 (C.A.).
[56] *Ibid.*
[57] R.P.A. 1983, s.144.
[58] Helmore (1967), pp. 91–94.
[59] R.P.A. 1983, s.145.

has occurred, the election is void, a by-election must be held, and the candidate will be ineligible for election for a period of years depending upon the nature of the practice and whether it was committed by the candidate personally or by his or her agent.[60]

(b) The Grounds for Petitioning

Although the discussion has thus far referred to the commission of corrupt or illegal practices, election petitions brought on this ground are, even in the context of a relatively small number of election petitions, rare. Broadly speaking, petitions fall into three categories: those questioning the *ab initio* eligibility for candidature of the successful candidate; those questioning the candidate's entitlement to be elected in the light of the election campaign (raising allegations of corrupt or illegal practices); and those questioning the election on the ground of some administrative irregularity. We consider each in turn.

(i) *Ab initio* ineligibility. *Ab initio* ineligibility cases are uncommon, because the criteria required to be satisfied before one can become a candidate are, as has been seen in Chapter 4, not particularly onerous, whether one is considering parliamentary or local government candidatures. The *Bristol South-East Election Petition*[61] case, involving the eligibility of Mr. Anthony Wedgwood-Benn, Viscount Stansgate, for membership of the House of Commons, is the best-known example of this type. Mr. Benn had for some years been the elected member for the Bristol South East constituency when he succeeded to the hereditary title of Viscount Stansgate. The House of Commons resolved that Mr. Benn had thereby ceased to be qualified for membership of the House, and a writ was ordered for a new election. Mr. Benn was nominated as candidate and subsequently won this election. His defeated opponent successfully challenged this result by election petition. The case turned on the question as to exactly when, if at all, Mr. Benn had ceased to be eligible for membership of the House of Commons, in light of the fact that Mr. Benn had refrained from applying for, and did not receive, a writ of summons to the House of Lords. It was held that the ineligibility arose immediately upon accession to the peerage, which the courts could establish by evidence other than, or in addition to, the writ of summons to the House of

---

[60] *Ibid*. ss.158–9.
[61] [1964] 2 Q.B. 257.

Lords. Thus Mr. Benn had not been eligible for election, and the petitioner succeeded.[62]

A similar result was obtained in the *Armagh* case.[63] This arose out of elections to the Northern Ireland Assembly under the Northern Ireland Act 1982. The Northern Ireland Assembly Disqualification Act 1975 mirrors the House of Commons Disqualification Act of the same year by providing that "a person is disqualified from membership of the ... Assembly who for the time being is ... the member of the legislature of any country or territory outside the Commonwealth." The election was conducted under the proportional representation system of voting, and Mr. Seamus Mallon was one of six successful candidates for the Armagh constituency. An election petition was brought to challenge Mr. Mallon's election. The petition succeeded, on the ground that some months previously Mr. Mallon had been appointed to membership of the Senate, the upper chamber of the Parliament of the Republic of Ireland. Once this had been established (Graham (1984), pp. 77–83), the Election Court had no option but to declare Mr. Mallon's election void, he being a person disqualified from membership of the Assembly by virtue of his concurrent membership of the legislature of a non-Commonwealth country.

The remedy obtained by the petitioners in the *Armagh* case distinguishes it in an important respect from the *Bristol South East* case. In the latter, the unsuccessful candidate petitioner not only challenged Mr. Benn's election, but sought to have himself declared the victor. Prior to the election the petitioner had made strenuous efforts to bring to the attention of the electorate the fact that Mr. Benn was ineligible for election. He therefore argued that individual electors, having been given notice of that fact, must, in so far that they had voted for Mr. Benn, be taken to have deliberately thrown their votes away, and that he, having the next highest number of valid votes (as the only other candidate), was entitled to be returned. The court agreed. The voters, having been made aware of Mr. Benn's incapacity in law, had voted for him at their peril, and the court had no option but to regard the votes as having been deliberately

---

[62] See also, *Re MacManaway* [1951] A.C. 161 (request to Privy Council for advice: held, Church of Ireland priest disqualified from membership of the House of Commons, having received episcopal ordination), *Herbert v. Pauley* (1964) 62 L.G.R. 647 (local government election held void, successful candidate found not to have satisfied any of the criteria for candidature now set out in the Local Government Act 1972, s.79(1)).

[63] *Armagh Election Petition, McCusker v. Mallon,* reported in Graham (1984).

wasted. Therefore, the petitioner was declared elected. In the *Armagh* case the position was at first sight very similar, in that the ineligibility of Mr. Mallon for election had been widely advertised to the electorate before the election. Nevertheless, the result of the petition was only that Mr. Mallon's election was held void. No declaration was made that the petitioner had been elected. The reason for this was that, as previously mentioned, the Armagh election was conducted on the basis of proportional representation, and Mr. Mallon was one of six winning candidates from a total of 15. Any of the other candidates could have brought a petition, yet the mere fact that a successful challenge had been made could not of itself entitle an individual petitioner to the seat when Mr. Mallon's votes became available for dividing up between all the other candidates. In these circumstances the election was merely held void, and a by-election was ordered to fill the vacancy.

(ii) Campaign offences. In principle the commission of corrupt or illegal practices in electoral campaigning renders the election void.[64] A successful petition on these grounds does not entitle the petitioner to the seat. A new election will have to take place to fill the vacancy.

The number of petitions brought alleging corrupt or illegal practices is now very small. The last successful petition in respect of a parliamentary election was brought as long ago as 1923,[65] although the *Richmond* case in 1981, in respect of a local government election, was also partially successful (albeit not to the extent that the election was declared void). A number of reasons may be suggested for this paucity of petitions. First, there can be no doubt that the processes of electioneering have become markedly less illegitimate. The overt corruption which characterised much Victorian campaigning has entirely disappeared in the face of a more highly educated electorate, an electoral campaigning law which, even if significantly flawed by omission, provides a coherent framework for constituency electioneering, and the development of national media attention which would not allow such practices to go unremarked upon.

Secondly, our electoral law provides an escape route for those who may inadvertently have committed illegal (as distinct from corrupt) practices, allowing them to pre-empt the possibility of becoming respondents to election petitions. An application may

---

[64] R.P.A. 1983, s.159(1).
[65] Butler (1963), p. 57.

be made to the High Court, to an Election Court or, in certain circumstances, to a county court for relief from the consequences of committing an illegal practice, payment, employment or hiring.[66] Relief, which is discretionary, may only be granted if the illegality arose out of "inadvertence or from accidental miscalculation or from some other reasonable cause of a like nature," and if the candidate shows that there is no want of good faith.[67] Thus, for example, an accidental overspending above the expenditure maxima, whether caused by carelessness not amounting to recklessness,[68] by reliance on incorrect official advice,[69] or even by ignorance of the law,[70] may be made the subject of an application for relief. In the *Richmond* case the respondents, having been found guilty of illegal practices of overspending and submission of an untrue return, obtained relief from the Election Court which had heard the election petition.

But perhaps the most important reason for the paucity of petitions alleging corrupt or illegal practices relates to the nature of petition proceedings. As was previously mentioned, these cases are fought out as private actions. Although the Director of Public Prosecutions or his representative attends the hearing of all petitions alleging corrupt or illegal practices, and may have functions to perform if corrupt practices are held to have occurred,[71] the D.P.P. plays no part in initiating the petition. Thus, unsuccessful candidates must initiate petitions, and in practice this will almost certainly mean candidates who have been authorised to do so by, and have received financial backing from, their parties.[72] It has long been recognised that it is hardly in the interests of the parties to seek to overturn their opponents' victories by election petition:

> "This is not because malpractices are never suspected ... but because the process of petitioning is expensive and uncertain. As one senior official said: 'If we lost a seat by

---

[66] R.P.A. 1983, s.167(1). The D.P.P. must be notified of any such application, and may attend and make representations at the hearing: R.P.A. 1985, Sched. 4, para. 56.

[67] R.P.A. 1983, s.167(2)(*b*).

[68] *Re Bedwellty Election, ex p. Finch* (1965) 63 L.G.R. 406.

[69] *Re Wakefield Election, ex p. Harrison* (1966) 64 L.G.R. 383.

[70] *Re Richmond (East Sheen Ward) Election* (1969) 67 L.G.R. 415.

[71] See, for example, R.P.A. 1983, ss.161–2.

[72] For an example of an election petition brought by an unsuccessful non-party candidate, see *Barrett* v. *Tuckman, The Times,* November 5, 1984, in respect of a European Assembly election. The petition failed.

one vote and I could clearly prove illegal practices by the other side I wouldn't try. It would cost perhaps £5,000 and they might be able to show that our man had slipped up in some way. But worse than that, it might start tit-for-tat petitions and no party could afford a lot of them. On the whole, we're both law-abiding and it's as well to leave each other alone.' "[73]

The figure of £5,000 would today require to be multiplied several times. It is now merely the sum for which petitioners must give security when first presenting a parliamentary election petition.[74]

In some respects this is unsatisfactory. It makes little sense to leave a framework of electioneering law to be enforced by parties which have good reason for not initiating petitions, save in rare or exceptional circumstances.[75] In 1948 the Committee on Electoral Law Reform recommended that the costs of petitioning be reduced by placing the responsibility for pursuing such proceedings in the hands of a public official, once a prima facie case had been established by a private petitioner:

> "Irregularities at elections should not be regarded as a private wrong which an individual must come forward to remedy, but as attempts to wreck the machinery of representative government and as an attack upon national institutions which the nation should concern itself to repel."[76]

This recommendation was not adopted, but in any event its adoption now might not be very significant, as parties would presumably still be reluctant to initiate the procedure. After all, as we have tried to show, all the parties are engaged in a silent conspiracy to circumvent the expenditure rules, and it is in the interests of none of them to bring these practices out into the open by way of petition.

[73] Quoted in Nuffield (1959) study, p. 280.
[74] R.P.A. 1985, Sched. 4, para. 48.
[75] Such as the Communist Party's long-standing objection to its small allocation of television broadcasting time, which led to the election petition in *Grieve* v. *Douglas-Home* [1965] S.L.T. 186. The reasons for bringing the *Richmond* petition are unclear – Williams speculates that the local Conservative Association was under severe pressure from Conservative Central Office following a series of poor performances in "natural Conservative" territory (Williams (1982)).
[76] Cmd. 7286, para. 54.

(iii) Administrative irregularities. Petitions brought on the basis of administrative irregularities in the conduct of the poll are more common than either of the other two categories. Section 23(3) of the 1983 Act provides:

> "No parliamentary election shall be declared invalid by reason of any act or omission by the returning officer or any other person in breach of his official duty in connection with the election or otherwise of the parliamentary elections rules if it appears to the tribunal having cognizance of the question that—
> (a) the election was so conducted as to be substantially in accordance with the law as to elections; and
> (b) the act or omission did not affect its result."

This section applies equally to European Assembly elections; section 48(1) of the 1983 Act provides an equivalent for local government elections. In *Morgan* v. *Simpson* the Court of Appeal held that this negatively-framed section should be expressed in positive terms, thus:

> "A (parliamentary, European Assembly or local government) election *shall* be declared invalid by reason of any act or omission of the returning officer or any other person ... if it appears to the tribunal having cognizance of the question that the election was *not* so conducted as to be substantially in accordance with the law as to elections or that the act or omission *did* affect the result."[77]

As Lord Denning went on to observe in that case,[78] this formulation permits of three possibilities. First, an election may be declared invalid if it was not so conducted as to be substantially in accordance with the law as to elections. The only case since the Ballot Act 1872 which clearly falls into this category is the *Hackney Election Petition* case,[79] where the administrative arrangements for the poll were such that two polling stations never opened and other stations were closed during various times of the day so that over 5,000 potential voters were disenfranchised. In 1974, an Election Court in *Gunn* v. *Sharpe*[80] appears to have held that an election in which 102 votes (out of a total of over 6,000 votes) were disallowed as cast

[77] [1975] 1 Q.B. 151, 161.
[78] At 164.
[79] (1874) 31 L.T. 69.
[80] [1974] Q.B. 808.

on ballot papers lacking the official mark was not so conducted as to be substantially in accordance with electoral law. However, in *Morgan* v. *Simpson* Lord Denning expressed the view that that case should properly have fallen into a different category, discussed below.

The second and third possibilities are that the election *was* conducted substantially in accordance with electoral law, but that nevertheless there was administrative error. If the error was not such as to affect the result of the election, there can be no question of invalidity. For example, an improper refusal to permit a recount,[81] provision of inconsistent or uncertain guidance to voters as to votes to be cast,[82] or permitting unauthorised persons to attend the count[83] have all been held not to render the election invalid. Conversely, if the administrative error *was* such as to affect the result, then the election will be declared invalid. Erroneous decisions by the Returning Officer as to the validity or invalidity of votes,[84] or failure to affix the official stamp to ballot papers,[85] can be sufficient to render the election invalid if they were such as to affect the result.

Once the matter is put in these terms, it can be seen that there is a far greater likelihood that petitions on this ground will be brought in respect of local government elections. The disputes are normally about the admissibility or inadmissibility of a limited number of votes, and the petition must show that the allegedly erroneous decisions on admissibility would have affected the result of the election. This is more likely to occur, if the number of disputed votes is small, only where the total number of votes cast is small, as in a local government election; in parliamentary elections, where constituencies are normally in excess of 60,000 voters, winning margins will generally exceed the numbers of disputed votes and so render the bringing of petitions pointless.

Disputes as to individual votes are determined by a process of scrutiny.[86] The petitioner is required to list the votes which he contends were wrongly admitted or rejected, giving his grounds.[87] The validity of each vote is then considered, and the

---

[81] *Levers* v. *Morris* [1971] 3 All E.R. 1300.
[82] *James* v. *Davies* (1978) 76 L.G.R. 189.
[83] *Re Kensington North Election Petition* [1960] 1 W.L.R. 762.
[84] *Re South Newington Election* [1948] 2 All E.R. 503.
[85] *Morgan* v. *Simpson* [1975] 1 Q.B. 151; *Gunn* v. *Sharpe* [1974] Q.B. 808 (and see *Morgan* v. *Simpson* at 164); *Ruffle* v. *Rogers* [1982] 2 Q.B. 1220.
[86] For details, see Halsbury's Laws, (4th ed.) Vol. 15, paras. 924–40.
[87] R.P.A. 1983, s.139(6).

court's judgment given. At the end of the process the court amends each candidate's total vote in the light of its decisions on the disputed votes. Where the result of the scrutiny is to produce an equality of valid votes as between candidates, the court must resolve the election by ordering the drawing of lots.[88]

(iv) Conclusion. Although discussion of election petitions has certain legal interest, in practical terms they are of minimal significance. They relate to a structure of law on election campaigning which as we have seen is flawed by its constituency-based assumptions and its consequent inability to take account of national campaigning. Furthermore, even within this restricted framework they play a limited role. As we suggested, it is not in the parties' tactical interests to pursue their opponents' candidates by way of election petition, and the structure of the law, as interpreted by the courts, is such as to dissuade potential petitioners concerned with administrative irregularities. Having said this, however, we would not want to suggest that the law of election petitions is that part of electoral law most ripe for reform. To argue this would be putting the cart before the horse. If there are inadequacies in our electoral campaigning law they are concerned less with inadequate or inappropriate methods of enforcement than with the unrealistic nature of the rules to be enforced. While the major parties quietly conspire to circumvent the spirit of the rules, we need hardly be surprised that they equally conspire to render insignificant the enforcement mechanisms which are effectively placed in their hands.

[88] For an example, see *McGuiness* v. *Ashby* (1984) (unreported).

CONCLUSION: THE REFORM OF ELECTORAL LAW

The system of electoral law which we have described appears likely to come under increasingly critical scrutiny in future years. Developments in campaigning techniques are accounted for with growing difficulty within the framework of the present expenditure rules. The inadequacies of present mechanisms for the registration of voters have recently been recognised, and reforms urged (Pinto-Duschinsky and Pinto-Duschinsky (1987)). The delineation of constituency boundaries continues to be controversial. In addition, a series of larger questions is posed by the possibility that some measure of proportional representation may be adopted. We conclude by surveying some of the electoral law reform issues which might ensue from this renewed interest in the operation of the electoral system.

(1) ELECTORAL REFORM

We are not concerned here to argue the case either for or against the introduction of a system of proportional representation. Rather, we intend briefly to look at some of the alternative systems which have been proposed, and to try to assess what changes in present electoral law might be needed if they were introduced. Obviously, the detailed changes in electoral law would depend upon which new electoral system was introduced; having said that, it does seem to be the case that voter registration law is unlikely to require substantial revision purely because of the introduction of a new system, and we leave it out of account here.

(a) List Systems

The essence of list systems is that the voter votes for a list of candidates nominated by the party. In the "purest" form of the list system, which operates in Israel, the votes for each party's list are calculated on a nationwide basis, and the parties obtain numbers of seats in the legislature directly in proportion to their votes in the country. In some versions of the list system the voter can place the candidates of his or her preferred party in a preferred order, whereas in others this is not permitted.

The introduction of a list system into the United Kingdom would represent a very considerable degree of "nationalisation" of the electoral system. Candidate selection would cease to be a primarily local function, as national or regional party headquarters would construct their candidates' lists for large areas of the country. In West Germany, which operates a modified form of the list system, this accretion of power to the central party organisations has been made the subject of legal regulation, but it has been truly said that there might be strong opposition to legal control of parties' internal organisation if a list system were introduced in Britain (Oliver (1983), p. 117). Quite apart from candidate selection, the "nationalisation" of the electoral process would necessitate a fundamental reconstruction of our electoral expenditure laws. Constituency electioneering would cease to exist (since there would be no constituencies), yet, as we have seen, our present campaign law is based upon the assumption of constituency activity. The regulation of national campaigning and expenditure raises very difficult practical problems, but this nettle would have firmly to be grasped if a list system were to be introduced.

One consequence of a list system would be that we could dispense with the activities of the Boundary Commissioners, since there would be no constituencies for them to draw. Opponents of list systems have argued that such systems be rejected precisely because their introduction would be wholly incompatible with our traditional commitment to geographically-defined constituencies. The report of the Hansard Society Commission on Electoral Reform (Hansard Society (1976)) was designed to meet this objection. The Commission proposed a modified list system whereby three-quarters of M.P.s should continue to be elected through constituencies, and that the remainder of the House of Commons be composed of "Additional Members" drawn from defeated candidates and offered seats so as to bring the composition of the House of Commons more closely into line with national voting patterns. This avoids the excessively centralising tendencies of pure list systems, in that candidates would continue to be selected by local parties and local constituency electioneering would continue. It would, however, require the Boundary Commissioners to draw substantially larger constituencies than now, and further difficulties would ensue in determining exactly which failed candidates would become Additional Members of the House of Commons. The proposals have attracted very little support (for further criticisms see Oliver (1983), pp. 118–119).

(b) Preferential Voting Systems

Preferential voting systems operate within geographically-defined constituencies, and for this reason seem more likely to be adopted in Britain if there is to be electoral reform. Under these systems voters indicate their preferences among the various candidates by numbering them 1 (for first preference), 2, 3, and so on until there is no preference. In specified circumstances determined by the particular form of preferential voting system adopted, a voter's first preference may be discounted and the vote transferred to his or her second preference. The process continues until the required number of candidates has been elected.

The two forms of preferential voting systems most commonly discussed are the Alternative Vote system and the Single Transferable Vote system. Under the Alternative Vote model, single M.P.s are elected from geographically-defined constituencies. If any candidate wins more than 50 per cent. of the first preference votes validly cast, he or she is declared elected and the process is complete. If no candidate achieves this on the first count, the votes of the candidate with the lowest number of first preference votes are redistributed in accordance with that candidate's supporters' second preferences. This process continues until one candidate achieves an overall majority as against all the other candidates. The candidate is then declared elected. Introduction of this system would require only a modification in the voting and counting rules. Constituency boundaries would continue to be drawn as now, candidates would continue to be selected by a predominantly local process, and constituency campaigning would continue. Because of the relative simplicity both of its introduction and its operation, the Alternative Vote has attracted considerable support, but, from the point of view of electoral reformers, it is defective in failing to provide for representation in Parliament in any way proportional to first preference votes when aggregated nationally, (see, for example, Butler (1963), pp. 192–194). For this reason the Single Transferable Vote (S.T.V.) system has become increasingly favoured. Properly operated, it can produce a high measure of proportionality between seats and votes, at the expense of some complexity and substantial amendments to electoral law. As has already been explained, the system is in operation both for Northern Irish elections to the European Assembly, and for Northern Irish local government elections, and we do therefore have a legislative model already available. Furthermore, in 1982 the Liberal/S.D.P. Alliance Commission on Constitutional Reform produced a detailed plan for constituency changes which would be necessary if S.T.V. were to be introduced (Liberal/S.D.P. Alliance 1982).

The Single Transferable Vote differs from the Alternative Vote in that it requires the delineation of constituencies which normally elect not less than three candidates. A Boundary Commission divides the country up into multi-member constituencies, and candidates who, either on first preference votes or on redistribution of losing candidates' votes, obtain the necessary quota of votes are declared elected. There are various methods of calculating the quota, but that which has been adopted for European Assembly elections in Northern Ireland is the "Droop quota." The total number of valid votes is divided by one more than the number of seats to be filled, and to the result of that division is added one.[1] To give a simple example, where three candidates are to be elected and 1,000 valid votes have been cast, any individual candidate must obtain 251 first preference and transferred votes to be elected (1,000 divided by three-plus-one, and one added to the result). Transfer of votes between candidates is required either "when the vote is not required to give a (preferred candidate) the necessary quota of votes" (because that candidate has already obtained a sufficient number of votes to satisfy the quota), or "when, owing to the deficiency in the number of votes given for a prior choice, that choice is eliminated from the list of candidates."[2] The Electoral Reform Society has produced detailed guidance on counting procedures (Newland and Britton (1976)).

The introduction of S.T.V. would obviously require substantial changes in voting and counting rules, as the European Assembly Elections Regulations for Northern Ireland illustrate.[3] Of even greater importance, however, would be the changes in constituency boundaries which would need to be introduced to create multi-member constituencies. The larger the constituency, the greater is the proportionality between voters'

---

[1] European Assembly Elections (Northern Ireland) Regulations 1986, S.I. 1986 No. 2250, Sched. 1, rule 44E.
[2] European Assembly Elections Act 1978, Sched. 1, para. 2(2)(*b*).
[3] S.I. 1986 No. 2250, Sched. 1, rules 44A–44M.

preferences and candidates elected (Newland and Britton (1976), pp. 6–7). On the other hand, excessively large constituencies would further dilute the territorial relationship between M.P.s. and electors. Boundary Commissioners would therefore need to be given a clear indication of appropriate constituency sizes. In the case of the Northern Irish District Electoral Areas Commissioner, the initial statutory guidelines permitted the creation of electoral areas composed of between four and eight district wards. The result was that there was a significant number of four-ward electoral areas, and minority representatives continued to experience difficulty in securing election. The guidelines now require the construction of electoral areas comprising between five and seven wards.[4] In its proposals for the introduction of S.T.V. in the United Kingdom, the Liberal/S.D.P. Alliance has argued for an optimum number of 4/5 members per constituency (Liberal/S.D.P. Alliance (1982), p. 16).

Quite apart from constituency size, the principles of delineation of constituency boundaries would need to be considered. The Northern Irish Commissioner, working under the aforementioned revised guidelines on size, took into account a number of factors: existing community identities, his desire to form local government constituencies in which the differing sections of each community could secure representation, and a wish to avoid groupings that would create electoral areas split by natural geographical barriers.[5] The Liberal/S.D.P. Alliance has proposed, in respect of parliamentary constituency boundaries, that these should be based upon "natural communities," and has published a scheme which it claims marks a return to the traditional ideas of representation of boroughs and shires (Liberal/S.D.P. Alliance (1982), pp. 9–10, and pp. 16–25). These constituencies would be created by using the existing parliamentary (single-member) constituencies as building-bricks. As the Alliance concedes, it is frequently difficult to reconcile the demands of respect for "natural communities" with ideals of close proportionality between votes and seats which a large number of five-seat constituencies might produce. In such circumstances the Alliance gives priority to "natural community" considerations, and is willing to countenance the

---

[4] See S.I. 1984 No. 360 and S.I. 1985 No. 169. See also McKee (1983), pp. 178–184 on the political consequences in the Republic of Ireland of three, four or five member constituencies.

[5] Hansard, H.C. Deb. Vol. 71, col. 816 (January 21, 1985).

creation of constituencies electing only three, two or even one M.P. if necessary, at the expense of strict proportionality.

A further set of changes in electoral law would need to be made consequent upon the fact that, under S.T.V., with its multi-member constituencies, a number of candidates from the same party would be fighting for election in the same constituency. Candidate selection would probably continue, as now, to be within the province of local parties, but once nominated, it seems quite likely that a party's candidates would wish to fight joint campaigns. This raises issues of election expenditure. Would the candidates be required individually to observe expenditure maxima, and would their expenditures be recorded individually? And what is the maximum expenditure to be? Until 1948, when the last of the two-member parliamentary constituencies was abolished, candidates running a joint campaign were assumed to benefit from economies of scale, and their expenditure maxima were reduced accordingly. That position continues in respect of local government, as section 77(1) of the R.P.A. 1983, discussed in Chapter 5, makes clear. It is at least arguable that the present expenditure maxima are too low, and that an extension of section 77(1) to parliamentary campaigns conducted under S.T.V. would be unfairly restrictive. Be that as it may, there ought in any case to be provision for joint submission of expenditure returns by candidates of a party who conducted joint campaigns.

Another electoral law problem arises out of the fact that S.T.V. constituencies would normally be at least four times as large as the present single-member constituencies. It would be reasonable to assume that a minimum of 10 candidates might be nominated for four-member seats. As we have seen, local televison and radio coverage of individual constituency contests is already rendered more difficult by section 93(1)(b) of the 1983 Act, which permits individual candidates effectively to veto their opponents' participation in a television or radio programme. We have already criticised this subsection, and have suggested that it may be in breach of the European Convention on Human Rights. Even more will there be cause for complaint if a single candidate in an S.T.V. constituency is able to prevent at least nine other candidates from making their cases. The repeal of this subsection should be an essential element in any legislation to introduce the S.T.V. system for parliamentary elections.

(2) ELECTORAL LAW REFORM WITHIN THE PRESENT SYSTEM

The result of the 1987 General Election has meant that there is very little likelihood of any measure of proportional representation being introduced for several years. Our attention therefore turns to considering what electoral law reforms might properly be considered within the context of our present plurality ("the first past the post") system. We assume that the proposals made by the Home Affairs Committee on the Redistribution of Seats[6] will be accepted, and that proper notice will be taken of recent research demonstrating inadequacies in the voter registration system (Pinto-Duschinsky and Pinto-Duschinsky (1987)), although we doubt whether any improved administrative procedures will go far to counteract the enhanced "avoidance problem" likely to be produced by introduction of the "poll tax." We approach the question of reform from a slightly different angle, that of institutional responsibility for the proper maintenance of the electoral system.

In our Introduction we made reference to MacKenzie's acute perception of the "systematic" quality of electoral systems (MacKenzie (1967), p. 19). That quality has not been recognised in this country in matters of institutional responsibility for the maintenance of the system. As we have seen, responsibility for the delineation of electoral area boundaries reposes in the various Boundary Commissions for local government and parliamentary constituencies in the four countries of the United Kingdom. The Home Office, on the other hand, takes responsibility for electoral law reform and for voter registration procedure. The regulation of campaigning practice is largely left to the parties themselves, both because there is no governmental agency formally charged with this responsibility, and because of the peculiarity of the election petition process, which effectively requires legal action to be taken by defeated (party) candidates. We suggest that there may be a case for drawing together these various responsibilities and placing them in the hands of a single agency (which, for convenience, we shall refer to as the Elections Commission).

The benefits which might flow from such a reorganisation of responsibilities are these. First, a greater degree of co-ordination between the various agencies might ensue if they were brought together under a single control. There have been problems for

---

[6] (1986–87) H.C. 97–I.

example, in integrating the work of the Local Government Boundary Commissions with that of the Commissions for parliamentary constituencies,[7] and there appears to be scope for greater co-ordination in respect of at least the substantive reviews of local government electoral boundaries and the reviews of parliamentary constituency boundaries (which boundaries are, as we saw, heavily dependent upon local government ward, county and London borough boundaries). Again, voter registration initiatives in particular localities might with advantage be co-ordinated with interim boundary reviews for those areas.

Secondly, there is merit in the idea of an agency which has overall responsibility for a continuing review of electoral law, but which is formally free from the government of the day. The reform of electoral law inevitably has political consequences, whatever shape that reform takes. Home Office proposals for substantial reform, no matter how badly needed, will always be regarded with suspicion as designed to advance the interests of the government of the day. Reform initiatives advanced by an independent agency would not be open to the same objection. The "independence" we advocate would not be an independence from politics—we have already had occasion to mention criticism of the parliamentary Boundary Commissioners in this respect—but an independence from the government of the day. Indeed, we would envisage that the ruling body of this Elections Commission would contain nominees of the various parties, who would bring practical experience of the electoral system to the Commission's activities.

The model we have in mind here is the Commission for Racial Equality. That body's statutory remit requires it, *inter alia*, to keep under review the working of the race relations legislation and to draw up and submit to the Home Secretary proposals for amending it.[8] Further, the Commission is empowered to issue Codes of Practice offering practical guidance as to the elimination of racial discrimination and the promotion of equality of opportunity in employment.[9] We suggest that the Code of Practice technique might be of great assistance in achieving better regulation of constituency electoral campaigning. The Election Commission might be empowered, in consultation with

---

[7] *Ibid.* p. 87.
[8] Race Relations Act 1976, s.43(1)(c).
[9] 1976 Act, s.47(1); and see the Commission's Code of Practice on Race Relations in Employment (1983).

the political parties, to prepare a code of electoral campaigning practice, regularly updated, providing guidance on permissible and impermissible campaign tactics, on conventions to be observed in the preparation of expenditure returns (for example, on the appropriate level of expenditure to be returned for the use of computers in constituency campaigning), and offering straightforward guidance to the requirements of election law. We appreciate that the various parties and pressure groups already advise their own activists in certain of these matters, but we see merit in the idea of there being a set of ground rules for campaigning, agreed between the parties and widely publicised. An independent agency of the type we have suggested would be in a far better position than a government department such as the Home Office to produce a generally accepted Code.

The question of *enforcement* of existing electoral campaigning law would also become the responsibility of the new Commission, in the same way that the Commission for Racial Equality has enforcement powers in respect of race relations law.[10] Enforcement by way of election petition is fundamentally flawed: "legal provisions mean nothing if enforcement of the law is left wholly in the hands of those who profit by breaking it" (Mackenzie (1967), p. 19). It is suggested that to entrust this responsibility to a government agency, albeit one independent of the government of the day, would provide that necessary public element in the enforcement of the law which was advocated by the Committee on Electoral Law Reform in 1948.[11] We do not believe that electoral law is regularly breached, and we would expect the Election Commission primarily to be concerned with "fire prevention" through its code-making activities rather than "fire-fighting" through enforcement of the law, but we do believe that the political parties have a vested interest in keeping these matters quiet, and that this is not necessarily conducive to the health of our democracy. A respected independent agency, specifically committed to maintaining and enhancing the quality of our electoral democracy, would be a worthy enterprise, regardless of the structure of the electoral system whose operation it would be required to supervise.

As for the substance of our electoral law, we believe that there is now an overwhelming case for legislation regulating expendi-

---

[10] 1976 Act, Part VIII.
[11] Cmd. 7286.

ture on national campaigns. Ewing has described the various proposals which have been advanced over the years to achieve this (Ewing (1987), pp. 97–102). Two recent developments make a further attempt imperative. First, there is the proliferation of campaign advertising, especially in the press. When, as in the period before 1979, the national party campaign consisted almost exclusively of the use of broadcasting, controls on national expenditure were largely unnecessary because broadcasting facilities were available at minimal cost. In contrast, in the 1987 General Election the Conservative Party spent in excess of three million pounds on advertising alone, and was able far to outspend the other parties in this respect. If we are to retain any conception of elections as fair contests between the parties, we must ensure some measure of equality of opportunity in parties' access to the electorate. If that means imposing some limited restraint upon one party, we think that that could properly be defended as necessary in a democratic society. Money must not be allowed to distort the electoral process by allowing one party disproportionate opportunities to make its case, to the disadvantage of the others.

Secondly, we are concerned about the role of interest groups in election campaigns. Such groups' active participation is not new, but the introduction of computer technology makes possible an interest group "direct mail" involvement in the 1990's which could dwarf previous interventions. At local level, interest group involvement must be authorised by a candidate's agent. A case can equally be made for requiring that participation in the national campaign in a way which appears to be designed to affect support for a political party should be authorised by that party, and count against that party's national campaign maxima. We do not underestimate the complexities of drafting a law which will both restrain the political power of money and yet recognise legitimate claims by interest groups for freedom of speech and the ability to participate in the electoral process. We do believe, however, that as the new technology becomes both more sophisticated and more widely available, the absence of any regulation of third-party intervention leaves the electoral system open to an improper degree of influence by pressure groups. That we should avoid.

The British electoral system has many strengths, not least of which are its efficient administration and a remarkable absence of corruption. We believe that it satisfies the criteria advanced by Butler, Penniman and Ranney for the identification of a "democratic general election," and which will serve equally well as a test of the existence of "free elections." We also believe that this position would be further enhanced by the introduction of the reforms we have suggested. They are the logical next step to achieving an electoral system in which ideas and arguments, rather than financial muscle, carry preponderant weight.

BIBLIOGRAPHY

Barnes, G.P. (1985), "The General Review of Parliamentary Constituencies in England 1976–1983," Vol. 4, *Electoral Studies*, 179.

Barnes, G.P. (1987), "The Use of Computers in Redistributing Constituencies," Vol. 6, *Electoral Studies*, 133.

Birch, A.H. (1964), *Representative and Responsible Government*.

Birch, A.H. (1971), *Representation*.

Birch, A.H. (1985), "The Theory and Practice of Modern British Democracy," in J. Jowell and D. Oliver (eds.), *The Changing Constitution*.

Blake, R. (1985), *The Conservative Party from Peel to Thatcher*.

Blumler, J. (1977), "The Intervention of Television in British Politics," Appendix E to the *Report of the Committee on the Future of Broadcasting*, Cmnd. 6753.

Blumler J., Gurevitch M., Ives J. (1978), *The Challenge of Election Broadcasting*.

Bogdanor, V. (1982), "Reflections on British Political Finance," Vol. 35, *Parliamentary Affairs*, 367.

Bogdanor, V. and Butler D. (1983), *Democracy and Elections*.

Boulton, C. (1986), "The Almost–General Election in Northern Ireland, 1986," *Public Law*, 211.

Boyle, A.J. (1986), "Political Broadcasting, Fairness and Administrative Law," *Public Law*, 562.

Brock, M. (1973), *The Great Reform Act*.

Brockington, R.A.A. (1984), "The Returning Officer's Discretion," Vol. 148, *Local Government Review*, 808.

Bromhead, P. (1986), "The Real Shape and Effect of Electoral Disparity," (unpublished).

Brown, W.J. (1899), "The Hare System in Tasmania," Vol. 15, *Law Quarterly Review*, 51.

Bruce, A. and Lee G., "Local Election Campaigns," Vol. 30, *Political Studies*, 247.

Busteed, M.A. (1975), *Geography and Voting Behaviour*.

Butler, D. (1955), "The Redistribution of Seats," Vol. 33, *Public Administration*, 125.

Butler, D. (1963), *The Electoral System in Britain since 1918*.

Butler, D. (1986), "The Changing Nature of British Elections," in I. Crewe and M. Harrop (eds.), *Political Communications: The General Election Campaign of 1983*.

Butler, D., Penniman, H.R., Ranney, A. (1981), *Democracy at the Polls*.

Byrne, T. (1985), *Local Government in Britain* (4th ed.).

Constitutional Reform Centre (1985), *Company Donations to Political Parties: A Suggested Code of Practice*.

Craig, J.T. (1959), "Parliament and Boundary Commissions," *Public Law*, 23.

Crewe, I. (1986), "Saturation Polling, the Media and the 1983 Election," in I. Crewe and M. Harrop (eds.), *Political Communications: The General Election Campaign of 1983*.

Curtice, J. and Steed, M. (1983), "Turning Dreams into Realities: The Division of Constituencies between the Liberals and the Social Democrats," Vol. 36, *Parliamentary Affairs*, 166.

D.H.S.S. (1981), *Care in the Community: A Consultative Document*.

De Smith, S.A. (1955), "Boundaries between Parliament and the Courts," Vol. 18, *Modern Law Review*, 281.

Edinburgh University Politics Group (1982(a)), "Do Party Workers Matter? The Evidence from Crosby," Vol. 35, *Parliamentary Affairs*, 143.

Edinburgh University Politics Group (1982(b)), "Learning to Fight Multi–Party Elections: The Lessons of Hillhead," Vol. 35, *Parliamentary Affairs*, 252.

Erskine May (1983), *Parliamentary Practice*, (20th ed.).

Ewing, K.D. (1987), *The Funding of Political Parties in Britain*.

Gordon, I. and Whiteley P. (1980), "Johnston on Campaign Expenditure and the Efficacy of Advertising," Vol. 28, *Political Studies*, 293.

Gostin, L. (1977), "Electoral Registration of Patients in Mental Hospitals," Vol. 74, *Law Society's Gazette*, 776.

Gower, L.C.B. (1979), *Principles of Company Law* (4th ed.).

Graham, E. (1984), "The Armagh Election Petition," Vol. 35, *Northern Ireland Law Quarterly*, 76.

Gudgin, G. and Taylor P.J. (1979), *Seats, Votes and the Spatial Organisation of Elections*.

Gunter B., Svennevig M., Wober M. (1986), *Television Coverage of the 1983 General Election*.

Gurevitch M. and Blumler J. (1982), "The Construction of Election News," in J. S. Ettema and D. C. Whitney (eds.), *Individuals in Mass Organisations: Creativity and Constraint*.

Hadden, T. (1977), *Company Law and Capitalism*, (2nd ed.).

Hall, P. (1987), "Flight to the Green," January 9, 1987, *New Society*, 9.

Hanham, H.J. (1971), *The Reformed Electoral System in Great Britain 1832–1914*.

Hansard Society (1976), *Report of the Hansard Society Commission on Electoral Reform*.

Helmore, L. (1967), *Corrupt and Illegal Practices*.

Hood Phillips, O. (1970), *Reform of the Constitution*.

Hughes, P. and Palmer, S. (1983), "Voting Bishops," *Public Law*, 393.

Ivens, M. (1986), "Industry and the 1983 General Election," in I. Crewe and M. Harrop (eds.), *Political Communications: The General Election Campaign of 1983*.

Johnston, R.J. (1986(a)), "A Further Look at British Political Finance," Vol. 34, *Political Studies*, 466.

Johnston, R.J. (1986(b)), "Places, Campaigns and Votes," Vol. 5 (Supp.), *Political Geography Quarterly*, S105.

Johnston, R.J., and Taylor P.J. (1986), "Political Geography: A Politics of Places within Places," Vol. 39, *Parliamentary Affairs*, 135.

Judge, D. (1980), "British Representative Theories and Parliamentary Specialisation," Vol. 33, *Parliamentary Affairs*, 40.

246 Bibliography

Kavanagh, D. (1970), *Constituency Electioneering in Britain*.

Le Lohe, M.J. (1987), *A Study of Non–Registration Among Ethnic Minorities*.

Le May, G.H.L. (1979), *The Victorian Constitution*.

Liberal/S.D.P. Alliance (1982), *Electoral Reform (First Report of the Joint Liberal/S.D.P. Alliance Commission on Constitutional Reform)*.

Linton, M. (1986), "Political Parties and the Press in the 1983 Campaign," in I. Crewe and M. Harrop (eds.), *Political Communications: The General Election Campaign of 1983*.

MacKenzie, W.J.M. (1967), *Free Elections*.

Maitland, F.W. (1963), *Constitutional History of England*.

McAllister, I. (1985), "Campaign Activities and Electoral Outcomes in Britain 1979 and 1983," Vol. 49, *Public Opinion Quarterly*, 489.

McKee, P. (1983), "The Republic of Ireland," in V. Bogdanor and D. Butler (eds.), *Democracy and Elections*.

Minkin, L. (1986), "Against the Tide: Trade Unions, Political Communication and the 1983 General Election," in I. Crewe and M. Harrop (eds.), *Political Communications: The General Election Campaign of 1983*.

Munro, C. (1976), "Elections and Expenditure," *Public Law*, 300.

Newland, R. and Britton F. (1976), *How to Conduct an Election by the Single Transferable Vote*.

Norton, P. (1980), "The Qualifying Age for Candidature in British Elections," *Public Law*, 55.

Nuffield (1945), *The British General Election of 1945*, (by McCallum and Readman).

Nuffield (1950), *The British General Election of 1950*, (by Nicholas).

Nuffield (1951), *The British General Election of 1951*, (by Butler).

Nuffield (1959), *The British General Election of 1959*, (by Butler and Rose).

Nuffield (1964), *The British General Election of 1964*, (by Butler and King).

Nuffield (February 1974), *The British General Election of February 1974* (by Butler and Kavanagh).

Nuffield (October 1974), *The British General Election of October 1974* (by Butler and Kavanagh).

Nuffield (1983), *The British General Election of 1983* (by Butler and Kavanagh).

O'Leary, C. (1961), *The Elimination of Corrupt Practices in British Elections 1868–1911*.

Oliver, D. (1983), "Reform of the Electoral System," *Public Law*, 108.

O.P.C.S. (1982), *The Electoral Registration Process in the United Kingdom*.

O.P.C.S. (1987), *Electoral Registration in Inner–City Areas 1983–84*.

O'Shaughnessy, N. and Peele, G. "Money, Mail and Markets: Reflections on Direct Mail in American Politics," Vol. 4, *Electoral Studies*, 115.

Peele, G. (1982), "Political Consultants," Vol. 1, *Electoral Studies*, 355.

Pinto–Duschinsky, M. (1981), *British Political Finance 1830–1980*.

Pinto–Duschinsky, M. (1985), "Trends in British Political Funding 1979–1983," Vol. 38, *Parliamentary Affairs*, 328.

Pinto–Duschinsky, M. and Pinto–Duschinsky S. (1987), *Voter Registration: Problems and Solutions*.

Pugh, M. (1978), *Electoral Reform in War and Peace 1906–1918*.

Ranney, A. (1979), "British General Elections: An Introduction," in H. R. Penniman (ed.), *Britain at the Polls 1979*.

Ranney, A. (1981), "Candidate Selection," in D. Butler, H. R. Penniman, A. Ranney (eds.), *Democracy at the Polls*.

Rawlings, R.W. (1986), "Parliamentary Redress of Grievance" in C. Harlow (ed.), *Public Law and Politics*.

Rose, R. (1974), *The Problem of Party Government*.

Rowley, G. (1975), "The Redistribution of Parliamentary Seats in the United Kingdom," Vol. 7, *Area*, 16–21, 279–281.

Rush, M. (1969), *The Selection of Parliamentary Candidates*.

Seymour, C. (1915), *Electoral Reform in England and Wales 1832–1885.*

Stewart, J.B. (1975), "Problems for Electoral Registration Officers," *Scots Law Times,* 65–68, 241.

Stewart, J.B. (1980), "A Survey of Electoral Registration Cases," *Scots Law Times,* 250.

Taylor, P.J. and Gudgin, G. (1976) "The Myth of Non–Partisan Cartography," Vol. 13, *Urban Studies,* 13.

Taylor, P.J. and Johnston, R.J. (1979), *Geography of Elections.*

Taylor, R. (1986), "C.N.D. and the 1983 General Election," in I. Crewe and M. Harrop (eds.), *Political Communications: The General Election Campaign of 1983.*

Turpin, C. (1985), *British Government and the Constitution.*

Vincent, J. (1976), *The Formation of the British Liberal Party 1857–1868.*

Walker, C.P. (1982), "Prisoners in Parliament: Another View," *Public Law,* 382.

Waller, R. (1983), "The 1983 Boundary Commission: Policies and Effects," Vol. 4, *Electoral Studies,* 195.

Wallis–Chapman, A.B. and Wallis–Chapman, M., *The Status of Women 1066–1909.*

Ward, L. (1987), *Talking Points: The Right to Vote?*

Whiteley, P. (1986), "The Accuracy and Influence of the Polls in the 1983 General Election," in I. Crewe and M. Harrop (eds.), *Political Communications: The General Election Campaign of 1983.*

Williams, D., *The Richmond Judgement and its Implications.*

Young, A., *The Reselection of M.P.s.*

INDEX

249